WRITE THE PERFECT BOOK PROPOSAL

10 That Sold and Why

2nd Edition

Jeff Herman
and
Deborah Levine Herman

John Wiley & Sons, Inc.

New York • Chichester • Weinheim • Brisbane • Singapore • Toronto

This book is printed on acid-free paper. ∞

Published by John Wiley & Sons, Inc.
Published simultaneously in Canada

This publication is designed to provide accurate and authoritative information in regard to the subject matter covered. It is sold with the understanding that the publisher is not engaged in rendering professional services. If professional advice or other expert assistance is required, the services of a competent professional person should be sought.

Library of Congress Cataloging-in-Publication Data:

Herman, Jeff
    Write the perfect book proposal: 10 that sold and why / Jeff Herman & Deborah Levine
Herman.—2nd ed.
        p. cm.
    Includes bibliographical references and index.
    ISBN 0-471-35312-4 (pbk.)
    1. Book proposals. I. Herman, Deborah. II. Title.

PN161 .H47 2001
808'.02–dc21   00-047764

Printed in the United States of America

10 9 8 7

Contents

PREFACE TO THE SECOND EDITION

We are happy to present to you this second edition of *Write the Perfect Book Proposal*. In the years since we wrote the first edition, we have sold hundreds more titles and have learned more about what makes a book proposal work. We have also seen changes in technology and in the publishing industry that we feel should be passed along to our readers or to first-time students of book proposal writing.

If you want to write nonfiction, mastering the book proposal is a must. Since our first edition, proposal writing has become more sophisticated, and editors and agents expect more from submissions.

Even if you have a completed manuscript to present, a proposal is considered more effective. Agents and editors are receiving more submissions than ever. They need to be able to skim through the material quickly to determine which projects deserve further investigation.

Writers today are expected to have more marketing savvy. The exceptions created the rule. Publishers are spending less of their resources on promotion, so it is up to the writers to give legs to their own books. When an agent or editor considers a book proposal, he or she is going to look at marketing ideas and access to book sales as a major plus. In the last decade alone certain books separated themselves from the others into bestseller status through the major efforts of their writers. Not everyone is able to achieve a bestseller through sweat, but there is a greater desire on the part of those making acquisition decisions to find projects that have that potential.

While there may be more challenges facing writers today, there are also more advantages. During the years since our first edition, so many more people have acquired personal computers. Word processing is much easier and more reliable, and printers are affordable and high-quality. Can you remember faded typewriter ribbons and dot-matrix printers? Can you remember waiting minutes per page for a printout?

Perhaps the biggest advantage writers have today is the Internet. There is an entirely new world when it comes to research. You can spend all night looking things up while your cat sleeps on your lap and your coffee warms your innards.

The "Competition" section of your proposal is now a piece of cake. Before the Internet and online booksellers, you had to go to the bookstore or *Books in Print* to see what the competition might be. We once proposed a book to a publisher who had just published a book with an almost identical title. If we had had the Internet back then, we might have been spared the red face. After all, we are supposed to know better.

There are many opportunities for writers to improve their craft and to learn the business of writing. It will be exciting to see what new developments there are by the time we write our third edition.

ACKNOWLEDGMENTS

We are very grateful to our clients who generously allowed their exemplary proposals to be used in this book. In alphabetical order, they are: Julie Andres, Jordan E. Ayan, Tony Burroughs, Gene Busnar, Jennifer Carney, Gary W. Carter, Richard M. Contino, Bruno Cortis, John Fanning, Kathryn Lance, Vicki Lenz, Rosemary Maniscalco, Jill Podjasek, Jeff Slutsky, and Mark Slutsky.

We have the highest regard for our first editor, Steve Ross, our second editor, Judith McCarthy, our third editor, Chris Jackson, and our most current, Gerry Helferich and Chip Rosetti, and John Simko. All writers should be so fortunate.

Amanda White, our loyal and capable associate, has earned our respect and gratitude.

I would like to acknowledge my co-author, Deborah Levine Herman, for sharing in the development of this material. I would also like to thank Deborah for changing her name to mine since our first edition went to print.

Jeff Herman

I want to thank Jeff Herman for having the faith to throw me head first into the water, knowing all the while I would have to learn to swim. And I also thank Jeff for jumping into the water with my three children and me so we could all swim together.

Deborah Levine Herman

INTRODUCTION

The Importance of the Nonfiction Book Proposal

The nonfiction book proposal is an important tool to help you arouse a publisher's interest and acquire a contract and royalty advance to write your book. At its best, the proposal can function as a sophisticated sales brochure. The more impressive it is, the greater your chances are of selling your book to a publisher, and the higher your advance is likely to be. That alone should be incentive enough for you to create the very best proposal you can.

Thousands of writers each year fail to find a publisher because they write mediocre proposals, even though many of them would have gone on to write successful books. The proposal process must be taken seriously; it's the price of admission to being a published author.

If you want to circumvent the proposal stage, you *can* write your entire manuscript before approaching any publishers. But such a time-consuming effort is speculative and doesn't guarantee your finding a publisher to buy your book. Furthermore, writing a full manuscript without a contract overlooks the chief advantage of being a nonfiction writer: If you write a proposal, you can sell your book and have a portion of the advance in your bank account before you've invested six months to a year of your time writing the manuscript.

The Contents of a Proposal

In a basic sense, a proposal tells a publisher what your book is about, why it should exist, and why you should be the one to write it. It should also explain why the book will be successful.

Through the years, a certain proposal protocol has evolved, and every proposal is expected to follow a roughly prescribed format. Fortunately, it's a reasonable and sensible format that seems to work well for both writer and publisher. Of course, no proposal method is carved in stone. Many successful writers take creative detours with great results. But if you're new at this, it's probably best to start developing good habits by working within the conventional style.

In brief, these are the elements that a proposal is expected to contain:

1. Title page
2. Overview
3. Author background
4. Competition section
5. Markets section
6. Promotions section
7. Chapter outline
8. Sample chapter(s)
9. Collateral attachments (optional, as an addendum to author background)

The sequence of items 3 through 6 is flexible, though if you have a particularly impressive background, you will want to highlight that by bringing it close to the front.

How This Book Works

When you look for a job you need a résumé to get job interviews. You can listen to the experts' rhetoric about the dos and don'ts of creating such a document, but nothing serves better than the books that contain a variety of *real* résumés. These samples clearly reveal each document's successes and failures—you don't have to reinvent the wheel.

This is the concept for this book. A book proposal is to publishing what the résumé is to the job search. By far the very best way for you to learn how to write a book proposal is to see proposals that have succeeded. It's a great advantage for you to see where these proposals were strongest and where they were weakest.

We have selected and critiqued 10 of the finest proposals on a variety of topics that we've had the privilege of working with. Each of the chosen 10 resulted in a publishing contract for the writer. Now you will not have to reinvent the wheel.

In walking through these proposals with us, you'll see a wide variety of formats, aesthetics, and styles of expression. But you'll also see that each of them clearly shows why it deserves to be a book. This exposure to a variety of successful styles will help you eventually to find your own.

Section One provides brief chapters that explain each section of the proposal and also gives advice on other issues you may encounter as a writer. Section Two contains the actual proposals. Some have been shortened to fit in the book. At the end of the book, you will find brief appendices of book proposal terms, suggested reading, and useful web sites.

We welcome all comments about this book and look forward to hearing from you.

Jeff Herman
Deborah Levine Herman
The Jeff Herman Literary Agency, LLC
332 Bleecker Street
Suite G-31
New York, NY 10014
www.JeffHerman.com

All Aspects of the Proposal— And Some Advice Thrown In

CHAPTER 1

The Concept
Shaping Your Idea

A good idea is the foundation for any nonfiction book proposal. It's the intangible product you're trying to sell to a publisher. Good ideas are everywhere. But it takes a keen eye and know-how to shape an idea into a book proposal and ultimately a sale.

Finding Your Hook

What makes an idea good? Innovation and a focused target market give any idea an edge—or hook. Finding a hook is the process of taking a complicated idea and describing it in terms that resemble a "soundbite" teaser for . . . the next Oprah Winfrey show. Your hook is the focal point from which your book proposal can be formed. This hook must be intriguing enough to pull an editor's attention away from your competition.

As you scan the universe for book ideas, you have to find just the right focal point. But your book idea does not have to be entirely original. If you can write a unique or superior treatment of a particular subject, it doesn't matter if there are similar books on the market. If you're confident, innovative, and can meet the competition head on, you might have what it takes to convince a publisher.

The first thing to consider when choosing an idea for your nonfiction book proposal is whether the idea can be expanded into a book. Many ideas can sustain a CNN factoid, but not a 200-plus-page book.

Some ideas can support only a magazine article. Magazines are good places to introduce concepts, but books require much greater depth.

Targeting Your Market vs. Market Saturation

Even if your idea can fill the pages of a book, the key consideration is whether anyone would buy it and read it. If you want commercial success, you must think commercially. The mating habits of obscure sea creatures may appeal to a certain segment of the population, but a book on the subject would not be a hot topic at most dinner parties.

If you want to write for the commercial market, you have to be aware of the possibility of market saturation on any given subject. When you're forming a book idea, you should first research the topic to see what's already out there. Go to a bookstore; go to a library and check *Books in Print,* a periodically updated publication available in book form and CD-ROM that contains extensive listings of books by category.

If there are complementary books but yours can fill a unique and necessary gap, move forward. If you can't find anything that would separate you from the fold, move on to another subject. Don't be overly alarmed about books that are old and not currently being distributed. Many very good books simply have been ahead of their time. If a subject is important enough it can often be cleverly resurrected in an updated format.

If several books in your topic area appear suddenly in the bookstores—from different publishing houses—take this as a good indicator of market saturation. For example, after the first books on codependency appeared on the shelves, we received innumerable book proposals on different aspects of this recovery movement. While there are still territories yet uncharted, we found publishers tired of the subject and reluctant to see anything more.

The Makings of a Good Idea

One way to spot a potentially marketable idea is to be aware of popular trends. But being tuned in to what is happening now is not enough—you have to be able to gauge where the public's interest may be when your book comes out. Nothing is more dated than a time-sensitive idea whose time has passed.

Keep in mind that the publishing industry operates at least six months to a year ahead of the bookshelves. Spotting trends and potential new markets requires an almost visionary quality. You can get around the "I can't stand to hear another word on that topic" syndrome by being creative. If you can distinguish yourself through a new approach to the material, you can still write in a somewhat saturated topic area. Start your own bandwagon; don't wait to jump on someone else's.

Spot trends and then try to stay ahead of them. Spotting trends also requires a good understanding of popular interests. Do not rely solely on the electronic media to reflect trends in the types of books people want to read. One does not necessarily offer an accurate guide to the other.

Popular culture magazines are helpful in seeing developments in the reading public's interests. They are often more immediate and should be included in your research. Even "rag magazines" such as the *National Enquirer* reflect popular taste and are useful for getting a sense of what people find interesting. Some people say the readers of the rags don't buy books. They are discounting the people who read them at the checkout or those who sneak them home so their neighbors don't find out.

Don't forget the Internet. Writers today are fortunate to have such a limitless resource. You can check which books are hot sellers or can check out newsgroups and chat rooms. The Internet offers a tremendous amount of information at your fingertips.

Trips to the library and bookstore will help you, but your greatest wealth of ideas will come from leading your life. Attend workshops and lectures that interest you. Pay attention to the questions people ask and the topics they focus on so you can get a handle on what kinds of books they might need. Look to your own profession and what you know best. If you are passionate about something, you can develop it into a book idea.

Once you find your hook and begin to shape your idea, you need to look at it objectively. If it is a thesis that can be expanded and fleshed out to support an entire book, then review the following questions:

- Why would anyone want to read this book?
- Who is my target audience?
- What is my unique hook in 25 words or less?
- Can the hook support an entire book?
- Will I be telling my readers anything they don't already know?

For example, if you're like most of us, the straight details of your life would not sustain a book. But if you can tell a good story or spin a good yarn, you can certainly liven up your book with entertaining anecdotes. You then need to put your anecdotes into a context that will serve as your hook.

Sharpening Your Focus

To shape an idea into a book proposal, you need to refine and polish it so it can be communicated in a logical fashion. Nonfiction writing is intended to convey information. Do not try to be literary. Concise and readable means that no one has to refer to a dictionary after every paragraph. In nonfiction, there should not be several shades of meaning, as you would find in classic literature. Narrative nonfiction may use creative techniques, but with the exception of examples, the proposal should stick to basic, clear language.

Having a focused idea is imperative. An unfocused idea is one of the main reasons why a book proposal will be rejected. Aside from your hook, you'll need to state your expanded thesis in one concise paragraph.

If you can't convince someone of the book's merit in six lines or less, you need to be more focused. We've seen some exceptionally talented people waylay their careers with unfocused book ideas. Even the best lecturers and speakers in the world can't find a publisher for a bad book. If your idea would only lead to something self-serving or dull, give it up and start again.

You need to be both objective and flexible in the writing business. You need to be tenacious and persistent, but not stubborn. Do not try to force a bad idea into the system. If you become too emotionally attached to an idea, you may not see a better one when it comes along.

Sometimes a book idea has a gestation period of many years before it's ready to be born. Don't give up if some of your efforts never seem to go anywhere. Keep a file of good ideas that need more time to develop. With time, you might acquire the insights or ingredients to make them work. Let the book grow with you as you learn how to package and market yourself.

When you have an idea for a book, you should see where it takes you. Good ideas can have a life of their own when you give them a chance to thrive.

CHAPTER 2

The Title

Creating an Image

Coming up with a title for your work is no trivial matter. A smart title can greatly multiply a book's sales, while a poor title can have the opposite effect.

You might prefer to believe that what truly matters is what's between the pages—and you'd be absolutely right. But when it comes to selling your work, your title has substantial power.

For a demonstration of how important a title is, stroll through your supermarket and pay special attention to the soap and cereal products. A close examination of ingredients and prices will reveal that most of the competing products are remarkably similar. When quality and price are essentially equal, it's title, packaging, and overall image that determine market share. Popular brand names such as Ivory, Tide, and Total were not selected arbitrarily. Companies spend quite a bit of time and money on idea-bouncing, research, and testing to develop titles like these. They work because they trigger a positive image in the consumer's mind. The most successful titles, regardless of the product, bypass the intellect and go straight for the emotions.

That infamous automobile the Ford Edsel, which got its name through nepotism, not merit, was poorly rated by consumers and was short-lived in the marketplace. But even with good ratings, the car's title probably would have doomed it. The name "Edsel" simply doesn't appeal to the imagination.

Guidelines for Nonfiction Titles

Here are some basic guidelines to use when naming your book:

The title should be relevant to your primary thesis. Don't hit the consumer with riddles or incomprehension. When scanning bookstore shelves, the consumer's eyes and mind are moving as quickly as any computer. Your book only has a few seconds to get its foot in the door. Develop a title that will make sense to virtually all English speakers and will state lucidly what the book is about.

There are important exceptions to this guideline, for which there are a variety of explanations, including luck. A prime example is the bestselling career book *What Color Is Your Parachute?* by Richard Bolles. (Initially, skydivers may have thought this one was for them.) A book may succeed in spite of an incongruous title, but it's always smarter for your title to be an asset, not an obstacle. As a general rule, clarity is best.

The title should not contain more than five words. A title with more than five words requires the consumer to start thinking instead of feeling. "What's wrong with that?" you may legitimately ask. Perhaps nothing. It may sometimes even become a big advantage.

But if the choice were ours, we'd go for the gut whenever possible, and leave the brains alone. Once the sale is made and the actual reading begins, the brain will have enough to do. But brains are not what usually spur people to buy things. Why would they? Brains don't even have nerve endings.

You need not feel overly constrained, however. Immediately following your title comes the *subtitle*. Here's your opportunity to elaborate intellectually upon your title. We've seen many successful subtitles go beyond 10 words. And that's fine—because if the consumer makes it to your subtitle, that means your title probably worked.

The suggested five-word limit for the main title isn't a hard-and-fast rule, of course. Many excellent titles are much longer. Some titles, because of the subject, simply have to be longer.

Two successful titles that meet the word-count guideline are *Think and Grow Rich* by Napoleon Hill, and *The Power of Positive Thinking* by Norman Vincent Peale.

An example of an excellent title that seemingly breaks this rule is *How to Win Friends and Influence People* by Dale Carnegie (seven words). However, those first four words pack an emotional wallop and win instant attention. In other words, going beyond five words can work if the first few words provide the emotional grabber.

The title should create a motivating visualization. Studies show that humans think in pictures—our minds translate everything we perceive into pictures. That's why it was never a contest between radio and television. The best communicators (and sometimes the most dangerous) are the ones who can make people *see* and *feel* what they are saying.

You want the consumer to scan your title and visualize your promised message in a favorable way. The book *Sales Power* by José Silva and Ed Bernd Jr. achieves this. Upon scanning that title, a salesperson would probably visualize gaining access to and closing big accounts. Such an image would be a motivating factor to buy the book.

For the same reasons, you have to be careful not to trigger negative or threatening images. For instance, it would have been a big mistake for Silva and Bernd to have titled their book *Stop Losing Sales.* Such a title would likely just evoke the image of the consumer's stomach and head hurting.

Titles for Biographies, Histories, and Exposés

Most of the titles we've used as examples so far are in the how-to/self-help realm. The rules are slightly different for titles in such areas as biography, current affairs, investigative works, and the like—though it doesn't hurt to apply the principles given above. You still want your title to create a dramatic and relevant visualization of the subject. However, impulse sales tend to be less important for books outside of the how-to/self-help categories. Sales for books in these categories are often driven through word of mouth, reviews, advertising, and publicity.

All the President's Men (about Richard Nixon and the Watergate cover-up) by Carl Bernstein and Bob Woodward falls in this category. The authors' timing and credentials couldn't have been better. It happens to be a good title because of the Humpty-Dumpty connection, but in this particular case, the book was not title-dependent. It would have succeeded even with a poor title because the authors were widely known for uncovering the Watergate affair, the subject matter was timely, and the media gave almost obsessive attention to the scandal.

For a biography, a frequently used option is for the title to capture something personal and recognizable about the subject, and then to use the subtitle to identify the person by name. *The Last Lion: Winston Spencer Churchill* is a good example of this kind of title.

Titles for Noncommercial Books (Textbooks and Books for Professionals)

The rules here are much different than for commercial titles. A slick title would probably be unhelpful—perhaps fatal. If you wrote a textbook for freshman physics majors, *Introductory Physics* would be an ideal title. For these books, staid, unprovocative, right-to-the-point titles are preferred. It would be unwise to name such a book *Einstein's Revenge*.

Final Caveat

Be aware that the title you create may not be the title your book ends up with. Publishers virtually always demand final discretion over titles. As the author, you have the right to try to persuade them, but the final decision is theirs. Publishers figure it's their job to know what works, and they legitimately assert that if they have to sell the book, they should get to name it. But don't fret; they—and their savvy marketing staff—often come up with titles that sharpen a book's focus and boost its sales.

CHAPTER 3

The Overview

Writing Power Paragraphs

Almost every editor at every publishing house has a stack of book proposals or manuscripts waiting to be reviewed at any given time. If you start your proposal with a powerful statement, you can distinguish yourself from the pack.

The overview portion of your proposal is—or should be—that powerful statement. The overview is your first opportunity to grab an editor's attention and presell your idea. This first impression will strongly influence the potential for an ultimate sale.

The overview should convey these four major points:

1. What your book is about,
2. Why your book should be written,
3. How you plan to write it,
4. Why you are the best person for the job.

Leading with Your Best Shot

Writers are sometimes too close to their project to be objective about its presentation. They assume that an editor will read between the lines and see how great their book is going to be. Don't conserve your energy here in order to save the "important stuff" for the outline or the sample chapter. The overview can open—or close—the door for you.

In general, the overview should contain a synopsis of your proposed book as well as any persuasive material that supports your case. It's a sales tool much like a prospectus. View it as your opportunity to have five minutes of a publisher's undivided attention. If you had just five minutes face to face with a publisher, what would you say?

Your lead paragraph is important. There are many possibilities for a powerful lead paragraph that will catch an editor's attention. But powerful does not necessarily mean fancy, creative, or clever. In nonfiction, you are not trying to impress an editor with your mastery of five-syllable words or metaphoric didacticism. You are trying to communicate information.

If your book calls for it, you can use some of the same techniques you'd use in writing a magazine article:

- An anecdotal lead—one that tells a story leading into your book idea,
- A startling statistic that would support your thesis,
- A clear and concise statement of exactly what your book is about.

The last approach is usually the safest and most effective. If you haven't said what your book is about by the third paragraph, you're pushing your luck and trying the editor's patience.

Using Powerful Techniques of Structure and Style

Think of each paragraph in your overview as a sound bite of information. Each should be short and to the point, while conveying only one idea at a time.

Your first paragraph should be your strongest, with each subsequent paragraph supporting your case.

The length of an overview can vary from 2 pages to 10 or even more. It depends on the complexity of your subject. If your writing is tight, persuasive, and well thought out, detail will be an advantage at this stage of your presentation. If you tend to ramble and repeat pertinent points, then edit your material down to a shortened version.

If you cover the basics, you can still be creative in your overview. Where appropriate, include examples and anecdotes so the agent or publisher will get an immediate sense of your voice. You don't want to tell what you are going to do without also showing how it will be executed.

Do not pontificate. Impress the editor with what you have to say and how well you say it, but do not include extraneous information intended only to impress. This usually conveys an image of amateurism and will dilute your effectiveness.

Take risks. Some overviews are so understated that they don't do their job of enticing the editor to read more. When you've found a strong hook for your book proposal, you should make every statement in your overview reflect the strength of your idea and the confidence you have in your ability to carry out the task.

Do not be boring. No matter what your subject matter, you must find a way to make it appealing. If your writing shows a total lack of passion, why on earth would anyone else develop any enthusiasm for it?

Do not be grandiose. Agents and editors see so much material that puffery is not going to impress them. Find a good balance of effective writing, persuasion, and appropriate confidence.

After you write your first draft, put it aside for a while. Then look at it again and see if there's any way you can turn up the volume.

Some final points: Always choose active over passive voice in your proposal writing, and never say anything negative about yourself or your idea. You can't turn a bad idea into something it is not, but you can make sure a good idea gets noticed.

CHAPTER 4

The Markets Section

Who Will Buy Your Book?

We know you want to write the book. But do we know who will buy it? In the markets section, you will answer this question by justifying your proposed book's commercial existence.

For example, if you're proposing a sales book, you'd want to present documented data about the number of Americans who earn all or part of their income through sales, and cite available figures pertaining to any expected growth in these numbers.

It's best to present this information in a visually accessible way, such as using bullets (■) to highlight each point. Remember, a book proposal is similar to a sophisticated sales brochure. The most effective way to communicate important information is to make it as easy as possible for the editor to absorb it without diminishing its substance. The more arduous it is to read something, the less useful it is as an efficient sales tool—even if the document contains important facts.

If you don't already know everything about your market, several sources can provide up-to-date and comprehensive data. Many public and university libraries have reams of government data on file, such as the latest U.S. census results. University research studies, private polling organizations, and industry trade associations are excellent sources for recent facts. You are expected to be an expert on your subject, so investing in extra research will not be a waste of time. The additional knowledge will likely be helpful when you begin writing the book.

Some subjects require a more extensive markets section than others. For instance, business-oriented editors should already know about the market demographics for sales books. If you're proposing a sales book, your markets section will be more like protocol than revelation to a knowledgeable editor (though you should always present it as if your editor knows nothing). But if you're proposing a book in a more obscure or arcane subject area, you'll be expected to go to greater pains to prove that a sufficient market base exists for your project.

It is rare, if ever, that the markets section alone will carry or demolish the entire proposal. But there are definitely ways that it can either enhance or diminish the proposal's effectiveness.

Some potential enhancers:
- Presenting strong visuals that make it easy for an editor to glean and comprehend the facts.
- Liberally using genuine facts that are relevant to your subject and help support your expertise.
- Presenting relevant facts that even an expert editor may not know—and suggesting several potential secondary markets.
- Describing professional societies or trade associations that underscore the numbers and vibrancy of your targeted market(s).
- Showing an overall sensitivity to the fact that your book needs and will have your commitment to earn its existence and make it successful.

Some common diminishers:
- Claiming that your friends and relatives all love the idea. When pitching your work to editors (and agents), pretend that you're a product of spontaneous birth of unknown origin. You have no relatives, no friends, and no literate pets.
- Making improbable or irrelevant claims. Doing so will damage your credibility.
- Sweeping, unfocused generalities. Most editors know that there are more than 50 million adult women in America—but few if any know how many buy drugs to treat PMS.
- Failing to address the obvious competition. If you do this, you may appear to be a charlatan, sloppy, or both.
- Making stuff up. It's too easy to get caught—and it's not a nice thing to do anyway.

In the end, you want the editor to feel secure that your book won't end up overstaying its welcome in the publisher's warehouse. The markets section of your proposal establishes who will potentially buy your book. It is a realistic assessment of natural markets that flow from your thesis. It reflects what direction your book will take regardless of how you and/or the publisher plan to promote it.

The markets section is often blended into the promotion section. However, we have found that it gives greater clarity to separate markets and promotion as a matter of focus. In "Markets" you are strictly describing to whom you are writing. You are painting a clear picture of why the book should exist.

In the promotion section we will show you how to develop an overall strategy to bring your book to the marketplace. Therefore we are renaming what has often been referred to as marketing, as simply "markets." "Marketing" connotes strategy. We want you to think in terms of marketing and what you can do to sell, sell, and sell. But you will have plenty of room to explain your marketing ideas under "Promotion."

CHAPTER 5

The Competition Section
What Else Is Out There?

Many excellent manuscripts are never published simply because there are too many other books like them already in print. Some writers become intimidated by similar books in the marketplace and give up on their idea. Others present their ideas without distinguishing them from what is already out there and are dismissed by agents or editors as being nothing new. There is nothing truly new if you think about it philosophically. However, what is new is how you approach a subject and present it. "Great minds think alike." If you have an idea, it's safe to assume that many others have had it, have it now, and will have it soon enough. Only a fraction of those who think of it will attempt to turn it into a book. But you are fortunate. You are reading this book. If you have a completed manuscript, by researching the competition you can cut your losses and redraft/reposition your manuscript according to what the market will bear.

If you are writing a proposal from an idea alone, you can

- Make an assessment of the viability of your idea.
- Determine how to turn competition into an opportunity to persuade.

In the competition section of a book proposal, you can acknowledge the books that are most similar to yours, and then show how yours will distinguish itself in the marketplace. Like a zealous lawyer, you will plead your case showing precisely why existing books on the subject:

- Complement yours,
- Show there is a market,
- Don't actually compete at all.

Step 1: Make Sure You're Familiar with the Competition

There is a good chance your editor knows about the competition. If not, he or she soon will. Editors won't acquire a book before doing their own basic research. If the editor discovers that you've omitted some key titles, your expertise and credibility may become suspect.

Also, by knowing the competition, you'll be better able to navigate around it and create your own unique identity. Editors are quickly turned off by an approach that has been sung by too many others too many times and too many places before. The editor wants to be the last one to the party. Their careers depend on carefully selecting books that can make an impact in the marketplace. A recycled idea may only be able to collect the crumbs of those who got there first.

Take us as an example. We wanted to write a book about proposal writing (you're reading it). But we knew it wouldn't be wise to employ the same instructional formulas that others have already published. After some thought we stumbled upon a fresh twist that everyone else missed. The competing proposal books are rich in theory but poor in example. We've always felt that the best way to learn is by example, not commentary. Using the wide array of sample résumé books as our model, we developed and proposed a parallel concept for this book: lots of real and successful sample proposals, supplemented by our critiques and essays.

In other words, while we entered a relatively crowded category, books for writers—a situation that our research confirmed—we came up with a concept that had no competition because there was and still is nothing else like it. We emphasized this strongly in the competition section of our own proposal.

When you begin the process of refining your idea in light of the competition, you always look first to what you have to say. A book must always start with its own central point. Never try to write a book to fit a gap in the market unless it is something that reflects your own passion. That said, look at your idea and determine how to present it in an innovative way. The competition section of your proposal is an opportunity to persuade. Keep it concise, but treat it with respect.

If you're unfamiliar with and uncertain about the competing titles in your area, there are several ways you can fill that gap:

- Ask your local bookseller. Don't ask a clerk; ask the person who actually runs the store and orders the inventory. Browse.
- Ask your librarian.
- Check *Books in Print,* a periodically updated publication available in most libraries as well as many bookstores that has extensive listings according to category.
- Check on-line booksellers.

Step Two: Using the Competition Section to Persuade in Your Favor

If many successful competitive titles are in print, that means there's a healthy book-buying market for the subject. Frequently, once a lucrative market segment is discovered, publishers will step all over each other to throw books at it. This practice will often oversaturate the market's ability to reasonably absorb everything that's being published, and many titles will fail. Eventually things will settle down, and supply and demand will become more synchronized.

Sales books are a good example of an ongoing lucrative market. There have been some big books that generated a sales-book feeding frenzy, but the market seems to have settled into a very steady pace. If you're proposing a sales book, for example, you'll want to mention a few successful titles that are a most similar—and state the primary factors that distinguish your proposed book from those titles. Then emphasize that the impressive ongoing success of the sales category shows a vibrant demand for these books, and that it's prudent for publishers to continue to introduce new and innovative products for this market—which is what your book will do.

Don't overwhelm your editor or agent by listing everything that's in print. Many books in print are effectively dead as far as sales activity is concerned. In addition, it would be wasteful to discuss obscure or unsuccessful titles, since (a) they're really not competitive, and (b) if they're unsuccessful, you may end up condemning the marketability of your entire category. Instead, concentrate on two to six of the most successful and visible tides.

Step Three: Directly Confront a Lack of Competition

Be very careful. There are many subjects for which the book-buying market is exceptionally specialized (e.g., horse breeding, managing mortuaries). If there is no competition, you don't want to leave the impression that there is no market. Instead, you want to make the editor think there is a sizeable *untapped* market out there that nobody has yet had the foresight to service. And by acquiring your book, the publisher will now have exclusive access to it. (Incidentally, there is a decent market for books on both horse breeding and mortuary science. But most of these titles are not sold in traditional bookstore outlets. If the kind of book you wish to write falls into a less commercial category like this, you'll have to seek out a specialty publisher.) By the way, if you do not find any books on your subject, you should be aware that there could be a good reason. Maybe no one wants to or will ever want to read a book on the subject. Never be afraid to return to the drawing board. Many of the most successful writers have come up with ideas that seemed very good to them at the time, but nevertheless had to be scrapped.

Remember that you want the competition section to reinforce what is special about your book, and create the image that your project will have its own place in the sun regardless of how crowded the category may seem to be.

A few final thoughts:

- Keep your competition section concise; three to six titles should be enough.
- Never sound catty. It is not to your benefit to distinguish competition by saying the writer of a book is a no-talent nincompoop. Nor is it wise to say anything about a competitive book's lack of quality (i.e., it stinks).
- To describe a book you feel lacks the quality of your own, use such phrases as "lacks detail," "not comprehensive," "difficult for the average reader to understand," or whatever you feel you must say to get it off your chest.
- You can better distinguish your book by talking about its positive aspects and what it has to offer the reader. A positive statement is always more persuasive than a negative statement about another book. You don't want to sound apologetic or defensive. Because a book exists that is similar to yours does not mean your book can't find a successful niche. As long as there are readers, there will be a need for new books. And all subjects can be considered from many perspectives.
- Be confident but not grandiose. Never make statements implying that there is no competition because no one has ever been as brilliant as you.

CHAPTER 6

The Promotion Section

What Can You Do to Help Your Book Sell?

The promotion section of a book proposal is the most difficult to assign a precise definition because it is where you can be the most creative. If you do it well, it can push your book over the top. Publishers think in terms of numbers and what you bring to the table.

The promotion section is where you state ways to promote the book upon publication. In practice, publishers tend to do very little to promote the majority of the titles they publish. You are free to offer a rational wish list (including getting on *Oprah*), but this is not going to catch a publisher's eye, unless, of course, you are already a regular guest or are a celebrity in your own right.

However, there are at least two ways to make this section go beyond pie-in-the-sky filler.

Specifying What You Can and Will Do

If you plan to use the book as a marketing vehicle to promote you, your company, and/or your cause, and you've got your own substantial budget to do it, then this section may be the most important part of the proposal.

It's not uncommon for businesspeople to buy themselves onto the best-seller list by hiring a public relations firm, buying ads, networking with powerful people, or buying a large number of copies of their book to either give away or resell at public appearances. If you are one of these people, then the promotion section should be a detailed and extensive plan that leaves nothing out. Of course, you'll be expected to promise all this in writing as part of your contract; but you'll be able to leverage an above-average advance. While mainstream publishers shy away from obvious vanity deals, they're attracted like bees to honey to authors who have the wallets and egos to virtually guarantee their publisher a sizable profit for editing, printing, and distributing the book.

Here are some other examples of efforts, less grandiose than the previous approach, that you can list in this section:

- If you're a public speaker, perhaps you can sell a significant number of autographed books at your events. State approximately how many events you do a year and what the average attendance is. If you've sold a large number of other books you've authored, you'll want to state how many.
- If the media frequently interview you for your expertise, you can probably get your book mentioned much of the time, perhaps even displayed on camera. List many of the important broadcast and print interviews you've had during the past year, and emphasize that these valuable contacts can be capitalized on once the book is published.
- If you're well connected and can get prominent people and celebrities to endorse and help promote your book, list them in this section.

Creating Innovative Ideas That You Can Help Implement

Any mortal can suggest a 10-city media tour, to which your editor will usually respond, "Uh-huh," while thinking, "Fat chance, Charlie." Your challenge is to go beyond the usual and give the promotion section genuine teeth. Fortunately, you can pull this off even if you have limited resources.

To get your juices flowing, here's what other writers have done in their promotion sections (always be careful to distinguish your suggestions from binding commitments that you're prepared to have inserted into your contract).

- Organize a contest relevant to the book.
- Call up all the bookstores within a 100-mile radius of your home and persuade (beg?) them to stock your book. If you succeed, expand the radius another 100 miles.

- Persuade large corporations to buy your books for their employees or to use as giveaways to potential clients.
- Promise to get yourself booked on radio interviews (by telephone) across the country.

The possibilities of what you can do are endless. Showing determination here may impress publishers. They appreciate authors who'll work to sell copies—as opposed to those who only complain about the publisher's promotional deficiencies. Research the Internet. Every day there are new opportunities for access to your carefully selected market and secondary markets. Locate web sites that could review or sell your book. List any relevant sales or places where your book could gain attention.

If your subject lends itself to this, try to become connected with appropriate web sites or create your own. Cross-promote with writers or organizations with similar interests and audiences. List what you find in this section.

If you have the resources, one of the best things you can do is hire a publicist. There are many levels of financial commitment. At minimum, you will learn many things about book promotion. You can also develop valuable contacts along the way. Don't forget to list that you have a publicist.

Read our book *Make It Big Writing Books* to learn many ways that top-selling authors have creatively promoted their books as well as promotion ideas from top book publicists.

The promotion section of your book proposal will build confidence in the potential for your book. A solid promotion section automatically builds a perspective of you as a hardworking, professional team player.

Publishing houses allocate only limited resources toward book publicity. There is a disproportionate allocation toward books they perceive as "big hits." Most books start out in the so-called middle range. However, by being creative in your promotion section, you not only persuade the agent or editor to consider your book a good risk, you also create a blueprint for how you will make your book a success once it finds its way to print.

CHAPTER 7

The Author Background Section

Presenting Yourself in Your Best Light

In the author background section, you will state why you are qualified to write the proposed book. Without reservation or modesty, you should reveal everything that reflects affirmatively upon you as an expert, a writer, a promoter, and a human being.

How Impressive Is Your Profession?

As with other aspects of the proposal, the importance of this section depends upon your subject. For instance, if you're proposing a business book, it's important to note your professional accomplishments, whereas if you're proposing a lighthearted trivia-type book, the fact that you're breathing may be enough. In all cases, you should list any writing experience you have—even if it was just garage-sale reviews for your local *Pennysaver.*

For many nonfiction subjects, having relevant professional credentials is the most important consideration. Publishers usually prefer to have M.D.'s author medical/health books and Ph.D.'s author certain self-help psychology titles, for instance.

Even if it's not directly relevant, it's generally a good idea to list your career experience. That's one way to say a little bit about who you are as a person. Obviously, if you have an exceptional background or are a celebrity, you can use this to leverage a significantly higher advance.

If Your Background Is Undistinguished

As with the example of the trivia book, in this case what you can write is more important than where you've been. Simply say whatever there is to say about yourself without seeming defensive or embarrassed. Even if you have never been published, if you are submitting a book proposal with a well-thought-out idea and good execution, you are a writer. Be confident and don't whine about anything, ever. Find a balance between egotism and saint-like humility.

Sometimes explaining your passion for a subject might be enough. However, if you're proposing a book about a subject that usually requires professional expertise, you'll be at a disadvantage. Your burden will be to prove that you have the requisite knowledge. Compensations include (a) a strong proposal and sample chapter(s), (b) strong promotability, or (c) getting someone with the relevant credentials to be your co-author.

Additional Materials

In addition to the author background section, there are various self-promotional materials that you may attach to the front or back of the proposal. These include:

- A formal résumé,
- Writing samples from magazines or newspapers,
- Publicity about yourself,
- Your corporate or self-promotional materials,
- Reviews or publicity about previous books.

The author background section can add favorably to the viability of you proposed book, but do not let it intimidate you. See how other authors have handled it, and use it as yet another opportunity to persuade. Anyone can find something positive to say about him- or herself.

CHAPTER 8

The Outline

Getting It Organized and Making It Persuade

Many nonfiction writers make the mistake of putting all of their energy into the prospectus portion of their book proposal package, and paying little attention to the chapter-by-chapter outline. The outline is as important as anything you will submit to a publisher—if not more so.

In fact, if you begin your process with a well-drafted outline, your entire book proposal is likely to be more focused and of higher quality than if you write the outline last. A chapter-by-chapter outline gives you the opportunity to iron out any bugs in your thesis and serves as a blueprint for the eventual writing of your book.

Tailoring the Table of Contents

When you write your chapter-by-chapter outline, begin with the table of contents. You need to focus some intense creative energy on mapping out your strategy. You can expect 10 to 12 separate chapters for a typical nonfiction book. This number will, of course, vary according to your topic, the level of complexity, and your book format.

If this is your first table of contents, you'll want to find a secluded spot away from distractions, and you'll need plenty of paper for rough drafts. You may want to prime your creativity pump by jotting down chapter topic possibilities before you try to put them into any particular order. Some people write chapter topics on 3" × 5" index cards so they can arrange and rearrange them until they find the most logical order.

Logic is the key to a good table of contents. The prospective editor must be able to visualize your book from a skeletal listing of chapter headings. One topic needs to progress logically to the next so the editor can see that your book will be well executed and complete.

When choosing chapter tides, keep in mind that clever is nice, but clear is better. If your inner muse cannot stand anything less than a quotable phrase for your chapter title, subheadings can help keep your table of contents on track. Make sure to keep both chapter titles and subheadings simple and relatively short.

Writing Chapter Abstracts

After you complete your table of contents, you can move ahead to your outline. If you plan to write a sample chapter, you need not write an abstract of that particular chapter as well. To keep your outline in proper order, do indicate that the sample is included.

The chapter-by-chapter outline consists of *abstracts* or *synopses* of each chapter. The level of detail should vary according to the complexity of your subject, but it's always best to include more rather than less.

The typical length for each chapter abstract is two pages or less. If you make each paragraph count, there's no need to make it any longer. A book proposal is intended to be considerably shorter than a completed manuscript. If you include too much material, it may become counterproductive, given the typical editor's limited time. Remember that this is only a rule of thumb. If your book is complex and requires more explanation, do not skimp simply to stay within these general standards.

A chapter abstract is an opportunity to show what you can do without having to do it all. It should be written in the best possible prose, with an eye toward holding a reader's interest.

You can view abstracts as mini-chapters or magazine articles. The most effective contain some substance while explaining what the chapter will include.

It is much less effective to show only what you intend to do without being specific. If handled correctly, a chapter-by-chapter outline shows an editor that you can follow through with some solid writing.

Sample book proposal Number 9, *Heart and Soul* (page 170), is one of our favorite examples of what a chapter-by-chapter outline can be. The author has included the right mix of projected intentions, good writing, and solid content. The abstracts are interesting to read, well thought out, and substantial. They're not too long, but they don't skimp in any way.

If you put enough effort into your chapter-by-chapter outline, you could eliminate the need for a sample chapter. However, the reverse is not true: A sample chapter never offsets the need for an outline.

Remember that an acquisitions editor makes a decision to purchase your book or not based on what you present. It's best for both of you if there are no major surprises down the road. Stingy abstracts leave too many unanswered questions. You don't want to make promises you can't keep, and an editor doesn't want to take a chance on you only to find out you can't deliver.

Starting with what could be the beginning of the actual chapter is a good structural idea for an abstract. You might want to include anecdotes where appropriate and other samplings of your writing style to be more persuasive.

The tricky aspect of an abstract in a book proposal is to make it more than just a condensed piece of the chapter. It's an opportunity for you to continue selling your idea. This is your chance to shine. You have the editor's attention. You do not want to waste any opportunity to show what you can do.

Faith may be important to the quality of your life, but you shouldn't rely solely on faith to secure a book contract. Even the most worthy writers have to sweat. If you take the time to write a complete, organized, and focused outline, you will maximize your chances for a sale.

CHAPTER 9

The Sample Chapter
Proving You Can Do the Job

Understanding an editor's point of view on book acquisition can help you see why a sample chapter is so important. It's one more ingredient the editor can assess to confirm that purchasing your book is a sound business decision.

Would you want to spend someone else's money on you? Acquisitions editors are given the authority to spend someone else's money. Would you want to do that on someone's word alone?

A sample chapter is considered an addendum to a book proposal, but you should never view it as an afterthought. A good sample chapter gives you an important opportunity to further persuade an editor and to sell your idea. It proves that you can deliver and shows how your idea will translate into a book.

Show the best you can do. Writing a good sample chapter requires that you incorporate all of your best writing techniques. Your chapter must be well organized and well written. In fact, it should be the very best you can do. About 20 to 30 double-spaced pages is standard, but this will vary according to your subject.

Treat the sample chapter like a magazine article with a beginning, a middle, and an end. Make it your best work by taking your time and by polishing it as much as possible.

We can't stress enough how important it is to invest your time and energy into developing a good sample chapter. Your book proposal will help you hook an editor, but a good sample chapter will help you reel that editor in.

A good sample chapter will also increase your chances for a more sizable advance. You are going to have to write a chapter eventually—so why not make it work for you?

CHAPTER 10

What About Fiction?

The Art and Science of Selling Fiction

Fiction and nonfiction work in very different ways. Publishers generally require that most or all of a fiction manuscript be written, or else they won't even consider reading it. This is especially true if you've never had a work of fiction published before.

Unlike nonfiction, fiction requires total upfront speculation by the writer. And the odds that you'll ever get the book published are scary. Nevertheless, countless people invest countless hours and many sleepless nights writing their fiction manuscripts. (If you're reading this chapter, you're probably one of those noble people, or may soon become one.)

Intellectually, these people probably are aware of the tough reality of trying to sell fiction. Fortunately, that knowledge doesn't extinguish their bold efforts. Almost every day, a new novel by a new writer is discovered and scheduled for publication.

Strategies for Selling Your Fiction

Once you have the manuscript finished, it's time to begin the journey to publication. As a first step, you should try to get an agent. A good agent will get your work the necessary access to editors, which is difficult to achieve without an agent. Access won't ensure publication, but nonaccess will ensure nonpublication.

There are many ways to get an agent for fiction. Most agents would like you to follow the protocol of initiating contact by submitting a one-page query letter with a two- to five-page story synopsis. Don't forget to include the self-addressed stamped envelope.

See chapter 12 on query letters for solid advice about this important step. The synopsis can be organized by chapter or just as an integrated overview. It should serve to capture your entire story in an exceptionally readable, enticing, and lucid style. You want to motivate the agent to request to see some or all of your manuscript.

This synopsis is important because most agents don't want to receive unsolicited manuscripts or chapters. They want control of what comes into their offices—many hefty manuscripts arriving at once can quickly take over office space. An agent once said that if you put two or more manuscripts next to each other, they'll breed like rabbits.

If you decide to (or maybe have to) sell your fiction to a publisher without the benefits of an agent, it would be wise to follow the same protocol. Send your query letter and synopsis to editors first. Unsolicited manuscripts sent to editors are likely to end up in the "slush" room, which can be a lot like being blasted into outer space without a spaceship. *The Writer's Guide to Book Editors, Publishers and Literary Agents* by Jeff Herman can help you locate the appropriate agents and editors for your book.

Other details to keep in mind:

- Use attractive, customized stationery, as opposed to unappealing computer paper.
- Personalize *all* correspondence so that your letter does not resemble junk mail.
- Use a good printer. The better it looks, the better you took.
- Send only manuscripts that are double-spaced and in good physical condition.

If you have won any fiction awards or have published any fiction, you can put together a mini–book proposal. This proposal can list your publications as well as your training. If your education is relevant, such as a degree in creative writing, or if you teach in this area, include this information.

If your background is exceptional and even peripherally related to your novel, include information about it in your miniproposal. For example, a coroner might be able to write an interesting crime novel. An insider in any out-of-the-ordinary circumstance can use his or her experience as a backdrop for a compelling work of fiction.

If you have a publishing track record in fiction or nonfiction, list it. If the numbers of books sold are impressive, list the statistics. If you have a unique plan for book promotion, explain it.

Even fiction writers can taper the advantages of a book proposal to suit their needs. Keep it short and simple, and do not use it instead of a good synopsis. Your synopsis, other than being a plot summary, is what will entice an editor or agent to want to read more. Keep it interesting, and don't hold back any surprises so you "don't ruin it for them." Giving away an ending is a good thing in fiction synopses, but still a bad thing to do to your friends.

CHAPTER 11

Writing Memoir and Narrative Nonfiction

Memoir and narrative nonfiction fall into a different category when it comes to a book proposal. Memoir is based on truth and one's life story and is highly dependent on quality of writing. Memoir writing is exciting for new writers and is often the reason they become writers in the first place. We all view our lives in the form of chapters. Each event unfolds in front of us and intertwines with our recognition and consciousness.

As we experience and survive our personal journeys, we want to share what we have learned. Some of us can do this effectively. Others of us may be legends in our own minds. No matter; even a dull life can be the stuff of which great memoirs are made if the storytelling is compelling enough. In contrast, the most exciting lives can be rendered impotent if the writing falls flat.

In approaching memoir, you must consider the techniques of any work of fiction. Even if you are talking about yourself, you must remember to develop your character, set the scene, and put your story into some kind of context. You can write in the first person, but you need to use creativity to tell your story in a way that will transport and engage your reader. Do not ramble, but rather create a logical progression of facts.

Many memoirs try to capture details of one's life that are simply not relevant to the pacing of the story. You can provide more detail than you might if you were telling a story at a gathering of impatient relatives. However, when writing a memoir, you are the one in control of the story. You can choose what details to add and leave out, You can edit your story without leaving out the pertinent facts that will explain why your story should be written in the first place. If you leave in every little detail, you will bore yourself to death before you ever have the opportunity to bore your reader, editor, or agent.

When you write memoir, think in terms of every detail you select having some purpose in moving the story ahead. If you include some fact, as in a good mystery, make sure you tie it in somewhere so it has meaning. Make sure it is relevant to something that breathes life into your story. Truth is truth, but memoir is in the eye of the writer. You can be creative and remain true to fact.

Narrative nonfiction is similar to memoir in that it puts fact in a context of fictional technique. A common example of this is true crime novels. There are many other examples of what is also known as literary journalism or faction. When this technique was introduced in such classic books as *In Cold Blood* by Truman Capote, it garnered much controversy. Those who are journalistic purists could not abide any form of perceived fabrication. Truman Capote was not present at the murders he wrote about in his book, so how could his descriptions from inside the minds of his characters be true? He created vivid dialogue and suspense. He drew his reader right inside the mind of a killer.

Narrative nonfiction allows the writer this license. Based on research and calculated suppositions, the writer can set the scene and use fictional techniques to bring the story to life. There are ethical considerations and limits. It is not considered appropriate to completely fabricate things. It is appropriate, however, to extrapolate a version of the truth based on available facts. To fictionalize something is to take its basic foundation and fill in what are still remaining gaps. A caveat must be made regarding whether the writer added facts that are not supported by any possible research.

Essays are narrative nonfiction. Humor could fall into this category as well. The most important aspect of narrative nonfiction is the voice. The writer connects directly with the reader. The prose does not simply convey information. It creates an experience. This experience is both emotional and intellectual.

Well, now that you know what memoir and narrative nonfiction are, how do you go about creating a book proposal format that will adequately convey what your book is? A book proposal for memoir or narrative nonfiction is the same as that for any other nonfiction book proposal, with the exception that it must convey the viability of the writing technique. The writing is more important than in a book that is topic-dependent because it is the writing that will sell the book to the readers.

If you are writing memoir, you will need to include in your overview a synopsis of the events that you believe warrant a book. What is it about your life that other people would want to read? Excerpt your style or a few key anecdotes. If your life has been visible, you are notorious, or you are a celebrity, you can write a proposal without having a completed manuscript. If your life experiences have been so unusual as to capture most people's imagination, you might not need an entire manuscript, but you will still need some solid sample chapters. If you are like most of us, you might want a completed manuscript available to back up your proposal upon request. We still recommend a proposal as opposed to a manuscript submission, as it is easier to handle. But if there is interest in your story, a publisher or agent might want to see the entire book before making a commitment.

Follow the standard format for proposals, steering away from global statements of comparison. A memoir stands alone. You can use some examples of successful memoirs, but because the books are so writing-dependent, it will not be as imperative for you to evaluate competition. If your memoir fits within a certain category such as recovery from a difficult disease or something of that nature, use this fact as a context or hook. You can then build your proposal around the hook, as opposed to relying solely on your writing.

In the matter of true crime, the proposal format you choose should include media clippings of the case. A case needs to be highly visible to sustain a book about it. Even the most notorious cases will not warrant a book unless the clever writer can make the execution of the story both interesting and compelling. If the reader does not care about the victim or perpetrator, he or she is not likely to buy or read the book. In evaluating true crime, the editor and agent will consider the visibility of the crime, how much attention it has received, if there are any unusual twists or a unique hook, and how well the writer has conveyed the story. A true crime book is like a good psychological thriller or mystery novel. It has to have a pacing that will sustain the reader's interest.

True crime proposals should follow the format of any other nonfiction book. In the author bio section you will want to fully explain your connection to the case, your access to information, and any relevant background.

Sample chapters are important, as in other book proposals where the topics do not immediately lend themselves to clear description.

We do not have an example of a book proposal that would fit the format of either memoir or narrative nonfiction. However, with the samples you have and the tools we have provided, you can create a format to fit your book. A book proposal is a living sales brochure. It does not contain boilerplate that you should substitute from one book proposal to another. You should consider your book carefully when working through the outline of the standard proposal. Taper your proposal to meet the questions the prospective editor and agent might have about this type of book.

You will need to show them the quality of the writing, the basis of your research, or the context of your life from which you are drawing your stories. You need to show how you plan to execute the book through a chapter outline, you need to show there is a market for your book, you need a plan of promotion, and you will need some sample material. Your job is to capture the imagination and the interest of your reader. Your voice is the key, and you need to be sure it is developed enough to meet the challenge. Be creative and incorporate suitable guidelines, and your proposal will be solid and effective.

CHAPTER 12

Query Letters, Submissions, and Sage Advice

Writers typically are immediate people. When we are pumped up about an idea, we want to pitch it to someone. However, as you have surmised, there is a protocol to follow in submitting your proposal or manuscript to agents and publishers. Our first piece of advice is to always have your proposal ready to go before you submit the concept to anyone. You don't need to be paranoid; no one will steal your idea. The book biz is not like Hollywood. You want your proposal ready because you may surprise yourself and pique someone's interest with your query letter. If you use the right technique, an editor or agent will read your query and request your proposal, and if it's not ready, you will miss an excellent opportunity to take your project to the next level.

By the way, don't even think about pitching a book by phone. Editors and agents will not consider a phone pitch. Aside from the inconvenience and intrusion into our workday, we do not want to be the sounding board for someone's undeveloped idea.

The first step in your submission process is the query letter. This is your opportunity to open the door to further consideration. It should be concise, one to two pages, and well written. The purpose of this letter is to entice the reader to want to see more. A query can be considered preselling your proposal to a prospective buyer. If an agent or publisher requests your proposal from your query, you know there is something in your hook that resonates positively.

Once you've mastered the nonfiction book proposal, you need to learn the vital skill of preparing the perfect query letter. The query is a short letter of introduction to a publisher or agent enticing him or her to want to see your proposal.

If you don't have an agent, you're going to have to develop a strategy to get a good one. If you want to go directly to the publishing houses, you still need to know how to get your foot through the door and your proposal on the right person's desk. A well-crafted query letter can help you leap over this first major hurdle on your way to a sale.

You can skip the query letter and boldly send an unsolicited (unrequested) book proposal to an agent or publishing house. However, you should still use the same techniques for an effective cover letter to include with your package. Keep in mind that your objective is to convince the recipient that your proposal will be worth the time it will take to read it and that you are professional, credible, and worthy of serious consideration as an author. If you submit a proposal without a query, your cover letter will give you an opportunity to persuade.

Before reading this book, you might have experienced a series of rejections in your effort to find either an agent or publisher. The problem may be in your approach, not your idea. Do not make the same mistake some writers have made of starting their query letters with "I'm tired of these people not wanting to see what I write . . ." or, "All these other agents/publishers have rejected me, but I know you will be different." If you were an agent or a publisher, would you want to take a chance on someone everyone else has rejected? Contrary to popular belief, agents and publishers have been known to give breaks to writers who might be considered long shots. Some of us do have hearts and can spot talent. But we are also human and not typically masochists. It's not good psychology to begin a query with antagonism or whining.

Think of your query as an advertisement. You want to make a sale and have limited space and time in which to do it. If you concentrate on a clear and to-the-point presentation of approximately one to two pages, you'll increase your chances of being taken seriously.

The goal of your query letter is to pique the interest of an editor who has very little time and probably very little patience. You want to entice him or her to ask for more.

The Query Package

You can put together what is called a query package. It should include your query letter, a short résumé, and media clippings or other favorable documents. Do not get carried away. Photographs of your children and pets or certificates of merit from local writing contests should not be included. Don't waste space in your query describing all of your supporting materials.

You can state at the bottom of your letter that there are enclosures or refer to them in a general sense in your introductory material. For example: "Enclosed are some supporting materials."

Include a self-addressed stamped envelope (SASE) with enough postage to return your entire package. This will be particularly appreciated by smaller publishing houses and independent agents.

Query/cover letters follow a simple format that can be reworked according to your individual preferences:

1. Lead,
2. Supporting material/persuasion,
3. Biography,
4. Conclusion/pitch.

Your Lead Is Your Hook

The lead paragraph in your query letter can either catch an editor's attention or turn her or him off completely. Writers sometimes mistakenly think that they have to do something dramatic to get someone's attention in a short space. If you're clever enough (do not take this as a challenge), a creative lead can be impressive, but it's safer to opt for clearly conveying thoroughly developed ideas. Get right to the point. The recipient of your letter shouldn't get the impression that you slaved over every word. That person really just wants to know why you're writing and what you have to offer.

Do not play it so safe, though, that you appear boring, stuffy, and factual. Determine what is most important about the book you're trying to sell and put this hook front and center.

The journalistic inverted pyramid is a good technique for a query letter. You begin with your strongest material and back it up with details in the subsequent paragraphs. It generally works better than beginning your letter slowly and picking up momentum as you go along.

Some possibilities for your lead paragraph are: using an anecdote; making a statement of fact(s); or using a question, a comparison, or a provocative relevant statistic.

Some writers tend to make glowing statements about the book's potential in the first paragraph without ever directly stating what the book is about. Remember that the most important bit of information you're trying to convey in your lead is the thesis of your proposal. Your letter may never be read beyond the lead if you do not have a solid hook.

Avoid bad jokes, clichés, unsubstantiated claims, and dictionary definitions in your lead. They're not effective and will make you appear amateurish.

Never be condescending; editors have egos, too, and the power to influence your future.

Supporting Material: Be Persuasive

After your lead, you'll want to include supporting material to substantiate your main idea. This could include some preliminary research or strong, convincing statements to back up your thesis.

This is also the portion of your query where you convince an agent or editor why your book should exist. Your goal is to sell your topic and your credentials while showing that you can back up your claims.

It's certainly acceptable to include a separate table of contents with your enclosures, but don't include this in the body of your letter.

If your query is directed to a publishing house, you could include a few lines demonstrating what the publisher will gain from the project. If you have brilliant and novel ideas for marketing that are realistic, include them.

It can be highly effective to state specific and unique avenues you might have for selling the book. Although the query contains much less detail than your book proposal, don't assume that editors will get the big picture later. If you don't entice them with your query, they'll never see the full proposal.

When rereading your letter, make sure you've shown that you under-stand your own idea thoroughly. Don't expect an editor to take the time to help you flesh out your thoughts. Exude confidence without being cocky, and make sure everything is grammatically correct.

Your Biography Is No Place for Modesty

The biographical information in your letter can be interspersed with, or placed separately after, your supporting material. Remember to toot your own horn in a carefully calculated, persuasive fashion. Include only relevant credentials that support the sale of your book. Don't waste space in your letter on too many extraneous details.

If, in order to be credible, your nonfiction book idea requires expert-ise, focus your biography on those qualifications that make you or a member of your writing team the best person to write this particular book.

You are not trying to impress anyone with how great a person you are. You are trying to show that you are qualified to do a particular job. The third-grade writing competition might have made your mother proud, but it has no relevance here.

Don't overlook nonacademic credentials that might correspond to your book topic. Often those experiences are more valuable than academic accomplishments. Any media or public-speaking experience should cer-tainly be highlighted.

There's no room for humility or modesty in the query letter. You need to find some way to make yourself compelling as an author in the same way ad agencies find ways to create excitement about toothpaste and other products.

Here's the Pitch

In the closing of your letter, reel them in. This means asking directly for the result you want: representation or a sale. Use strong statements like "I look forward to your speedy response." Do not hedge with phrases such as "I hope" or "I think you will like my book, but I'm not sure." This may be your only opportunity to go for the kill, and you have nothing to lose. Be sure to thank the editor or agent for his or her attention.

Finishing Touches

Edit . . . edit . . . edit.

Make sure your letter is aesthetically appealing. Use good letterhead paper and only black ink in your typewriter ribbon or printer. Your letter should represent you in the best possible way.

Making Submissions

Now that you know how to write the perfect query letter and book proposal, how do you know where to send them? You know that the best possible first step would be to find representation with a qualified literary agent. A literary agent has access to editors that you won't have. A reputable agent can get past the gatekeepers busy editors set up to keep aspiring writers from beating down their doors.

There are several ways to find the names and addresses of legitimate agents. Legitimate agents are those who actually sell books and who do not charge "reading fees" for their services. An agent is paid a commission for selling your work. A reputable agent will not charge an upfront fee to consider or represent your work. Some agencies charge for unrelated editorial services, but these services should have reasonable fees and must be completely separate from representation.

You can find the names of agents from:

- A reference book called *Literary Market Place (LMP)*. *LMP* is an expensive book, so you will want to look at it at the library. It lists everything related to the book publishing industry.

- A listing from the Association of Authors' Representatives (AAR), located in New York. Not all agents are listed, but those who are have agreed to meet certain standards of the industry as determined by their peers. Many legitimate agencies choose not to affiliate, so this is a good resource but not necessarily a measure of an agency's quality.

- The Internet. There are many web sites, some of which are listed in the back of this book, that will provide you with names of agents.

- The acknowledgments pages of books similar to your own. Most diplomatic writers list their agents and editors in the acknowledgments pages of their books along with their spouses, children, and everyone else they want to impress.

- Attending writers' conferences where agents are present. Quite often writers' conferences offer individual appointments with agents where you can pitch your projects and ask valuable questions.

Of course, we believe our annual book, *Writer's Guide to Book Editors, Publishers and Literary Agents,* is the best resource available in your search for an agent. We designed it to be comprehensive and easy to use, and we update it yearly to keep up with the ever-changing industry. We include a listing of agents that contains their preferences for representation as well as their personal interests and hobbies. This information is very helpful in finding common ground and determining if an agent would be a good match for you. Some entries include sample books sold and client lists.

You approach an agent with the same protocol as you would a publisher: query/query package with an SASE and proposal when requested. If you sign with an agent, he or she will make submissions on your behalf.

Finding an agent is sometimes the most difficult leg of your journey. If you are unable to sign with an agent, do not give up. It takes a little tenacity and know-how, but it is possible for you to sell your book on your own. If you know who is interested in the type of material you are proposing, you can query him or her directly. Since you know how to write the perfect query letter, there is a good chance your proposal will be requested. Now your perfect book proposal can do the rest.

We have gone one step farther for you. As you research where to send your query and proposal, you can look at our book *The Editors Speak,* which lets you into the mysterious minds of various editors. Learn how they think and you have a complete package. You have all the tools you need to have a thriving writing career. Now, there are no guarantees. But at least you have enough information. There are many things about writing and selling your work that you can't control. The choice to buy a book is very subjective and is influenced by many factors. We can only guess at what ultimately goes into the final decision to acquire a book. But there are many factors you can control with technique and confidence.

The nonfiction book proposal is just one important tool for your writing career. Learning to use it well will give you the professional edge that will set you above the competition. But there's a lot more to building a successful writing career than mastering the proposal craft. You must take charge of your career, and learn how to get the largest possible advances to support yourself.

Charting Your Writing Career

Writing careers are created. You can take the lottery approach, as one editor described it, which is to buy a ticket and hope for fame, glory, and cash through sheer luck of the draw. Or you can be in charge of your career, mapping out your course with precision and forethought.

If you're writing to enhance a primary professional career, you'll develop a strategy much different than if you're writing because you simply love to write. Psychologists, medical doctors, lawyers, and other professionals see writing a book as a means to build name recognition and a reputation as an expert in a particular area.

If you fall within this category, you'll enhance your chances of being published if you work on building your reputation before writing a book. You need to speak or write at every opportunity as well as to try carving out a particular niche that only you can fill. Specialization is the key.

For example, you may be the greatest psychologist in the world, but if you don't have an area of expertise or hook that can be summed up in 30 seconds, you aren't going to be able to publish a book in the commercial market.

If you want to write for the sake of writing, you need to recognize that wanting and doing are two entirely different matters. A career in writing requires self-motivation and very thick skin. Even if you think you have what it takes, our first bit of advice to you is: Don't immediately sell your belongings and move into a loft, and don't give up your day job unless you have a sizable trust fund. You want to be in control of your career. It's difficult to be enthusiastic and creative when you're scraping the bottom of your change drawer to buy dry spaghetti and a jar of Ragú.

A writing career can be monetarily rewarding, and you should always believe in your potential. You merely want to have a backup system to allow for the unexpected at the early stages of your career.

Even if you have a job you don't particularly love, you can use your free time to write as much as possible. Freelance writing and editing for magazines or public relations firms is a great way to build your credentials. Publishers want to feel confident that you can deliver what you promise. A solid clipping file shows a proven track record. Experience is also an advantage of an active freelancing career. The more you write, the better you become.

Once you choose to write full-time without any other source of income, our second bit of advice is: Learn to budget. This means time as well as money—but mostly money. If you want to write books for a living, you should learn to anticipate two months of circulation time to sell a book proposal to a publisher, if you are so lucky. Then expect it to take six weeks after that to get the contract, and six more weeks to get the first half of the advance.

The second half of your advance generally is paid when the publisher approves the manuscript for publication. This will depend on your deadline; some are nine months to a year. Royalties? Books are always purchased by the publisher at least a year before they're expected to reach the shelves. If your book earns back its advance, you still will not see royalties for quite some time.

Sowing Your Seeds Wisely and Widely

Smart writers stagger assignments and are always planting seeds for new projects. The more seeds you plant, the less time you'll spend contemplating marrying for money or running home to Mom and Dad.

If you choose to be a writer, whether or not you're actively in the business, *think* of yourself as a writer. View everything you do as an opportunity for new material. Look at the world with a critical eye, and always think in terms of trends and filling an information need for the mass audience.

Packaging Your Product—You

The best way to take charge of your career is to view yourself as a business, with *you* as the main product. Think about how you can best package yourself. Treat yourself with respect and take yourself seriously even if no one else does.

Above all else, have endurance. Some people get a sale the first time around and can learn as they go. Others have to learn the business by surviving rejection after rejection. Rejection is just a part of research and development. You need to refine your product until it's just right for the market.

Use your brain. Luck may be a part of everything in life, but a strategic approach raises the odds that you will succeed in the career you have chosen. You may lack experience, but anyone can improve with practice and objective self-evaluation.

Do not sabotage yourself with impatience. The worst thing you can do is to make a nuisance of yourself. If you call an agent or editor one day after they would have received your proposal, you're going to be seen as a potential "pain in the __ __ __." The next time you call, you might find that they're in a permanent meeting.

Your career may mean everything to you, but the writing business progresses in its own time. Keep yourself busy so you're not sitting by the telephone or mailbox. Who knows? Maybe someday the publishers will be waiting for you.

Landing a Bigger Book Advance

There are several strategies that can help to increase the worth of your book in your prospective publisher's eyes. The best advice we can give to obtain a bigger book advance is to find a good agent. However, finding an agent may be as tricky as finding a publisher. If you are unable to get past this proverbial Catch-22 at this stage of your career, there are several things you can do to improve your bargaining position with any publisher.

First, you need to understand what is meant by an advance and what purpose it serves for both writer and publisher.

What Is an Advance?
The advance is the upfront money the publisher pays the writer in exchange for the right to publish his or her book upon its completion.

The publisher is eventually repaid the advance money through the writer's future royalty and subsidiary rights income, if the book earns enough to make this possible. The writer is not required to return any money if the book does not recoup the advance, so the advance is essentially the money a publisher is willing to risk for the chance to publish your book.

If, for example, you receive a $10,000 advance for your book, you will not receive any more money until your share of the book's income exceeds $10,000.

What Does the Size of the Advance Mean?
The size of the advance is usually determined by what the publisher predicts the writer is likely to earn within the book's first year in print.

The advance is also a rough indication of how much attention and support the book will receive from the publisher. Naturally, the publisher will be much more concerned about the book for which it paid $100,000 than the one for which it paid $5,000.

There are no set rules in the advance game. Some publishers are stingy across the board, and small presses and university houses often don't have a lot of capital to speculate with. Many books never come close to earning back their advances, while other books perform well beyond anyone's expectations and earn back the advance several times.

That's why determining the advance is one of the most arbitrary aspects of the acquisition process.

The Writer's Road to Bigger Advances

Publishers are willing to pay a price that equals a perceived value. It's the writer's job to package herself and her material effectively, and to project as much potential value for the book as possible. There are several tangible and subliminal ways to accomplish this. The most obvious is to have good materials and credentials. A less obvious way is to radiate a persona of confidence, professionalism, and an overall winning image.

Here are methods you can employ to enhance the possibility of getting a higher advance:

Understand the contract—and negotiate. You don't have to accept the publisher's first offer. This may be the editor and publisher you want to work with, and that's fine. But you can still negotiate with them for better terms.

The first offer is rarely the final offer. Publishers, like all buyers in all businesses, will tend to offer what they think they can get away with. You have to show them what they *can't* get away with.

There are no set negotiating rules, but a little knowledge could get you a bigger advance. Before you even begin the submission process, we suggest you buy and read *How to Understand and Negotiate a Book Contract* by Richard Balkin and *The Writer's Legal Companion* by Brad Bunnin and Peter Beren. Both books will walk you through the typical book contract. No two publishers have identical contracts, but they do all contain similar provisions.

It's important for writers to recognize that every contract has "soft" and "hard" areas, meaning contractual aspects that the publisher expects give-and-take on, and aspects that can rarely be hedged by anyone.

Let's say an editor calls to say the publishing house wants to acquire your work and is prepared to pay you a $5,000 advance. Follow these steps:

First, ask questions:

- Find out in what format the publisher intends to publish the book (hardcover, mass market, or trade paperback). Each format tends to have a different royalty schedule, with hardcover earning the highest percentages and trade paperbacks earning the lowest. However, paperbacks often achieve greater sales volumes, thereby offsetting and perhaps surpassing the pcr-unit royalty difference.
- Find out whether the publisher pays royalties against list price or net receipts. This will make a big difference in your bottom line. If the

royalty is paid against list (the cover price), you'll know exactly what you're getting per sold copy. However, when you're paid against the publisher's net, your royalty is assessed against what the publisher receives per copy, which due to sales discounts can fluctuate between 40 and 50 percent of the list price. Obviously, your income will be higher (on a per-book basis) and more predictable when paid against list. To offset this, some publishers that pay on net will pay higher royalty percentages than the publishers that pay on list.

- Find out how large a first printing the publisher plans. (This may not be determined until much later.) The first printing will reveal the number of copies the publisher believes it can realistically sell within the first few months of publication.

- Find out what the publisher's "standard" royalty schedules are. Although each publisher has its own "usual schedule," the good houses tend to approximate each other. The typical hardcover schedule is 10 percent on the first 5,000 copies sold, 12½ percent on the second 5,000 copies, and 15 percent thereafter. Trade paperbacks tend to range anywhere from 6 to 8½ percent, and mass market from 8 to 10 percent. (These figures assume that royalties are paid against list price.) Depending on the situation, these percentages are open to discussion during the contract negotiations.

- Find out what subsidiary rights the publisher wants to keep and what percentage of such sales would be paid to you. The most common subsidiary rights are translation, world English, audio/video, software/electronic/CD-ROM, dramatization, and first and second serial rights. Retain these rights only if you intend to peddle them. Otherwise, if your publisher has an active subsidiary rights department, assign them to your publisher and negotiate favorable percentages of the income. Depending upon the right in question and the publisher's customary schedules, you can secure anywhere from 50 percent to 90 percent of the income pertaining to each right.

All these factors will influence your royalties down the road and should be taken into account when determining a fair advance. However, the publisher may not yet have definitive answers to all of these questions.

Second, say as little as possible: If you commit yourself too soon, you run the risk of binding yourself to an unfair situation, one the publisher would have been willing to negotiate. Buy yourself a few days to get educated and then come back once you know what you're dealing with.

Third, find out everything you can: Seek advice from experienced friends and colleagues. Try to talk to other people who write for the same publisher. See if their terms match yours.

Let's say you've discovered that the publisher tends to pay considerably more than the $5,000 advance offered you—perhaps $15,000 for books that are similar to yours. So, once you're confident and ready to play, call the publisher back and request $20,000 or more, and the game begins. Always be courteous, professional, and flexible. But remember, the publisher may not want to pay more than $5,000 for your book, period.

Get noteworthy people to promise endorsements or a foreword. How often do you pick up a book in a store and feel impressed by the laudatory endorsements from prominent people crowding the jacket? In fact, those endorsements may be the most important factor in helping you decide whether to buy the book.

The right endorsements add significant value to a book's commercial prospects. If you demonstrate to the publisher upfront that Lee Iacocca is prepared to write a foreword for your business book and that H. Ross Perot is ready to contribute a great blurb, that should be reflected in the advance.

Of course, you don't need only household names backing you up. Writs from people with the right credentials will also be effective—even if they're not famous.

There are many ways to get endorsements, but you must focus on people or organizations relevant to your material. For instance, Iacocca wouldn't be the most appropriate endorsement for a cookbook, but the White House chef would be.

Ask yourself these questions:

- Who do you know?
- Who do your friends know?
- Who do their friends know?

Don't be bashful; seek out and pursue all possible leads. Many noteworthy people are happy to endorse books that they believe in. In many cases, it provides valuable publicity for them, too. The hard part is reaching these candidates and getting them to notice your work. This may, like most endeavors in writing and publishing, require tenacious work—but it will often prove to be well worth the exertion.

Show the publisher all the flattering comments or commitments you've secured when you first submit the proposal. This will establish at the outset that significant people know you and your work, and are willing to vouch for it. This makes a favorable first impression, wins you more serious consideration from the publisher, and enhances your work's perceived value from day one.

When you sign with an agent or sell a book, always try to be a good client. If you have an agent, remember that all the time he or she spends talking to you about trivial matters is time taken away from selling your book. If you have things you want to discuss, make a list and try to do it all at once in an efficient and short conversation. This will be greatly appreciated, and your agent is more likely to take your calls without trying to think of new excuses to avoid you.

Your agent represents you and acts on your behalf, but does not serve at your behest. We have known agents who drop clients who are moneymakers simply because of the aggravation factor.

If you do not like or respect your agent, you do not need to stay in the relationship. Just be sure your unhappiness is not due to unrealistic expectations or impatience with the slow wheels of publishing or a lack of personal strokes. Your agent does not have to be your friend, but serves a very important purpose for your career.

Now that you have sold your book, you need to deliver a quality manuscript. You have been contracted by the publisher to do a job and deliver a product. One of your main obligations is to meet your deadlines. Writing a book is time-consuming, and you have to plan well so you have enough time to complete the job. Your publisher is not your parent. You won't be scolded or grounded for not handing in your work. Face reality and let someone know if you anticipate any problems. If you communicate honestly rather than making excuses, editors, salespeople, and your production department can adjust the schedule accordingly. If you do not let anyone know, your agent can't help you, and you put yourself at risk of breaching your contract, with consequences that could have been avoided. There are situations when a manuscript is going to be unavoidably late. Be upfront. Editors are not the enemy. They have nearly as much invested in the success of your book as you do.

Follow your editor's advice. Although your ego is invested in the beauty of your words, you will find that most editorial changes are for the better. After you scrape yourself off the ceiling, look at the changes objectively and only appeal those you feel are the most heinous to your sensibilities.

We have offered you tools to help you on your way. But the best advice we can give you for your writing career is to always be proactive. Too many talented people are limited by a lack of focused motivation, confidence, and tenacity. Keep at it, and you will rise to the level of your own potential.

10 Proposals That Sold —And Why

Introduction to Section Two

Here are 10 real, successful, though slightly abridged, nonfiction book proposals accompanied by out critiques. We didn't include sample chapters, press clips, and other collateral materials. While it's invaluable for you to incorporate these materials as part of your total package, presenting them here would have gone beyond the scope of this book

PROPOSAL 1

10 Habits of Naturally Slim People

... and How to Make Them Part of Your Life

by
Jill H. Podjasek, M.S., R.N.
with
Jennifer Carney

The author made this one easy for us. Not only did she come to us with an excellent concept and proposal, but she also had an offer in place from Contemporary Books, with whom we negotiated the contract on her behalf. The authors graciously credited their success to our first edition of *Write the Perfect Book Proposal.* Of course, we are willing to accept the accolades.

1. A mission statement is not necessary, as it should be apparent from your main thesis. The first paragraph in this proposal sets an idealistic tone, which can work against you if you appear to be more concerned with having an impact on the world than in producing a commercial book. Most authors who are passionate about their work feel it is a type of mission, but if this seems to be your main focus, it might create an image that you have unrealistic expectations. Are you a "legend in your own mind"? This translates into "hard to work with." Publishers are also used to seeing grandiose statements that are never matched by the manuscript.

2. This statement is clearly lofty and will likely be ignored altogether.

Proposal for: *10 Habits of Naturally Slim People*

Contents

I. Mission Statement

It is our belief that each and every piece of literature that is published has a mission. A work of nonfiction is a very special coming together of people, experiences, ideas, and skills coalesced into a tangible, readable product. It is our hope that this work will enlighten and improve, in some small way, the mind, body, and spirit of the human population.

The Mission of *10 Habits of Naturally Slim People* is threefold:

1. To expose the self-defeating beliefs, thoughts, and actions that compose what we call "Diet Mentality" and provide the reader with a new understanding of the mind–body connection that will lead them away from dieting as a means of weight management.

2. To describe the natural eating and exercising instincts that all people were born with and how naturally slim people utilize these instincts to maintain their weight, free from worry and obsessions.

3. To identify the thoughts and beliefs that cloud many people's access to a naturally slim body and to educate readers about how to change those thoughts and beliefs in a way that will allow them to become naturally slim.

II. Overview

3. This is a good start. It is a strong statistic with a provocative contrast.

Americans spend over 32 billion dollars a year on diets and diet related products, yet we are the fattest nation in the world. Part of the reason we have come to this place is the process of dieting itself. Research shows that . . . Diets Don't Work, at least not long term. Only 2–3% of dieters can ever expect to maintain their weight loss for over three years. in fact, chronic dieters may add 5–10 pounds to their weight every time they diet. According to studies done at Harvard Medical School, constantly losing and gaining weight, or "yo-yo dieting," is more hazardous to our health than being slightly overweight. Considering these facts, what should people who are overweight do? Should they keep dieting, but in moderation? Should they just give up? Should they just accept themselves the way they are and "Be Happy"? Current literature is lacking in answers to these questions. However, the Center for Positive Life Changes in Denver, Colorado, is not. The answer to reaching and maintaining an optimal body weight lies in developing a totally new mentality . . . the mentality of a naturally slim person.

This new mentality begins with the knowledge that we are all born loving and enjoying our body *and* we are all born normally and naturally slim. Every one of us was born with natural instincts to tell us when, where, what, and how much to eat to maintain our body at optimal weight. These instincts are meant to be used throughout our entire life, not just in infancy. In fact, our bodies would be perfectly capable of maintaining a slim, healthy weight throughout childhood, adolescence, adulthood, and aging, if we would stop getting in our own way! Many people, as they grow up, adopt belief systems that sabotage their natural instincts at every turn. Beliefs gathered from parents, the media, teachers, and others block our ability to access our own natural instincts. During the past three years of working with chronic dieters and studying naturally slim people we have come to the the realization that:

Those among us who are healthy and naturally slim have maintained intimate contact with the natural instincts of infancy. Specifically, naturally slim people remain in touch with their own innate wisdom in the areas of self-love, self-nurturing, food, water, hunger, thirst, satiety, and exercise.

In order for overweight men and women to return to their naturally slim state they must develop new attitudes and skills. The best way to do this is to study a master and model his or her beliefs, thoughts, and behaviors. Unfortunately, the majority of the American public views any person with a slim body and a food plan as a master and this is just not so! Many of these "masters" are quite unhealthy and UN-naturally slim. Instead of maintaining their optimal body weight with very little effort, these "masters" lead and promote a life consumed with weighing oneself measuring foods, counting fat grams, avoiding hunger, using artificial sweeteners, following food plans and exercising as much as humanly possible. . . . This is LIVING??? True masters of the art of being slim do not fight their body. Thoughts of food and numbers on scales consume little if any of their time. Eating is a pleasant interlude that fuels their body for getting on with life. These people are "naturally slim." They have never dieted, never had a weight issue, follow very few if any eating guidelines, and truly do not understand what all the fuss is about. Every overweight person has known someone like this and has secretly lusted after their genetic code. Sadly, most overweight people believe they can *never* have what naturally slim people have and this is not true. If one

---

4. The author should refer to the book here and not to the Center. The book is what is being proposed. This is where a strong statement should be made that the book offers solutions to the issues that have been raised. Remember that your purpose here is to help an editor or agent see the potential in your book.

5. For example: "*10 Habits of Naturally Slim People* tackles these issues head on."

6. This may encourage a skeptical reader to ask about people with physical conditions. The writer should anticipate such questions by confronting them head-on or by indicating that the subject will be treated later on.

7. Here the author could have said, "At the Center for Positive Life Changes," as it supports the thesis and provides credibility.

8. This is an excellent thesis statement. The fact that the information leading to these solutions stems from research at the Center should be used to support the thesis. The logical order is:

- State the problem;
- Tell how the book solves it;
- Show how you support your claims through examples.

9. This statement could be more provocative by giving veiled examples of diet gurus. The term *master* is potentially too esoteric for the general public. A more common term would be *guru,* but this is not a major issue. You just want to be aware how certain words create an overall feeling for a book.

10. This statement is discouraging. Remember, editors and agents often choose to look at certain proposals because of personal interest. Do not assume your editor or agent does not have the problem you are writing about. Assume he or she does. This sentence can be reframed and made clearer, such as, "This book can let you in on this mystery." When you say, "These people never had a weight problem," it automatically puts the reader on the defensive. He or she is thinking, "Well, what's wrong with me?"

studies healthy, naturally slim people and then models their beliefs and behaviors, one will find a blueprint for permanent weight loss.

During the past three years we have been studying naturally slim people. We have followed them around, eaten meals with them, and asked them hundreds of questions. Our book, *10 Habits of Naturally Slim People,* is the culmination of this data collection. Each of the 10 habits has its own chapter and each chapter provides awareness exercises and resources for the reader who wants to study a particular habit in depth. *And How to Make Them Part of Your Life* is the second half of the title and it is equally important. Knowing what these ten habits are and making them a permanent part of one's life are two very different things.

Samuel Smiles, an author and philosopher during the 19th century, wrote,

"Sow a thought, you reap an action,
sow an action, you reap a habit,
sow a habit, you reap a character,
sow a character and you reap a destiny"

One of the reasons traditional weight loss programs fail to produce permanent weight loss is that they focus on changing external actions rather than the thoughts and beliefs that *cause* those actions. Most diets dictate, "Change what you eat." "Exercise more." "Cut fat grams." "Reduce calories." Participants in these programs are unable to make the actions a lasting part of their life because they do not have the belief system and thought patterns to support them. This book not only exposes the negative effects of dieting and gives readers 10 habits to adopt instead, it also introduces a totally new [12] concept called Psych-K™, psychological kinesiology, that allows people to make permanent changes in their belief systems with very little effort.

From our beliefs, flow our thoughts. From our thoughts, flow our actions. When we incorporate the beliefs of a naturally slim person into our subconscious mind we cannot help but think and act like one. The results??

A naturally slim body for life!!

III. Biographical Information

Jennifer Carney, a nurse by profession, spent most of her nursing career in [13] psychiatric nursing. Her avocation was and still is studying the effects of the mind–body connection on lifestyle behaviors. Having a weight issue herself, Jennifer became involved with Weight Watchers. She lost 75 pounds and became a group leader. However, for the 5 years she was a group leader, her conscience was constantly plagued by the unnatural way she and her co-

[13] workers kept their weight off. Starving and bingeing, counting jelly beans, making guacamole from puréed asparagus, and being continuously obsessed with food and weight. Some of her acquaintances even resorted to bulimia to keep their weight down so they would not lose their jobs. Three years ago she turned her back on what she considered an unhealthy industry and started the Say NO to DIETS, Say YES to LIFE! program. Here she melded her extraordinary ability as a motivational speaker with her integrity and devotion to people. At this time she began her current quest to educate the public about the mind–body connection as it relates to weight issues. She is currently the Director of the Center for Positive Life Changes, a nonprofit corporation dedicated to helping people plant the seeds of positive change in their lives.

[14] **Jill H. Podjasek, M.S. R.N.,** also a nurse, spent most of her nursing career in hospitals caring for critically ill patients and teaching graduate students. Jill began honing her writing skills when she was asked to do major writing assignments for four different hospital committees! Later she wrote several book chapters, a 100-page Master's thesis on nutrition, and several magazine articles. Her avocation has been writing and nursing research. She met Jennifer at a Say NO to DIETS, Say YES to LIFE! class and they immediately connected with synergistic results . . . the motivational speaker and the motivated writer. Jill chairs the board of directors for the Center for Positive Life Changes. She is an asset to the Center, developing educational and marketing materials, conducting research studies, teaching classes, and writing from firsthand knowledge and experience.

Jennifer and Jill collaborate closely on the content of their writing projects while Jill does the actual writing. They are dynamic, singularly and as a team, in public appearances. They have been in the newspaper, on radio and television and hosted a three-part local cable TV series entitled *Say NO to DIETS, Say YES to LIFE!*

[15] IV. Promotion and Competition

[16] With over 45 years of combined experience in weight loss, weight gain, diet centers, exercise programs, foods, drinks, supplements, and fasts, we have come to the conclusion that there are three tenets a weight management program must embrace in order to produce healthy, permanent results:

[17] 1. **A weight management program must be user friendly.** That is, you do not have to buy special foods, drinks, or supplements. You do not have to carry around special salad dressing or artificial sweeteners in your fanny pack and you do not have to fill in little boxes or look up fat grams or calories before you take a bite of food. People who

---

11. This seems patronizing. If you are writing about something that is painful to your reader, be careful not to sound above it all. Even though it is clear in the bio that the authors understand the issues of weight, they should make sure that they keep a tone of understanding throughout the book.

12. We need more information on Psych-K long before this. Is this something they invented? Is it a core concept in their work? How is it used? If it is original to them or a main portion of the book, it should be more prominent.

13. This is an excellent example of tapering a biography to fit the thesis. She effectively points out the significant personal experiences that led to her writing this book. She does not draw attention to any credentials that may be lacking, but rather leaves us with the impression that we can trust her expertise.

14. This bio sketch seems a little apologetic. It might be better to simply list writing experiences in the form of a résumé to avoid sounding unsure of her ability to write this book. It is not

relevant to indicate that she is an asset to the Center, as once again it causes us to wonder if we should have doubts. It is also not necessary to indicate who does the lion's share of the writing. The image to convey is that of a solid team effort where no link is weak.

15. This should be called "markets and competition."

16. This would be a good place for a startling statistic about how much money is spent each year on weight-loss programs.

17. This is a very good explanation of the foundation principles of the book. It could have been summarized in the overview, with expansion here. It is always a good idea to repeat important points if you can do so without seeming redundant.

18. It would be better to phrase this, "We believe . . ." because you don't want to be grandiose. Or you could say, "We have not found any books or programs . . ."

19. Use the title of the book here. You always want to keep the title up front and center as much as is reasonable.

are overweight want to feel "normal." They really, truly, down deep [17] in their heart do not want to spend every waking moment thinking about eating or not eating something or feeling guilty if they do. People who are overweight deserve to have a life just like everyone else. Even though they, themselves, sometimes feel unworthy of it.

2. **A weight management program must be respectful of each person as an individual spirit, with a mind and a body.** People who are overweight are not just bodies that need to be starved and whipped into shape, and they are not people with weak minds who just need to take control of themselves. They are three-dimensional people just like everyone else. Any weight loss approach that does not address the spirit and mind as well as the body of each individual will not be permanently successful. Knowledge of good nutrition and fat-burning foods is only a very small part of the path to becoming and staying slim for life.

3. **No weight management program, no matter how "user friendly" or "respectful," can be successful for life unless the persons involved in the program have a set of subconscious beliefs that support it.** Our psychology is a belief-driven system; *Belief* > > > > > *Thought* > > > > > *Action*. If we jump in and change an action without changing the beliefs that have produced it, the performance of the new action will diminish over time because it has no foundation to support it.

There is no single book or program on the market today that takes all [18] three of these tenets into consideration except for ours. Therefore, as far as [19] we are concerned, we really have no competition. However, in deference to [20] the millions of dollars spent on the current wave of diet and fitness books, we have reviewed them all and addressed specifically five of the best-sellers:

Fit for Life II by Harvey and Marilyn Diamond. Harvey and Marilyn have mellowed and become even more balanced in this, their second book. Food, air, water, sunshine, exercise, and love are areas they address as necessary to be fit for life. These do indeed nurture the body, mind, and spirit, and this is a book we recommend to our clients. However, what they do not address is tenet #3. People can read all the wonderful, natural books on fitness they can lay their hands on and never make the suggestions part of their life.

Why are people unable to make these sensible changes? Aren't they serious? YES, they are serious and they are seriously frustrated because they don't understand why they can't make the changes either! Our book tells why. It also offers a natural approach to losing weight and keeping fit along with a method to change unhealthy beliefs and assimilate new behaviors into everyday life.

Perfect Weight **by Deepak Chopra, M.D.** This book, along with *Fit for Life II*, is one of the most balanced books on weight loss available today. It is user friendly, it refers to natural healthy foods, and it approaches optimal body weight as an interaction among the spirit, the mind, and the body. We recommend this book to our clients also. However, it does have boxes and charts to fill in, which often threaten ex-dieters, and the frequent references to Aryevedic medicine and body typing can be confusing to the general public. Dr. Chopra does not give his readers information on how to change the beliefs that are creating their unhealthy behaviors.

Eat More, Weigh Less **by Dean Ornish, M.D.** Dr. Ornish has done a lot for people seeking to lose weight. He has diffused the myth that starving oneself is the answer and that the quality of food we eat is of utmost importance. However, he spends a lot of time on recipes and very little time on what really causes people to get fat. That is, the use of food as a substitute for love, comfort, and self-worth. Until people develop a sense of self-worth and learn to care for themselves in ways that don't include overeating, they cannot assimilate this good scientific information and put it to use on an everyday basis. Dr. Ornish ignores tenet #2 and tenet #3, making his program very unbalanced.

The McDougall Program for Maximum Weight Loss **by John McDougall, M.D.** Like Dr. Ornish, Dr. McDougall presents good, scientifically based information about food, fat, and exercise. However, his book is sorely lacking in the mental and spiritual aspects of eating behaviors. Dr. McDougall has a list of what he calls "excuses" for not following his program and basically tells readers to stop being fearful of change and buckle down. We see his so-called "excuses" as very real and very limiting beliefs. These types of negative beliefs, engraved in a person's subconscious, can keep that person in conflict and unable to follow any health program.

Stop the Insanity **by Susan Powter.** Ms. Powter espouses "get angry" as a motivation, eat mass quantities of high-bulk, low-fat food, breathe, and exercise. Breathing and exercise are healthy, getting angry and eating huge amounts of foods are not. We have very little respect for a person who would actually recommend that you eat 32 baked potatoes instead of one chicken breast. I don't care how low-fat it is, it is body abuse to eat those amounts of food when your stomach is only the size of your fist. Anger as motivation is physically unhealthy and cannot have a lasting positive effect. This program does not respect the individual's mind, body, and spirit, and, like the others, gives little consideration to supporting behavior changes with a foundation of positive beliefs.

20. We don't believe it is ever a good idea to state that there is no competition, especially in a crowded area such as diet and health. All the books on this subject are potential competition. It is better to address the issue of competition by stating what this book offers. Then you can list the most direct competition. Don't claim to have read everything on a subject. It is probably not humanly possible and is certainly not necessary. Make a more reasonable statement that after extensive research you have discovered certain similar titles that indicate the market for your book, but that your book distinguishes itself for the following reasons.

21. You might not want to use the phrase "have no respect." It sounds too judgmental. All these descriptions can be slanted more positively toward what this book does rather than what the other books don't do. Otherwise it is very well done and concise.

10 Habits of Naturally Slim People is written by two women who have been and done it all when it comes to weight loss. Now we have researched what to do instead. I repeat, *There is no book on the market that offers information on all of the following issues while remaining user friendly and respectful:*

- Why overweight people are normal.
- How we become fat and why we hold on to it.
- How to change beliefs that support holding on to fat and resisting a healthy lifestyle.
- Three-dimensional nutrition, food for the body, the mind, and the spirit.
- The process of change, what to expect and how to embrace it.

V. Marketing

[22]

It is a given that a publishing house of your size has a marketing department and marketing plans. However, we feel that the authors of a book need to be invested in the marketing of the book also. It is our passion to reach as many people with weight issues as possible, hoping to make a positive impact on their lives. Therefore we are willing to invest a sizable amount of time and energy into marketing our book.

Weight loss is a hot topic, health and getting back to nature are hot top- [23] ics along with books on the mind–body connection. This book will appeal to the readership in all four of these areas.

Radio Talk Shows

We have at our disposal a national listing of radio stations that will review new [24] books and do telephone interviews with the authors. We feel that the expense incurred mailing copies of the book to each of these stations could be justified by the fact that we could trigger the beginning of a national grass roots demand for the book. We have contacts at all local radio stations and can easily get on air coverage in the Denver area.

Classes and Workshops

We conduct classes and workshops locally and have a party interested in financially backing a national effort. We would recommend or require the book at each of our classes and workshops and have it available for sale on site.

Newspaper

Getting local coverage would be very easy; we have contacts at all of our major newspapers. We would look to the publisher for help nationally.

---

22. This should be titled "Promotion."

23. This material belongs under "Markets," which addresses who will buy the book. This section would be enhanced by books-sold statistics, and by looking at health club memberships, diet group memberships, and magazines on the subject, which would establish a clear potential market. Of course, with this subject, some of that will be assumed, and the most important thing an editor or agent will be looking for is if there is anything new here. So if the author has some unique potential market, this would be the place to describe it.

24. This material should be under "Promotion." It is not impressive to state that you have a list of radio stations or magazines that will do interviews or reviews. You need a more direct statement such as that you have made a target list of relevant magazines and radio stations that often cover this topic. If you can, do some preliminary research into possible media outlets. Your statements about promotions have to be more than what-ifs and wish lists. If you have a publicist or have had success promoting

Television Talk Shows and Newsmagazine Shows

This book is a fresh approach to the problem of being overweight and has a much greater chance of coverage by national television than the latest exercise or diet fad. It is especially suited for review on television because [25] Psych-K™, the technique used to change overweight beliefs to naturally slim beliefs, can actually be demonstrated on the air.

Videotapes

Because Psych-K™ is most easily taught in visual media, we hope to follow the book very shortly with a videotape. Rob Williams, the creator of Psych-K™, has a basic videotape out and he has agreed to help us with one specifically [26] for *10 Habits of Naturally Slim People*. The videotape would refer people to the book, and the book would refer people to the video.

Audiotapes

[27] This book could easily be formatted to a series of audiotapes that, like the videotape, would refer people to the book, and the book could refer people to the audiotapes.

Book Signings and Lecture Tour

[28] Either Jennifer or I could be available at almost any time for travel and signings if the publisher does advance work that makes it worthwhile. Locally we have contacts at Tattered Cover and Hatches and could easily get signings there.

VI. Chapter Outline

Table of Contents

something else using this avenue, explain it here. Although it shows you have good ideas, a statement that is not backed up will have no weight.

25. This is only the second time Psych-K is mentioned. If this is original and demonstrable, it should have been given more attention as a hook for promotion. Something like that with a built-in following is a major bonus. It translates into potential.

26. This is the first explanation of Psych-K and its creator. We need more information on what it is, how connected the authors are to the creator, and whether they have permission to use the idea. An immediate question will be, Is the Psych-K creator's promises to help the authors a serious gesture that will stand the test of money and contracts, or is it one of those "let's do lunch" kinds of things? The author should anticipate the questions and include the answers in the proposal.

27. These ideas for cross-promotion are great.

28. It is best not to state what you will do "if." In the "Promotion" section you want to suggest things you *can* do above anything the publisher might do. It would be fine to state availability, but we suggest you avoid the limiting statement that the publisher must make it worthwhile. There is reference to local bookshops that are probably unknown to the editor. Describe them, and their potential attendees, or just say you will set up local and regional book signings.

29. This is a wonderful and well-thought-out Table of Contents that gives a good sense of how the book will be executed. There is terrific order and a logical progression of chapter titles. The titles are clear and direct.

30. This introductory paragraph has done a good job capturing the writer's voice. The outline contains passion and enthusiasm even in an abbreviated form.

Introduction

When we wage war against ourselves, we can never win. Yet, for decades, we **30** have taken up the battle of the bulge and waged war against our own physical bodies. Somehow, we keep thinking, if we can bend, starve, exercise, or suction our physical body into shape, the rest of our life will follow. Guess what? It doesn't work that way. Why? Because we are not just *physical* bodies. We are three-dimensional beings. Beings with a body, a mind, and a spirit. Understanding and utilizing the mind–body connection is essential to making permanent changes in our lives. This includes changes in what we eat and how much we weigh, as well as changes in how fulfilling our lives are. Jennifer and I have traveled the road of chronic dieting and chronic nondieting and are delighted to share with you the joy of becoming and remaining naturally slim.

Each chapter in this book will contain in-depth coverage of one topic **31** and will include: data and conclusions from our own research, facts and quotes from outside sources, and anecdotal experiences, both our own and those of our clients. This lively combination will take readers from the world of experts telling them what to do into the world of self-responsibility. They will learn to recognize their own instincts and their ability to know what to do. At the end of each chapter there will be a short exercise for the reader to carry out. Completing these "hands on" exercises will help the reader bring the concepts presented in each chapter into their own lives. We hope that many chapters in the book will stimulate readers to increase their knowledge about health and the mind–body–spirit connection. Therefore, at the end of each chapter, we will list several subject area references.

31 This book is about much more than becoming slim. Each and every chapter serves as a jumping-off point for the reader's personal growth.

31. This is a very good overall synopsis of what the book will do. It is a clever device to use the "introduction" portion of the outline to convey so much supportive information.

Chapter 1

32 Diet Mentality: The Mind–Body Connection That Keeps You Fat

Over 32 billion dollars a year are spent in this country on diets and diet-related products. However, the weight of the average American goes up each and every year. We, as a country, are just beginning to understand that no matter how healthy the food choices may be on any given weight-loss program, the actual process of dieting is making us fat. Permanent weight loss is achieved by LESS THAN 5 percent of dieters on any given program. The experience of gaining and losing of weight over and over again, sometimes called yo-yo dieting, is very stressful on the body and has been proven to decrease longevity.

32. This is a good statistic. It automatically brings the reader into the meat of the book.

The restriction of food intake recommended in most diet programs actually works *against* our body's ability to lose excess fat. Metabolically, our body interprets dieting as a famine. Our brain, in an effort to save our life, sends out messages to the rest of the body to slow down metabolism and conserve fat. Psychologically, the high of losing weight is countered by the low of gaining all the weight back and then some. Chronic dieters frequently get sucked into a negative spiral of Dieting >>> Weight Loss >>> Weight Gain >>> Guilt >>> Body Hate >>> Poor Self-Image >>> and More Dieting. Self-image and slimness become insidiously linked in the dieter's mind and, in a desperate struggle to gain self-esteem, they stay endlessly mired in the no-win process of dieting.

33 This chapter will address the psychological and physiological effects of dieting, the diet–binge cycle, the role of self-esteem in weight gain and weight loss, and how to begin to break out of diet mentality. Also included will be a definition of optimal body weight and the reader will be asked to truly assess whether they need to lose weight. And if not, why do they continue to diet?

33. This paragraph tells you what else to expect. It is a good teaser.

Chapter 2

Infants and Children: Slim by Nature

"We're not all looking to be models, some of us really need to lose weight. If diets don't work, what do we do?" This is a very valid question that we hear every day. It is true, a person who is at his or her optimal body weight or within 20 percent of it has less health risks than an obese person. They also feel subjectively better and can more easily participate in the vigorous activities that make life fun! These are all very good reasons for wanting to be slim. However, the way to become slim and remain so permanently cannot be found in the latest "thirty pounds, thirty days, thirty dollars" scheme that is posted by the roadside. The answer can, however, be found inside ourselves, by rediscovering the natural instincts we were born with and bringing them back into our consciousness. Think of the mind and body of an infant. Infants know when they are hungry and insist on eating right then. They also know when they are satisfied and there is no way anyone can force another drop of formula into their mouths. They eat small amounts, about the size of their tiny tummies, and they eat every two to four hours. As they grow a little older they still are very sure about when, where, what, and how much they want to eat, if adults don't interfere. They also look at their little naked bodies, potbelly and all, and think they are the greatest thing that has happened since sliced bread! We can learn a lot from these tiny, naturally slim people, including how not to diet. Every one of us was born with these same instincts; we just need to unearth them from deep within our mind–body system.

This chapter will review in depth the eating habits of infants and children and identify when, where, and how people begin to lose touch with their natural instinctive eating habits.

Chapter 3

Naturally vs. UN-Naturally Slim Adults

Our conscious and subconscious mind are both exposed to a myriad of experiences between infancy and adulthood. These experiences create the belief system that we operate out of every day of our lives. This includes how we treat our body, how we cope with stress, and the habits we develop around when, where, what, and how much food we eat. Having made a commitment to never diet again, we decided to look for "what to do instead" by looking for *masters of slimness,* adults who have been slim all of their lives. We interviewed all the slim adults we knew and then we started interviewing strangers. During our interviews we found two types of slim people: (1) *The UN-Naturally Slim,* those who focus 90 percent of their waking hours counting fat grains, exercising, and agonizing about their body; and (2) *The Naturally Slim,* the people who just "followed their instincts" and found questions like "How do you know when to eat?" extremely funny. In the chapters that follow, we have condensed our data into ten habits that were common to each and every one of the naturally slim people we interviewed. We have found, over the past three years. that modeling the beliefs and habits of naturally slim people creates a slow, gentle weight loss and permanent lifestyle change that can keep a person slim for life.

This chapter will address the important dichotomy we found when we interviewed people who were slim. Some slim people are extremely unhealthy and should not be used as mentors or role models. Our readers will learn how to distinguish these two types, do their own research work, and choose a healthy role model to follow.

Chapter 4

Habit #1—Keep Your Life Priorities Straight

An overwhelming number of healthy, naturally slim people have a keen sense about what is important in life. Words like love, commitment, purpose, and happiness come up often when they talk about themselves, their vocation, their relationships. They see exercise and nutritious foods as a part of good health, but they are not obsessed with them. Many people have taken on the goal of weight loss, or obtaining and maintaining the perfect body as the driving force in their lives. They see the shape of their body as the sole reflection of their status and worth. Overweight men and women constantly tell us, "If I could just lose this weight, then my life would be so much better." We say to them, "Why? If you do not know how to cultivate things like love, peace, joy, commitment, and purpose when you are a size 28 most likely you will not know how to at a size 8 either!"

We are all three-dimensional beings. We have a spirit or inner self, a mind, and a body. When we put our physical body as the top priority in our life we are missing two-thirds of the action, the most important two-thirds at that. In fact, if our spirit and our state of mind are congruent, our physical body will follow naturally.

In this chapter we will address the importance of putting weight loss in perspective. We will discuss what things might take the place of focusing on weight loss in a person's life and how that will promote health and weight loss rather than deter it.

Chapter 5

[34] Habit #2—Love Yourself: Body, Mind, and Spirit

The naturally slim people we interviewed genuinely liked themselves just as they were, imperfections and all. Overweight people tend to say, "When I lose all this weight, then I'll like myself." We have found the opposite to be true. Unless people who are overweight can at least accept themselves in a loving way, just as they are, they will never be able to lose the weight they want. Reaching your optimal body weight, naturally, without deprivation and abuse, is a kind and loving thing to do. If you hate yourself, you will not be able to do loving things like embark on a journey to become naturally slim.

34. Although there are some minor weaknesses in this proposal, the chapter-by-chapter outline is excellent. It is strong, well written, and substantial. It gives the agent or editor a clear vision of what the book offers and how it will look as a completed manuscript. It is very likely that it was the chapter outline that closed the deal.

Right now, you may not even be able to look in a full-length mirror without feeling disgust. A loving relationship with yourself takes time and nurturing. It is essential to move through the stages of introduction, acquaintance, like, and love just as you would with a partner. If you come to the stage where you love your spirit and love your mind and are at least able to accept your body, you are on your way.

Regaining a sense of self-love and self-respect are absolutely essential to the process of becoming slim for life. This chapter will explain the relationship of self-esteem to being stuck and unable to change even when you know you want to.

PROPOSAL 2

How to Get Clients

An Easy and Practical Program to Build Your Business

by
Jeff Slutsky
with
Marc Slutsky

Several editors made offers on this proposal, which was sold to Warner Books. It was published as a how-to popular business book in a quality paperback format with the same main title, *How to Get Clients.*

The proposal is well organized and captures the authors' expertise and special self-marketing skills, projecting energy, enthusiasm, and a nonintimidating "you can do this, too" approach.

The primary obstacle here was that there were many good books on the subject already in print. The authors didn't include a sample chapter, but in this case it didn't matter. The outline was well done, and the principal author had written three other commercially successful books.

1. This is what overviews are all about. In one tight paragraph, the authors completely describe what the book will do for the reader and show the publisher that there's a market for it. This paragraph reflects confidence and the ability to deliver.

What's *How to Get Clients* About?

How to Get Clients teaches and guides professionals and those responsible for marketing service-oriented businesses on how to build their client base. With this book the reader learns every aspect and skill needed to build a successful service business by getting clients who pay big fees. The readers discover how to identify or create their special market niche, how to initially contact the potential client, gather needed information about the client, make the presentation designed to get a positive decision, and even how to dominate the marketplace in their area. With consolidation, takeovers, restructuring, and mergers of major service organizations including the big eight (now big six) accounting firms, advertising agencies, law firms, insurance and financial institutions, and a host of others, hundreds of thousands of professionals have gone on their own or have joined smaller organizations. They must learn how to get clients to survive. This book is the answer to their survival.

2. While it's unusual to place the table of contents so early in the proposal, it's perfectly acceptable. By doing so here, the authors quickly deliver the program aspect of the book. Substance put this proposal over the top.

   Each chapter title is strong and effective. A publisher looking at this table of contents can visualize exactly how the book will be structured. This shows good organization and a logical progression of the material.

Table of Contents

Introduction

Chapter 1: Who Are Your Potential Clients and Why Do You Want Them?

Chapter 2: How to Discover and Develop Your Unique Market Niche

Chapter 3: 14 Ways to Establish Credibility That Make Clients Take Notice

Chapter 4: How to Make an Effective First Contact and Avoiding Wasting Your Time

Chapter 5: How to Dominate Your Marketplace without Spending a Fortune

Chapter 6: 10 Techniques for Avoiding Fee Shopping

Chapter 7: When Advertising Makes Sense and How to Do It for Less

Chapter 8: The Value of Free Publicity and How to Get It

Chapter 9: How to Communicate Persuasively to Get a "Yes"

Chapter 10: Proposals and Presentations: 5 Rules for Results

3. This introduction may not have been necessary because it seems to repeat information from the overview.

Introduction

How to Get Clients is a unique and complete marketing guide specifically written to help professionals develop a larger and more profitable client base. Most professionals have little or no marketing experience, especially in the complex and confusing area of selling services to new prospective buyers. Yet there are hundreds of thousands of professionals in numerous areas who have to get more clients to pay higher fees for their services if they are survive in the difficult times ahead.

The service economy is increasingly more competitive. As a result large

4 companies are restructuring, merging, and consolidating, leaving hundreds of thousands of highly skilled professionals to fend for themselves. Their only alternative is to go out on their own or team up with others in the same situation. While they are perfectly competent in their specific areas, they now have to take on new responsibilities, the most important of which is to get new clients so they can pay their bills. It's a matter of survival.

4. This shows a growing need for the material.

5 Who Buys *How to Get Clients* and Why?

Target Audience—The strongest target group most likely to buy this book is professionals who have gone out on their own or are given the responsibility of client acquisition in their present organization. It is also "must" reading for any aggressive corporate person who wants to climb the corporate ladder of any service organization because, while any trained professional can do the work for clients, it's the partners and future partners who actually bring the clients into the firm. Just a few service areas that use this information include:

5. This effective market section is focused and credible even without the reinforcement of statistics from respected publications.

Accounting/CPAs/Tax
Advertising/Public Relations
Architectural/Contracting
Business Consulting
Computer/Telecommunications
Finance
Franchising
Fund Raising

Insurance
Investments/Brokers/CICs
Law Firms/Legal
Manufacturing/Wholesaling
Medical/Dental/Hospitals
Research/Information
Retrieval

6   For example, in a recent issue of *Business Week,* an article entitled "For Law Firms, It's Dog v. Dog Out There"[1] stressed how the legal profession is becoming increasingly competitive. A sidebar article went on further to stress the need for sales and marketing. The article, entitled "The Latest Law Course: Marketing 101"[2], went on to say:

6. The quotations cited are on target and offer a solid foundation for the authors' marketing claims.

> For the lawyers, it represents a bold new step into the world of competitive business. Traditionally they had shunned overt marketing efforts because of ethical restrictions and professional biases. But the rules have eased. **In today's saturated legal market, firms are looking for every advantage they can find.**

Take a look at another high-end profession where sales and marketing are just now becoming a major part of the practice. The first item of the

---

1. *Business Week,* August 6, 1990. (Legal Affairs Section) "For Law Firms, It's Dog v. Dog Out There" by Michael Galen with Tim Smart and Geoff Smith and Keith Hammonds.

2. *Business Week,* August 6, 1990. "The Latest Law Course: Marketing 101" by Michael Galen, p. 58.

"Business Bulletin"[3] on the front page of the *Wall Street Journal* recently had the following:

> More lawsuits and the S&L crisis cause firms to take steps against exposure. The American Institute of CPAs tightens its membership rules. A national survey finds eight of 10 midsize accounting firms restrict services and 56% won't take clients considered "high-risk."

This means that with less clients to choose from, accounting firms are becoming more aggressive in going after the business they do want. For the first time, sales and marketing are becoming a vital part of a successful CPA firm.

7. The authors identify the key market segments likely to be attracted to the book, extending the market beyond the obvious and showing broad potential. "Field-proven techniques" are always great.

Anyone who needs to have clients to pay the bills needs this book. It makes no difference whether it's a branch office of AT&T or IBM or a single consultant with a part-time secretary, this book gives field-proven techniques needed to master the art of getting clients.

8. It was smart to itemize these benefits in a separate category.

Buyers' Benefits with *How to Get Clients*

1) Complete step-by-step program easily adaptable to any service organization.
2) Most effective, up-to-date, proven client acquisition techniques.
3) Easy to learn and use for *non*sales or *non*marketing people.
4) Ideas that are easily absorbed in the operation of the company.
5) Negates the need for expensive and perhaps ineffective outside marketing and sales specialists.
6) Puts the reader in control of his or her own destiny.
7) Features nine ways for the reader to get potential clients to initiate the contact, which saves time and puts the reader at a great advantage when negotiating fees.
8) Ideas and techniques are fun to read and easy to understand.

Publisher's Benefits

9. Itemizing the publisher's potential benefits in this way was a creative and bold move. But if you try it, make sure not to fill it with fluff, overzealousness, or signs of major egotism.

1) **A Proven Program**—You market a client acquisition book using ideas with a proven track record in the field, not only by the author himself, but by many of his clients and associates. The concepts get results, which makes the book a popular backlist title that is sure to bring you strong sales for years to come.
2) **Expandable**—This book, once proven successful, lends itself to sequels and special editions geared for a specific group that pays double or triple retail for access to this information.

10. Strong source materials bolster the authors' case.

_____

3. *Wall Street Journal*, "Business Bulletin," August 23, 1990, p. 1.

3) **Writing Track Record**—The principal author has three successful published books and one published audio album to date as well as several self-published projects including video and audio.

4) **Promotional Track Record**—The author delivers close to a hundred speeches a year to prominent associations and corporations, giving tremendous visibility for this book. The associations include the American Booksellers with additional exposure in *Publishers Weekly*.

What's My Background?

My background and abilities are ideally suited to make *How to Get Clients* a big success. My strengths, as I see them, are threefold:

1) *Solid professional credentials and practical experience*—I founded the Retail Marketing Institute over ten years ago after leaving an advertising agency for which I was promoted to Vice President at age 23. With a background in both traditional advertising and public relations I began to develop, discover, and adapt ways of using results-oriented, low-cost marketing to get us clients.

Over the past ten years, I have worked with many organizations of various sizes to develop their client acquisition program. While the material in *How to Get Clients* is simple and easily adaptable, it is based on actual success stories. There are no theories here, only proven programs that work and will work for the reader.

I know it works because I use it for my organization and my clients. I've also gathered many other ideas, stories, and strategies from the people who made them work. All of this has been presented in workshops and speeches hundreds upon hundreds of times all over the country and around the world. I have worked with organizations as large as AT&T, American Express, Firestone, Honda, CBS Records, Ramada Inns, Hilton, McDonald's, the city of Dallas, the state of Arkansas, and the country of India! I have also worked with organizations as small as Versatile Investments, Steven Trotter's Legal Clinic, Dr. Donald Pritt, Podiatrist, and Silvan Krel, C.P.A. The one thing they have in common is that they've paid thousands of dollars for this information.

Marc Slutsky started working part time with me about five years ago and then came on board full time three years ago. He has an education background with a specialty in special education. Many of the techniques he used to train his students have been incorporated into our program to make it as easy as possible for a business professional to learn and use these ideas.

11. "About the Author" sections are usually written in the third person. Some people find it easier to blow their own horn without using "I." In this case, first person is highly effective. The principal author makes a strong statement that amplifies his very impressive background without sounding arrogant.

12

12. This "About the Author" section's strength is that it doesn't miss an opportunity to persuade the publisher about the merits of the book. You don't need to list all of your accomplishments since kindergarten. Publishers are more impressed with credentials relevant to the potential success of your book.

13. It's a smart move for the author to bring attention to his previous books, and to highlight his proven ability to help sell substantial copies. Publishers like it when a prospective author with a good project has been successfully published in the recent past.

This past July I was awarded the CSP (Certified Speaking Professional) designation by the National Speakers Association. This title is held by less than 5 percent of the NSA membership. [12]

2) *A publishing track record*—To have a good idea is one thing; to turn it into a book is another. I know I can turn *How to Get Clients* into a great selling book because I have written three books to date that are. They are *Streetfighting: Low Cost Advertising & Marketing for Your Business*, *Street Smart Marketing*, and *The 33 Secrets of Street Smart Tele-Selling*.

Streetfighting (Prentice Hall, 1984)—After a couple of years I acquired the rights and the negs and now self-publish it. In one year, I personally sold out the remainder of the first printing, some 3,400 copies in hard cover after raising the price from $18 to $25. It was picked up by the Adweek Book Club and the Entrepreneur Magazine Book Club as well as promoted by many trade organizations to their members. It is a consistent seller for these groups.

The book is now in its sixth printing. With a newly designed dust cover and a new list price of $30, sales are still going strong with close to 50,000 copies sold to date. *Streetfighting* is an interesting, practical, and clever book that is the farthest thing from a textbook that you would ever read. It now enjoys the tremendous credibility of being recognized by many major universities and is required reading in many business schools and entrepreneur classes, including Indiana University, Northwestern, and the University of Deudlin in New Zealand. [13]

Since we sell *Streetfighting* ourselves, we know where people hear about it. Most of our book sales are referrals. Arby's received one promotional copy then ordered 150 more at full price, and we're still getting follow-up orders to this day. Chick-fil-A, a fast-food operation in Atlanta, ordered 500 copies and now buys *Street Smart Marketing* in quantity direct from the publisher as required reading for every single employee. Amoco Oil, Honda, H & R Block, U-Haul, Greyhound, Photo Marketing Institute, and the Retail Bakers Association are other examples of companies consistently ordering in quantity. Firestone bought 1,100 copies for each of their retail dealers, and Baskin-Robbins bought 3,200 copies in a special run for each of their franchisees.

Street Smart Marketing (John Wiley & Sons, 1989)—While *Streetfighting* is successful, *Street Smart Marketing* targets a much larger and more profitable market. The former was geared toward small, independent businesses. This newer book takes those same ideas, combined with four more years of new ideas, and gears them to the profitable corporate environment.

Street Smart Tele-Selling. The 33 Secrets (Prentice Hall, 1990) was just released. It's geared for the tens of thousands of corporations and businesses that need to sell to the business community. Prentice Hall also produced an audio cassette album with workbook under the same title. The book features a foreword by Robert L. Shook.

My first three books prove I can write in an easy-to-understand and very entertaining style, packed with useful ideas.

3) *A wealth of media exposure and experience*—When it comes to promotion and marketing, I practice what I preach. Not only do you get a quality manuscript, but you also get an author who is promotable and is a promoter. I know how to take advantage of opportunity and turn it into sales.

I'm a performer and do extremely well in an interview situation. In addition to the national publications in which I've been featured, including the *Wall Street Journal, INC Magazine, USA Today,* and *Success,* I've also received a great deal of exposure from dailies including the *Chicago Tribune, Chicago Sun Times, San Francisco Chronicle,* and a host of others. I've been on hundreds of radio and TV shows including CNN, *Nation's Business* on ESPN, WFYR in Chicago, WMCA in New York, and KMPC in Los Angeles, and was on KCBS in San Francisco four times.

One of the most exciting bits of exposure was when I was asked to be a featured speaker at the American Booksellers Association convention this year. As a result, *Publishers Weekly* did a feature story about me and my books, and ABA has invited me back for next year's convention in New York. In addition, I now am a presenter on a regular basis for the National Speakers Association. This is a trade association of some 3,500 professional speakers who collectively reach millions of businesspeople every year. Only a small percentage of our membership is invited to present programs to its members, and I do so on a regular basis. As a result, hundreds of speakers quote from my books, creating additional demand for them.

14. This shows verve and creativity. The principal author has demonstrated genuine confidence throughout the proposal, peppered with the facts to support his claims.

This author's promotion credentials are highly impressive. You can work to build your résumé, as he has—but don't overlook anything you already have in your favor. This author is affiliated with organizations that enhance his status in the field, and shows he has the respect of colleagues.

Delivery of the Book

The book will be about 50,000 words plus illustrations and charts. There will be 10 chapters, each of which includes several subheadings. The complete manuscript will be delivered February 15, 1991. I write with WordPerfect 5.1, and the diskette will also be made available if you so request.

Chapter Summaries

Chapter 1: Who Are Your Potential Clients and Why Do You Want Them?

Before you can begin to go after new clients you have to determine what type of clients you really want. This can be the most important step because oftentimes professionals make an effort to go after clients only to find out years later that they've pigeonholed themselves into a segment of the marketplace that is not very profitable.

The first step is to conduct a simple "internal capabilities audit" to see what your company's strengths and weaknesses are. By playing to your strengths and avoiding weak areas you'll be able to compete on a much stronger footing than your competitors.

You also have to develop some simple guidelines for your account acquisition program that tell you when to go forward and when to "dump out" of an effort. Developing ways for looking for "red flags" or potential trouble areas are critical at this stage before you invest too much of your time or money in getting the client. A few "red flags" include how fast they pay their bills, turnover of similar services, turnover of their personnel, etc.

In this chapter you learn:

15. This chapter-by-chapter outline is complete, yet not bogged down with too much copy. The authors start with a reflection of the book's voice, and list the chapter highlights clearly and concisely. It's very effective to itemize the various "missions" of each chapter like this. This outline gives the impression that there won't be any hot-air filler in this book.

The chapter summaries show exactly what you can expect. It is easy to visualize this book. This is also a clear blueprint for the writer.

1) How to identify the profitable clients from the ones that only talk a good game yet waste your time and eventually lose you money.
2) The 10 steps for determining just how profitable a client will be in the short term.
3) Three steps for determining the long-term value of this client.
4) Why some clients have a need to exaggerate their value to you and how to avoid this.
5) How to determine residual value of a client beyond fees.
6) The 17 red flags to watch out for in determining if a client is going to be more trouble than he's worth.
7) How to develop a plan for guaranteeing that your client base is complementary and avoids duplication of effort.

Chapter 2: How to Discover and Develop Your Unique Market Niche

After you've determined which types of clients are best for your situation, you need to go one step farther and ascertain your market niche. This is a critical step because it is a major factor that determines your fee levels. Generally, the more you are a specialist in a given area, the higher the fees. But you have to be careful not to pick a market that is limited in any way.

Your niche is governed by two factors: 1) the type of service you provide and 2) where you provide it. If you have a geographical territory, that in itself is a partial niche. A computer consultant, for example, may specialize in putting in complete systems for the medical profession and may further limit the niche by staying within a 100-mile radius from his home office. To expand, you then have three choices: expand your territory (which could have its downside); expand your market (find additional niches), which forces you into areas in which you may not have the same level of expertise; and/or provide more services to an existing niche, which also challenges your expertise.

In this chapter you learn:

1) How to discover the most profitable niche for you.
2) When it's time to expand and how to do it.
3) The five factors for determining when you're spreading yourself too thin and in danger of losing it all.
4) How to work your niche to maximize fees.
5) How to select a niche based on ease of marketability.
6) When to consider switching your niche and how to do it.
7) How to expand by offering new services to existing clients without losing credibility.
8) An overview of dominating your niche and keeping the competition at bay.

Chapter 3: 14 Ways to Establish Credibility That Make Clients Take Notice

Credibility is the key to not only getting clients to hire you but getting them to pay top dollar for your services. How you subtly "toot your own horn" is a major factor in getting the business by winning over the client. There are many ways in which you can get a client to "perceive" your credibility and feel comfortable paying you a premium for your services.

In this chapter you learn:

1) What credibility is and how it directly factors into your fee level.
2) The power of the client testimonial and how to get it.
3) How the right publicity can establish you as an expert in your field.
4) When writing a book is appropriate and how to do it without really writing it yourself.
5) Identifying your past "hidden" activities that help develop your credibility even farther.
6) How to put all your credibility elements together to create additional credibility.

7) How to effectively yet subtly use lack of credibility to give you an edge against the competition.

8) How to identify which elements of credibility are the "hot buttons" for your potential client and how to use them to your advantage.

Chapter 4: How to Make an Effective First Contact and Avoiding Wasting Your Time

The first contact is critical because you only get one opportunity to make a good first impression. That's why the first contact is often one that is not even noticeable by your potential client. You have to do your homework first. There's a plethora of information that can be gathered by phone from non-decision-makers that helps you greatly when you're ready to "engage." Once you do "engage" there is no turning back. It's close or be killed. You must handle this first encounter with all your options available to you for maximum maneuverability.

In this chapter you learn:

1) What valuable information you need before you "engage" and how to get it without exposing your position.

2) How to know when you're ready for your first encounter.

3) Why you need to use a "fact gathering" mission or "reconnaissance" mission before you're ready to make your major pitch.

4) How to structure fact gathering so that you position yourself for a "no-fail" return visit.

5) When the "dog and pony" show is more of a distraction than help and how to avoid its pitfalls.

6) The magic elements that every potential client wants to know.

7) How to get commitment from your client by presentation's end.

8) Five ways to get your client to pay for your research and presentation.

Chapter 5: How to Dominate Your Marketplace without Spending a Fortune

There are many ways a skilled professional can achieve a leading market position and make it difficult for competition to move in on your territory. It takes thought and effort but with a carefully planned program, you can easily dominate your "turf."

In this chapter you learn:

1) How to determine if your marketplace already has a leader and just how strong that position really is.

2) Seven ways to shut out your competition.

3) How to use trade journals or local news media to your advantage.

4) The power of public speaking in creating your leadership position.

5) How to work with a trade association.
6) How to avoid spending much time and money working with trade associations.
7) How to effectively use your printed support material, articles, newsletters, books, tapes, speeches, and other items to secure and maintain leadership position.
8) Why the leadership position allows you to get 10 to 100 percent higher fees for the same work as your nearest competitor.

Chapter 6: 10 Techniques for Avoiding Fee Shopping

When selling a service it is often common for clients to negotiate your fees heavily, playing your competition against you for the best price. Nobody wins at this kind of game and you need to avoid it completely. Selling on price is the weakest position you can take, especially in a competitive situation. You must build "value" for your services and help the client find solutions to problems, not just buy your services.

In this chapter you learn:

1) How to avoid fee shopping before it becomes an issue.
2) How to deal with the "price" issue when it becomes a major objection.
3) When to fight and when to flee.
4) What other problems arise later on in the client relationship when price is the major consideration in hiring you.
5) Ten ways to build high value to justify your price.
6) How to negotiate lower fees when appropriate without losing fee credibility.
7) How and when to add services that the client needs that also add extra profit to your bottom line.

Chapter 7: When Advertising Makes Sense and How to Do It for Less

Service organizations often spend fortunes on advertising, most of which is wasted. There is a time and a place to advertise but you have to know all the basics or you'll end up going under supporting your advertising. You also need to know that the only thing advertising can do is perhaps create some interest and get a potential client to contact you. What you do with that contact really determines the value of your advertising. Advertising itself does not sell clients—you do.

In this chapter you learn:

1) Which media make the most sense and why.
2) How to negotiate with media to save money and get better results.

3) What to say in your ad so that only qualified potential clients call you.
4) How to follow up an ad so you convert the interested client into a paying client.
5) How to track the results of your advertising.
6) When to consider direct mail, telemarketing, trade journals, yellow pages, etc., and how to use them for less money.
7) How to look for opportunities to barter with the media and not get stung.
8) The proper use of 800 numbers, computer dialing machines, marketing software, and business reply cards.
9) Three ways you can use a two-step process.

Chapter 8: The Value of Free Publicity and How to Get It

One of the best ways to support your business is with free publicity. It does many different things for you and has been mentioned briefly in previous chapters. Now it's time to get it in detail and put this tremendous tool to work for you.

You can't depend on publicity entirely, yet it makes a great supplement to your regular account acquisition program.

In this chapter you learn:

1) How to approach the news media so they want to do your story.
2) How to leverage your publicity long after the item has run.
3) How to handle the interview so clients know how to get in touch with you.
4) Five things to avoid when talking to the media.
5) How to handle negative publicity and why there is no such thing as "off the record."
6) When enough is enough and when too much is harmful.
7) How to determine which media are best for you and which are a waste of your time.
8) Why and when it's good for your business when you're just stroking your own ego.

Chapter 9: How to Communicate Persuasively to Get a "Yes"

The key to your success in getting clients is your ability to communicate persuasively to the prospective client. They have to understand the value of what you have to offer with the same intensity that you do. Selling is not a negative thing. It often brings to mind used-car salesmen in polyester sport coats selling lemons to unsuspecting buyers. That's unfortunate. Selling in the '90s is much more. It's a means of helping your prospective client understand how you are going to solve the problem and why they should be happy to pay top dollar.

In this chapter you learn:

1) How to get past the gatekeeper, the person who can't say "yes" but can say "no."
2) How to know when you're talking with the decision-maker and why you shouldn't waste your time with others.
3) How to control the conversation by asking questions.
4) How to use the "echo" in fact gathering and discovering client hot buttons.
5) Understanding the painful process of decision-making and working it to your advantage.
6) How to properly diagnose your clients' problems and then perform a "cashectomy."
7) How to turn a conversation around after you're on the defensive.
8) When it's time to get the commitment and how to identify client buying signals.

Chapter 10: Proposals and Presentations: 5 Rules for Results

The final stage is preparing and presenting the proposal. This should actually be the easy part if all the other stages were followed properly. Yet many things can still happen. To make sure there are no surprises, you have the client help you prepare the proposal. In this way they know exactly what they're getting. No surprises. Furthermore, a client is more likely to buy into a program in which they were involved.

In this chapter you learn:

1) How to get your client involved in the development of the proposal.
2) When it is appropriate to charge a fee for your proposal and how to use your "needs analysis" as a fee generator.
3) How to develop a proposal that is geared for what the client likes and not what you like.
4) How to balance the written proposal with the live presentation.
5) Why a "dog and pony" doesn't get the client.
6) How to structure the numbers so that you have maximum flexibility when it comes down to final negotiations.
7) How to avoid a competitive bid situation and why you'll always lose if you don't.
8) The "one bite at a time" proposal and how it makes it easy for the client to "give it a try," which gets you in the front door.
9) How to suggest "add-ons" that your client may want and provide extra dollars to your bottom line.

PROPOSAL 3

Black Roots

A Beginner's Guide to Tracing the Family Tree

by Tony Burroughs

Black Roots: A Beginner's Guide to Tracing the Family Tree

Contents

Overview

Black Roots: A Beginner's Guide to Tracing the Family Tree is the fun, easy-to-use, detailed, "how-to" guide people have been waiting for since Alex Haley's *Roots*. *Black Roots* is filled with live examples of records, photographs, documents, charts, and forms used in tracing family history and discovering ancestors. This comprehensive guide is based on the author's twenty years of successful genealogical experience and six years of teaching genealogy and lecturing around the country.

Alex Haley took the nation by storm with his book and mini television series, *Roots*. The book sold 1.8 million copies in the first eighteen months. The television series was the most watched program in history—seen by 130 million viewers. *Roots* caused a genealogical explosion and inspired thousands of Americans, black and white, to trace their family histories. *Roots,* however, was a novel—not a genealogists' "how-to" guide. While Haley's work *Roots* illustrated that African American genealogy is possible, *Black Roots: A Beginner's Guide to Tracing the Family Tree* explains how to do it. Now PBS will air a new ten-episode genealogy series beginning in January 1997 that will be the biggest genealogy program since *Roots*. *Black Roots* will not only be very timely, but the author will be the guest expert in the series' African American genealogy episode.

After the television series *Roots*, African Americans were left on their own to search for their ancestors by trial and error. *Black Roots: A Beginner's Guide to Tracing the Family Tree* fills this void. *Black Roots* is a practical, step-by-step

1. This proposal came with a nice graphic on the cover. If you decide to go beyond a simple cover with a nice font, be sure it is tasteful. Every aspect of a proposal creates a mood. If your topic warrants a nice graphic on the cover page, go for it. Just make sure it's clean and professional. It represents you. Make sure to include information about where to reach you on the proposal. Sometimes a cover letter is separated from the proposal, and the consequences could be really sad.

2. The material included here has been shortened from the original proposal, which was quite long. We have abbreviated other proposals as well.

3. This is a great first paragraph in that it clearly states what the book is about and establishes the author's *expertise.* It also hints at a market by reminding the reader of the success of Alex Haley's book *Roots,* which creates an immediate image of success.

4. This is a good follow-up statistic and supporting statement regarding why the book should exist. It establishes a need and meets it.

guide. For those who know nothing about tracing their roots, *Black Roots* offers the basics and progresses logically, with later chapters building on skills learned from earlier chapters. For those with experience, *Black Roots* reinforces the basics and explains procedures even the most experienced researchers have neglected.

Black Roots is based on twenty years of genealogical research experience and six years of teaching genealogy. My adult education class covers genealogy theory. Students work on their own families during class, using the methods taught in *Black Roots*. Students have located their ancestors in records or identified new ancestors during the course—so the methods have been proven in the classroom. As I lecture around the country and talk with other researchers, I continually update the methods and sources used in African American genealogy.

Black Roots explains genealogy theory and gives examples of records, [5] documents, charts, and forms used in the process. Readers are shown how records are interwoven and how one find can lead to another. Researchers learn where to search close to home, where to write for records, how to organize records, and how to analyze documents. *Black Roots* even gives information on preserving family records, photographs, and research documents. But genealogy is not just about records, it's about people, and readers get to know the people in *Black Roots*. The book shares personal vignettes and anecdotes that personalize both the records and the research.

Robert Burroughs, a brother to my grandfather I never knew, becomes [6] a central figure in the book. As the chapter on Family Records unfolds, Robert's personal belongings are discovered in a trunk. The items are examined and shown to have genealogical value and lead to other records.

One of the reasons Robert is unknown is that his life is completely contrasted with his brother who becomes a prominent and well-known attorney. Robert hangs with the wrong crowd and ends up robbing a bank and going to jail. Robert's circumstances are significant because everyone descends from varied backgrounds. Genealogy provides seeks to provide understand- [7] ing of differences and hopefully inspires those who are less fortunate and don't descend from kings and queens. We also realize everyone is found in the records, no matter what their background.

Other African American genealogy guides contain artificial case studies. [8] Unfortunately, these studies are not based on real genealogy where a researcher traced back from one generation to the previous generation. One such study uses records primarily from one library to highlight that collection. Another study was based on records that 'looked interesting" but proceeded on broad assumptions and omitted major steps in the research process. The problem with artificial case studies is that while they work in books, they do not prepare researchers for real problems they may encounter while researching.

5. The overview gives plenty of substance and establishes credibility. While some of the ideas will be described in greater detail in later portions of the proposal, questions are anticipated and answers are provided.

6. If handled correctly, it is worth repeating a good point. This makes a subtle reference to why Alex Haley's *Roots* was so successful by pointing out there will be interesting narrative support in what could otherwise be a dry subject.

7. Although no one may have noticed the redundancy in this sentence, you should always edit, edit, edit to catch simple typos and mistakes, and there are many typos in this proposal. Don't rely solely on Spell-Check or you will find some often hilarious and embarrassing results.

8. This raises an interesting issue and shows in a positive light how this book can take a researcher through potential pitfalls. This is very persuasive.

9   In addition to being a guide to African American family history research, *Black Roots* contains fundamental methods useful for all genealogists. Many non-African Americans have attended my lectures and read my materials. They have said the methods are sound and very useful for all genealogists.

10   *Black Roots* highlights some of the special problems, solutions, and sources unique to African Americans. All too often traditional genealogists say that African American genealogy is the same as any other genealogy until you get back to the slavery period. Records for enslaved African Americans were recorded under the slave owner's names with slaves only referred to by first names. This research is very different from traditional European American genealogy. However, African American genealogy is also different *after* the slavery period. If not, it would negate 130 years of U.S. history that include racism and segregation—two factors which influence African American genealogical research. The genealogical research process during this period is somewhat similar to European American genealogy, but there are nuances and traps that researchers can fall into if they negate this history. This is the new perspective that *Black Roots* addresses.

11 Author

Tony Burroughs is an internationally known, recognized leader in African American genealogy. In 1996 the National Genealogical Society awarded him the Distinguished Service Award for his contributions to the field of genealogy. With two others, he co-authored the *African American Genealogical Sourcebook* (Gale Research 1995).

    Mr. Burroughs has been interviewed many times on radio and television. When Alex Haley died in 1992, the NBC and CBS television evening news program in Chicago interviewed him on his thoughts on Haley's death. Next year he will be featured in episode seven of the forthcoming PBS series *Ancestors* as the African American genealogy expert. This program is slated to be broadcast to 351 national affiliates beginning in January 1997. It will be repeated at least four times over the next four years. He has also appeared in national print media from the *New York Times* to *Jet* magazine (see appendix).

    Mr. Burroughs has been teaching genealogy in the Adult Education Department at Chicago State University since 1990. He's also founder and president of Black Roots, a genealogical supply company. He served as president and vice president of the Afro-American Genealogical & Historical Society of Chicago, Inc., the second-largest African American genealogical society in the country. Under his leadership the organization grew in membership from sixty-five to over two hundred people while the treasury increased eightfold. The society came into national prominence while he was

---

9. This points to a secondary market, which flows naturally from the main market.

10. This gives a taste of the substance of the book and supports the author's credibility.

11. This is a wonderful author bio. It is well written, interesting to read, and shows he is marketable. Of course, his fabulous and relevant credentials don't hurt. This is a good example of tying credentials to the substance of the book. It also shows how ideas follow to build relevant credentials. There are always things you can do to develop credibility in your chosen area of expertise. If you are planning to follow up and build upon your proposed book, you will want to continue to map out a strategy to build up your reputation in the field.

president and received the Award of Merit for distinguished service to the genealogical community in 1993 from the Federation of Genealogical Societies, the national umbrella group for all genealogical societies in the country. He has served on the board of directors of two national organizations, the Federation of Genealogical Societies and the Afro-American Historical and Genealogical Society in Washington, D.C., the. largest African American genealogical society in the country. He is a member of the National Genealogical Society, the Association of Professional Genealogists, the Chicago Genealogical Society, and the Illinois State Genealogical Society.

Mr. Burroughs lectures at national, state, and local conferences. He has accepted invitations to speak from across the country in over twenty cities from Seattle and San Diego on the West Coast to Rochester to Washington, D.C., on the East Coast and throughout the Midwest. He was the James Dent Walker Memorial lecturer at the Federation of Genealogical Societies' conference in Richmond, Virginia, in October 1994. At the National Genealogy Society's national conference in San Diego, California, out of over 130 lectures, his was the only presentation on African American genealogy. He delivered his first international lecture in Chatham, Ontario, Canada in May 1995.

Competition

12. This is a strong foundation for assessing competition. It uses the thesis statement to offset any competition before referring to it.

There are only a few books in the field of African American genealogy. Most [12] existing works focus on sources as opposed to practical methods of research. None is directed toward beginners, and only one was produced by a major publisher.

Why *Black Roots* Is Different

13. This focuses on what is positive and unique about this book. He has not yet mentioned specific books, but the reader already has a sense of where he is heading. This is very effective because it does not sound defensive. It is a confident and reasonable approach to the subject.

Black Roots is different because the author came through the ranks of geneal- [13] ogy, reading the fundamental literature, attending classes, institutes, lectures, conferences, working with genealogical societies, and serving on national boards. He researched his own genealogy and shared his knowledge and expertise by teaching others for six years and lecturing around the country, learning the problems of others. He is very well respected in the industry, receiving the Distinguished Service Award from the National Genealogical Society.

A couple of books have been written on African American genealogy by nongenealogists, trying to catch on to its popularity. Some dwell on history and culture because the author is not well grounded in the science and methods of genealogy. Some try to be impressive by mentioning many different sources. But what good are sources if researchers are not told how and when to use them? Researchers need to not merely know the names of records, but where they are located, how to obtain them, what they contain, why they should be used, how to analyze them, their strengths and weaknesses, ins and outs of when to use them, and the priority and sequence of using different records. Beginners need to know how records can be used efficiently to progress from A to B to C.

14
1
Black Roots answers these questions. *Black Roots* goes into less sources, but more depth and detail so beginners really understand the process and the records. It only goes into sources beginners need. These things are not difficult, they just need explaining and good examples on how they're used. This book is fundamentally sound and the author makes things easy, interesting, logical, and fun.

- *Black Genealogy* by Charles L. Blockson (Black Classic Press, 1991 reprint of 1977 original) covers many sources, only some of which can be used in tracing African American family history. It is not methodological in nature and does not illustrate the fundamentals of beginning genealogical research.
- *African American Genealogical Sourcebook,* edited by Paula Byers (Gale Research, 1995) is primarily a source guide. This book includes three essays describing records and how to use them. It would be difficult for a beginner to learn genealogy with this directory. It is marketed as a library reference book. With its high price, it may discourage purchase by beginning researchers.
- *A Student's Guide to African American Genealogy* by Anne E. Johnson and Adam Merton Cooper (Oryx Press, 1996) focuses more on history and culture than genealogy. Beginning methods are covered ten pages.
- *African American Genealogy Workbook* by Nova Law (self-published, Legacy Publishing Co.) is primarily blank charts and forms with less than ten pages of text.
- *Slave Genealogy: A Research Guide with Case Studies* by David H. Streets (Heritage Books, Inc., 1986) is definitely not for beginners. This work only covers material for those who have advanced to researching slave ancestors.

15
1

16
1 Out-of-Print Works

- *Black Genesis* by James Rose and Alice Eicholz (Gale Research, 1978) is a directory with a few pages of essay. A section for novice researchers covers a page and a half.
- *Beginning an Afro-American Genealogical Pursuit* by Jean Sampson Scott (self-published, 1985) is a twenty-seven-page paperback book.

14. It is not what is intended, but this statement could sound like a potential weakness in the book. He is saying he uses fewer sources. While it is wise to address what is an actual flaw that will be readily recognizable by an editor or agent, don't give information that may be known only to you or true experts in the field. You have enough to overcome without drawing attention to items too detailed to be relevant to the ultimate decision to publish or represent your book. This statement could be made clearly but in a more positive fashion. For example, "*Black Roots* focuses on using basic sources so as not to overwhelm the beginning researcher." This is certainly not a significant problem in this proposal, but it is an important point to keep in mind when writing your own. Don't write as though you are confessing something. You know far more about your subject than anyone else. Unless the "weakness" could be fatal to the credibility of the book if unaddressed, leave it out.

15. What does this statement mean? Because of a typo, it is a non sequitur. Edit, edit, edit. Typos will not be fatal, of course, but

you don't want to send the message that you are careless about your work.

16. It is not necessary to refer to out-of-print books as competition.

In spite of its title, it only lightly touches upon fundamental genealogical research.

- *Case Studies in Afro-American Genealogy* by David Thackery and Dee Woodtor (Newberry Library, 1989) is a forty-three-page, paperback book with most examples limited to Newberry Library's collection.
- *Black Genealogy: How to Begin* by James Dent Walker (University of Georgia, 1977) is a fifty-two-page paperback book including many topics too advanced for beginners.

Market Analysis

17. This is a great market statistic.

18. This sentence might have been better in the previous paragraph, with the other relevant statistics.

19. This is very good. It anticipates a question an agent or editor might ask about the size of the audience and shows a clearly developing market for African American–oriented or –authored books.

20. This is a sentence floating in space. It would have been better placed in the material in the previous pages establishing the market. Instead, he could have introduced this anecdote with a sentence such as, "Here is an example of how strong the interest is in African Americans in tracing their family history." You want your statements to flow together logically for maximum impact.

Genealogy is great for hobbyists, mystery readers, researchers, treasure hunters, and curiosity seekers. It's great for people who like puzzles, game shows, detective shows, or research. It keeps people guessing and it's a never-ending quest. Once people start looking, who knows what they'll find?

The December 1995 issue of *Demographics Magazine* states genealogy is [17] one of America's most popular hobbies, practiced by close to half of American adults. Almost 113 million people state they are somewhat interested in their family history, whereas 19 million say they are seriously involved in researching. It was reported that the most popular suite at the June 1996 conference of Public Broadcasting stations in San Francisco belonged to *Ancestors*, a genealogy series to be broadcast in January 1997.

The primary market for *Black Roots* is composed of the African American middle class, senior citizens, and students. Younger people will use it to begin researching their families and interviewing their parents and grandparents. Senior citizens will read it to begin their searches and as a guide to record their memories and life stories. According to *American Demographics* 46 [18] percent or more of adults aged 25 to 64 are involved in genealogy.

According to *Target Market News*, book expenditures by black house- [19] holds rose 67 percent in 1994 to $297 million. Sales have steadily increased from 1992 when Terry McMillian (*Waiting to Exhale*) brought new buyers in the market. *Target Market News* says that growth is being fueled by the growing number of titles of African American interest and increased marketing efforts by major publishers.

Beginners, students, teachers, librarians, researchers, and professional genealogists continually ask me to recommend a good beginning guide for African American genealogists. Before *Black Roots*, there has been no comprehensive beginning guide to African American genealogy. This is virtually an untapped market due to existing books' failure to fill this void.

There is a strong interest in African Americans in tracing their family [20] history.

- On a freezing winter day in Chicago on February 22, 1992, hundreds of people waited in line in subzero temperatures to hear Dorothy Spruill Redford (*Somerset Homecoming,* Doubleday, 1988) and myself talk about tracing African American roots. Ms. Redford spoke of tracing her ancestry to the Somerset Plantation in North Carolina as well as researching the 471 slaves on the plantation. My story examined the problems and differences between the surnames of former slaves and those of their last slave owner to avert researchers from myths and assumptions. Before the program ended, 500 hundred people packed a 400-seat auditorium, 100 people sat and stood in the aisles all day.

- The head of Ready Reference at the Alabama State Archives recently stated they have had increasing numbers of African Americans in the archives searching for their roots.

- *American Visions,* an African American family and historically related magazine, added a genealogy column within the last two years because of increased demand.

- The Chicago branch of the National Archives has been acquiring more microfilm related to African Americans based on the increasing numbers of researchers interested in African American genealogy.

- Gale Research (Detroit) has had an increasing demand to reprint *Black Genesis* by James Rose and Alice Eicholz. It was published in 1978 and was the last major book on African American genealogy. Because of this demand, they decided to publish a new book, *African American Genealogical Sourcebook* (Paula Byers, ed., 1995). On the strength of my reputation and presentations that highlighted the book, sixty copies were sold at $69 each at three genealogical conferences. A dozen more could have been sold if more copies had been available.

A built-in demand exists for *Black Roots.* I wrote a significant portion of *African American Genealogical Sourcebook,* which is in most libraries in the country. This book will serve to presell *Black Roots.* There will be instant name recognition among most genealogists and genealogy librarians. Because *African American Genealogical Sourcebook* is a library reference book, beginning researchers will want something easy to read and affordable.

Secondary Market

More and more non–African Americans are interested in African American genealogy. They will make up a large percentage of purchasers of this book. There are many segments within this group and many reasons for their interest.

21. It is always good to put a number with a potential market. This can create an image that also translates into potential book sales.

22. What is the circulation of this magazine? This is easy to ascertain and would strengthen the statement. Of course, if there are only five people who read it (including you), you don't need to mention the number. In this situation, omission is not the same as lying (just don't tell your teenager, if you have one, about this particular loophole).

23. The author could consider making a bold statement about the implications for selling his book to a general audience at a less prohibitive price. Again, you are painting a picture of potential book sales.

24. This would be a good statement to place before the previous paragraph regarding the genealogical sourcebook. It is not clear that the author wrote a significant portion of the book. This information makes the point even stronger.

- Many teachers and librarians have African American students and patrons.
- Many genealogists are interracially married and want to research their spouse's line.
- Many genealogists are discovering they have African American ancestors in their background.
- Many genealogists have African American friends and coworkers and want to either research for them or introduce them to the subject.
- Genealogical lecturers are encouraged to be more inclusive in presenting lectures at conferences and workshops that include all ethnic groups.
- Many professional genealogists have African American clients.
- Many experienced genealogists have been doing their genealogy for years and are looking for new challenges.

Several lectures at national conferences and articles in national journals have already given the author name recognition in the non–African American genealogical community.

Black Roots will be used heavily in schools. Elementary students have been getting into the early stages of genealogy. In fact, the Boy Scouts have a genealogy book used to obtain a merit badge. I started with this book when I was twenty-six years old. It was originally published in 1973 and reprinted in 1988.

25. If you can find numbers to correspond with any of this, it is always effective.

Currently, some teachers are teaching genealogy by trial and error (often in Social Studies classes). *Black Roots* can be easily adapted to use as a classroom textbook in elementary and high schools. It is also most likely to [25] become a standard reference book in libraries around the country. *Black Roots* will become required reading for my classes at Chicago State University. It will probably become recommended reading for other programs and genealogical societies around the country.

26. This is excellent and relevant. It is clear this author worked hard to build his recognition and will continue to work to promote this book. The image is established that the author is focused and that this is his life's work. Don't be concerned if your book is merely something you want to write before you move on to some-

Promotion

In addition to promotion efforts by the publisher, the author's public speak- [26] ing engagements will greatly add to *Black Roots'* exposure and sales. Over the last couple of years, the author has presented workshops, and lectures in over two dozen cities in the United States and Canada and has presentations scheduled into 1997 and 1998. The opportunity to autograph books at these future events will enhance sales. Additional exposure will come from media coverage at speaking engagements, and genealogy articles slated for national publications (see letters in Supporting Material). Additional sales will come

26 from mail order catalogues of genealogy supplies, the directory *Genealogy and Local History Books in Print,* and vendors at national, state, and local genealogy conferences.

The PBS *Ancestors* series is scheduled to air four times in the next three years. Clips from the African American genealogy episode will also appear in a companion video. The author's chapter in the companion guide to the series will keep his name and image in the public eye

27 # Chapter Outline

1. **Introduction**
2. **What Is Genealogy?**
3. **Fundamentals: The Building Blocks of African American Genealogy**
4. **Organizing Before It Gets Messy**
5. **Preserving the Past and the Present**
6. **Managing Your Research**
   - Research to Do
   - Things to Do
   - Research Calendar
   - Correspondence Index
   - File Folder Contents
7. **Beginning Research Steps**
   Step 1. Oral History: The Most Important Thing You Can Do
   Step 2. The Family Archives: Researching Family Papers
   Step 3. Family Group Sheets
   Step 4. The Pedigree Chart
   Step 5. Records in Cemeteries
   Step 6. Records in Funeral Homes
   Step 7. Vital Records
   Step 8. Preparing for the Library
   Step 9. Social Security Records
   Step 10. U.S. Census Records
8. **Preparing for the Library**
9. **I Can't Stop Now: Continuing the Search**
10. **Appendices**
    A. Glossary
    B. Recommended Reading
    C. National Archives Branches
    D. African American Genealogical Societies
    E. Vendors

thing else. But if it is your life's work, any evidence of this is good to include. It translates into commitment and possible book sales. Don't make statements you can't back up, however. If it is not your life's work, don't say it is. This is not the same as omission. You will feel guilty, and you don't want that, do you?

27. This is a very clear and unintimidating Table of Contents. It is good to actually list this as the Table of Contents as opposed to calling it only an outline. You want to show that this is not just an example but is what the editor or agent can expect in the book itself. The author has handled his Table of Contents in the relaxed yet clear style he has used throughout the proposal. It is clear that this is how he will be approaching the book.

Chapter Summary

28

1. Introduction

This brief section explains how much fun genealogy is and how it is akin to game shows and treasure hunting. It doesn't cost a lot of money to start and anyone can do it. There is plenty to discover and if researchers go about it the right way, everyone will have success. The book is based on my twenty years of genealogy experience and six years of classroom teaching experience. Students have used these methods successfully in class. They also learn what they will get out of this book. The chapter ends by wishing researchers happy hunting.

2. What Is Genealogy?

This chapter of the book defines "genealogy" and presents an overview of the process. An analogy is drawn between genealogy and assembling a jigsaw puzzle, where every bit and piece is important. The science of genealogy and rules that govern the research are discussed.

What is not genealogy is explained. With the advent of computers, there are databases published disguising as genealogies. They contain a minimum of research on a surname, a family crest with some history of the crest, and a database of persons with the same surname. Most of the people in the database are neither related nor entitled to use the family crest. Many unsuspecting novices are attracted to these publications—they are attracted to the low price and the thousands of names in the book. One of my cousins was upset when his father lost a similar book. He thought the family history was lost. He was relieved when I explained the book had nothing to do with our family.

Genealogy is compared with history. Genealogy is related to history but distinctly different. A knowledge of history is needed to practice genealogy—the interdependence between the two disciplines is explained. This chapter discusses history in general and distinguishes among American history, African American history, local history, and family history.

The distinction between genealogy and African American genealogy is clearly discussed. There is a lot of talk among white genealogists about how to research African American genealogy. Unfortunately, most of this talk is based on theory instead of actual research. Some of the differences are discussed and several examples are cited.

The growing group of African Americans who have experience in tracing their family history are discussed next. Many have published articles and books, lectured, and organized groups of other African American genealogists. Many novices are unaware of these experienced researchers and the existence of formal organizations.

I also discuss problems and weaknesses people have that affect their ability to research genealogy. The lack of knowledge of history directly

---

28. These summaries are approached with an explanation of what they will do. The proposal is so strong and clear that the summaries don't need to be more comprehensive. The necessary level of comprehensiveness is greatly dependent on the detail and substance of the proposed book. If you have any doubt that the editor or agent will understand what you are going to write, opt for more detail, including some actual copy. For some books you want to do more showing than telling.

affects understanding of ancestors' lives, conditions, and surroundings. It will also affect the ability to trace them backward in time. Fortunately this weakness is easily overcome by reading and study. Genealogy provides a purpose and a focus in studying history that most people did not have in school. When people see their ancestors were actually involved in history, it comes alive. Then researchers begin to crave the same history they may have found uninteresting in school.

The chapter ends with a discussion of the bright future of African American genealogy. New methods, techniques, and sources are being developed every day.

3. Fundamentals: The Building Blocks of African American Genealogy

This chapter discusses the basics and compares the fundamentals in genealogy to another American pastime, baseball. Fundamentals are needed in any field—without them, participants are on shaky ground. Seventeen basic steps in African American genealogy are categorized as beginning, intermediate, and advanced. This chapter explains that this book concentrates only on the beginning steps.

Beginning Steps

1. Write your autobiography
2. Interview parents and older relatives
3. Locate and examine family papers, records, photos, and memorabilia
4. Fill out family group sheets
5. Fill out pedigree chart
6. Visit cemeteries and funeral homes
7. Obtain birth and death certificates, marriage licenses, and divorce records
8. Preparing for the library
9. Research Social Security records
10. Research U.S. Census records

Intermediate Steps

11. Preparing for the county courthouse and state archives
12. Research wills, probate, and estate records
13. Research real estate records
14. Research other city, county, and state records
15. Research military records

Advanced Steps

16. Research Freedmen's Bureau records
17. Research slave records

29. This seems like a throwaway. It might be better to list quality resources for this purpose. Otherwise, a statement of what this book covers might be enough. It may not be necessary to mention that other books will be needed to take the reader beyond, to more intermediate and advanced steps. This is not the concern of this author. If his book is not enough, then the reader will choose to go beyond what he can offer. Here is another good example of a professional assuming that the agent or editor is going to have the same sophisticated knowledge of the field as he does. He is writing what will be a commercial book for the general public. He is not writing a college text. He needs to change hats.

30. These chapter summaries work for a book of this nature, as they cover the details that will be included in the book. The details are less important for most editors or agents, but it is not a bad idea to give actual examples. It is also fine to include more anecdotes, which might pique the interest of someone who may never have considered the subject.

31. Although we were able to find a few areas that could be improved, overall this is a highly effective proposal.

Once readers have mastered beginning techniques, they should study [29] intermediate and advanced steps from other books and resources.

4. Organizing Before It Gets Messy

Organization is a key element in successful genealogical research. This chapter explains the need to organize research findings from the beginning. It suggests how to categorize records and documents for easy filing and retrieval. Organization is probably the most neglected aspect of genealogical research. Many researchers never bother with organizing their findings until it is too late. They get swamped with documents and notes and can't locate items they know they have collected. If they use a system from the beginning, it will work for them throughout their genealogical careers. Also, if they stop researching, someone else could easily continue where they left off.

A file management system is described in detail. This is an expandable system that can grow as researchers become more successful and put more time into their research. Pitfalls are also exposed in using notebooks, with which almost all novices begin. The intent is to avoid problems down the road by having beginners start correctly and understand what otherwise could take months or years to learn. Several diagram are used to illustrate the filing system (see appendix).

The chapter also covers tools and supplies needed for genealogical research and proper organization. They are broken down among basic, intermediate, and optional tools. These tools enable researchers to hold down costs by buying items as they need them. If they never advance beyond the basic level, they have not spent unnecessary money.

5. Preserving the Past and the Present

Records genealogists utilize have been around for hundreds of years. Some are in excellent condition, many others are deteriorating. This chapter explains the need for preserving existing records and gives tips on how researchers can preserve records they collect and create.

Most novices are unaware that paper deteriorates. A brief explanation is given of the manufacturing process of paper and why it deteriorates. Readers are introduced to long-lasting acid-free paper and file folders. The chapter concludes with information on preserving photographs. Although many families take snapshots of relatives, most people are unaware that everyday color photographs will not last a tenth as long as black-and-white photographs. Readers are advised to take black-and-white photographs at birth-[30,31] days, holidays, and family reunions. Tips are also included on using cameras in genealogical research.

PROPOSAL 4

How Saturn Reinvented the Customer Loyalty Wheel

"No Hassle" Steps ANY Business Can Use!

by Vicki Lenz

We sold this one to John Wiley & Sons. The proposal isn't the author's first draft, but she went the distance to create an exceptional proposal. Its strengths are clarity of purpose, a fresh approach, and the way it distinguishes this book from the competition.

1. This is not written in stone, but our preference would be to see a stronger thesis statement here. All of this material is effective and interesting, but it is not immediately clear that the information about Saturn is placed in a larger context. One statement would remove any question that the book is only about Saturn and is just a self-serving corporate publicity book. While the book was written with Saturn's cooperation, it has a greater usefulness for the standard business reader and therefore a much bigger market.

2. This paragraph would be enhanced by a definition of customer loyalty as it relates to many different industries. This would define potential markets.

3. This is an effective statement that clearly illustrates the importance of customer loyalty.

Overview

"Their no-hassle, no-haggle sales approach was refreshing. We have six Saturns in the family. Five of us are on our second Saturn. My wife of 25 years feels comfortable taking the car in for service by herself.

Your have to look at the whole picture: the car, sales, and service. What makes it special is that I feel I'm being treated like a human being. And that they care."

In an industry where customer loyalty rates typically range from 30% to 40%, Saturn Corporation excels at close to 60%. Pretty good for an auto manufacturer that has had only seven short years to develop repeat-buying customers. Saturn, the small-car wholly owned subsidiary of General Motors, is also the perennial leader in the J. D. Power and Associates annual sales satisfaction study. Saturn set out from the very beginning to be "a different kind of company," with "a different kind of car." They have changed the way cars are sold and the way business is conducted. Results include not only a profitable business, but also enthusiastic, loyal customers that keep coming back. Tom Peters, in his book *The Pursuit of WOW!*, describes what Saturn has created as an "almost cult-like devotion." Like the 44,000 owners and their families that made the trip (from all over the country) to Spring Hill, Tennessee, in 1994 for a "Homecoming"— just to eat barbecue, see where their cars were made, and meet the people who made them. And like the guy that had the Saturn logo tattooed on his leg.

Unfortunately, many major corporations now lose *half* their customers in five years. Companies that ignore these losses can expect a future of low growth, weak profits, and shortened life expectancy. On the other hand, increasing the number of customers a company keeps by as little as 5% can mean doubling profits. A study by Bain & Company, Inc., proves that this holds true for a wide range of industries including insurance, advertising, software, banking, and industrial distribution.

It's like a leaky bucket. As a company loses customers out of the leak in the bottom of the bucket, they have to continue to add new customers (an expensive process) to the top of the bucket. If the company can even partially plug the leak, the bucket stays fuller. It then takes fewer new customers added to the top of the bucket to achieve the same level of profitability. It's less expensive and more profitable to keep those customers already in the bucket.

This Book

4 *How Saturn Reinvented the Customer Loyalty Wheel* shows how to plug that leaky bucket and turn one-time customers into repeat-purchasing loyal customers, with the "Saturn style" of business as the role model. It progresses along the basics of a six-step Saturn buying experience—before, during, and after the purchase. It tells how a buying process ***should be***—for any product or service, from any size or type of business. Plenty of DOs and DON'Ts, straightforward tips and suggestions are offered. Each step of the way, facts and examples tell how Saturn has created—and continues to create—the atmosphere necessary for customer loyalty. Perspective is provided from the outside looking in, through quotes from customers that help tell the story and emphasize points. Further guidance for owners and managers on creating a customer-loyalty environment is provided in the last two chapters, including comments and suggestions from top Saturn management.

5 A simple writing style plus quick-reading format help make this book attractive to all those busy business readers out there waiting to buy it. Lots of subheadings, bullet-item tips, and offset quotes make it easy for readers to skim quickly for usable ideas.

6 This is the first how-to book on customer loyalty that uses one major, highly visible corporation as the role model.

Who Needs It?

Businesspeople in positions ranging from receptionist to customer service rep, from sales rep to manager, and from small business owner to CEO, will find something useful in this book. As competition continues to increase at the speed of light, and growth continues to be a tough challenge, all types and sizes of businesses—from AT&T to the entrepreneur—stand to benefit from increased customer loyalty.

Why Me?

7 As a marketing professional and speaker, I've observed and often mentioned "the Saturn style" of doing business. I even cited Saturn's Homecoming event in one of my earlier books. Enthusiastic Saturn customers started coming forward and sharing their experiences with me. When my own car needed replacing, I ended up buying a Saturn, which gives me firsthand experience and perspective as a Saturn customer.

I have the ability (and proven experience with my two previous books) to view things from both the corporate side and the customer side, then translate into easily understandable, how-to information and tips for businesspeople.

4. This is a clear thesis statement. While it can be repeated here, this is the type of statement we would have liked to see at the beginning of the proposal. In evaluating a business book, an editor or agent will automatically look for the book's usefulness to the reader. A business book needs to have a "what's in it for me?" component. It needs to offer information that will motivate, offer examples, or offer information that will assist the reader in reaching his or her goals.

5. This statement is a little too informal in the context of the general style of the proposal for our taste. If you are going to be informal, be informal throughout. Don't jolt your reader with an abrupt change of tone.

6. This would be a good place to make a strong supporting statement about Saturn. Never miss an opportunity to persuade, even at the risk of repetition.

7. This is a good example of integrating biographical material with persuasive information.

I have already created interest for this book through my interviews (in-[7] person, phone, written questionnaires, and e-mail) with hundreds of Saturn customers, plus Saturn team members and retail facilities, and even Saturn suppliers. The Saturn Corporation folks that I have met in the process continue to cooperatively provide necessary information for this book.

Plus, with my marketing and speaking background, I will intelligently and enthusiastically promote the heck out of this book!

Marketing

The Market

The primary audience for *How Saturn Reinvented the Customer Loyalty Wheel* consists of business managers, owners, CEOs, salespeople, customer-contact people, and entrepreneurs—in all sizes and types of businesses—who recognize the value of customer loyalty.

8. This is a great statistic. These numbers spark the imagination of potential editors and agents to envision a strong market for the book.

For example, the estimated 44,000 agents representing five major [8] insurance agencies, whose income grows through the creation of loyal customers. Industries that have undergone deregulation (or will), such as telephone, banking, and electric/gas utilities, that struggle to keep their customer base. A review of industry publications turned up hundreds of recent articles related to customer loyalty. Concerned industries include:

- small businesses,
- banking,
- hotels,
- catalog companies,
- grocery stores,
- computer industry,
- insurance,
- accountants,
- general retail,
- and even art galleries.

9. This is an excellent example of creative marketing. In a standard proposal, this would fall under "promotion." This statement translates into potential book sales and could leverage a higher advance. Even better would be an actual agreement with Saturn to buy a number of books. This is possible in some situations.

10. Excellent

A key market is Saturn Corporation. Saturn is team-oriented, and as of [9] December 1996 employed 9,591 people. This book is excellent training and inspirational material for team leaders and members throughout the company. Team members that I have spoken with indicated that if Saturn didn't supply the book for them, they would purchase it on their own.

Saturn has 369 retailers (dealers), including 35 in Taiwan and 61 in [10] Canada. They expect to add 21 dealers by the end of this year, and another 100 by early 1999. These retailers currently employ over 13,000 people. Retailers that I have spoken with indicated interest in making the book a

[10] "must read," particularly for their sales consultants. Other potential markets in this category include sales, marketing, and management people within:

General Motors Corp. (Saturn is a wholly owned subsidiary) and their divisions, plus their dealerships nationwide.

Competing automotive manufacturers and their suppliers.

[11] Another market is composed of over 22,000 national trade, business, and commercial associations with members as businesspeople that they are tasked with helping. What a great offering, gift, or renewal premium for members this book would make!

Additional outlets consist of specialty business stores (like Successories), office supply stores, libraries, business/training materials catalogs, and the Internet.

Also, the book is written in a style that will allow for individual chapters to be excerpted for serial form.

[12] The Book Vision

I have a vision for the book, based on experiences shared by businesspeople and customers, and my own preferences as a reader and businessperson. Here's what I've found and plan to deliver on—AND what I believe the readers of this book will appreciate:

not too long (just under 200 pages)

easy to read

affordable (trade paper, ranging in price from $12.95 to $14.95)

simple concepts

real customer stories

quick tips

easy-to-relate-to examples

I plan to obtain endorsements from top Saturn management and retailers, and possibly from Tom Peters and Harvey Mackay.

[13] Promotion

I believe the book should be given to customers that contributed stories for inclusion. People like to see their comments in print, and there's no doubt that these Saturn customers will enthusiastically spread the word about the book (the best kind of advertising!).

I plan to release information about the book over the Internet, to newsgroups, mailing lists, and car clubs that I participate in as a Saturn customer.

The topic of creating customer loyalty is a natural for discussion on

11. This is also excellent.

12. This section indicates an effective departure from the standard proposal format. Creativity is allowed. As you become more self-assured, you should experiment with different styles. A proposal is a living document. Don't feel hindered like a cook who only follows a recipe. As long as you include the necessary information, follow your muse. But be aware of creating the image you want to convey.

13. As indicated, some of the material in "markets" would be more logically placed under "promotion," which indicates how the author can enhance the sales of the book.

radio and TV (for business audiences), and I plan to advertise in *Radio-TV Interview Report*.

I will promote book signings with print and media exposure, and work to coordinate them with speaking engagements for businesses, Chambers of Commerce, Saturn retailers, and CarClubs. I anticipate corporate clients [14] buying books for meeting attendees, or back-of-the-room sales at my speaking engagements, for which I am planning 50 per year. I will also promote the book, through my own quarterly newsletter and planned web site.

A possible "spin-off" strategy to generate interest could be a "How does your business create customer loyalty?" contest, involving a simple entry form, panel judging, and prize awards (maybe even get Saturn to donate a car for the grand prize!). Entries could even be compiled and organized for use in a new book!

14. If the author has experience speaking to groups, it would be a good idea to indicate that here. It would support the plan for 50 lectures and give this statement more credibility.

Related Titles

No other book on the market deals with the combination of creating customer loyalty and the Saturn Corporation. Only two business books carry the Saturn name:

15. This title immediately puts the book into a framework. The author must clearly show the niche for her book.

Forming the Future: Lessons from the Saturn Corporation (Jack O'Toole, Blackwell [15] Publishers, 1996) is about industrial relations and how Saturn was formed, from O'Toole's perspective as a UAW member and one of the original group that developed the founding concept of Saturn.

In the Rings of Saturn (Joe Sherman, Oxford University Press, 1993) is another look at the beginnings of Saturn, including the problems GM faced and the effects of the Saturn plant on the surrounding community.

Not a corporate profile.

Various corporate profile books on the market, including the following two, may contain a type of customer-focus information but are typically directed at management only. They are told from the "inside" by CEOs, management, or consultants, and lack customer perspective.

16. This competition section is too comprehensive. This title does not need to be included, as it is not directly relevant.

Nuts! Southwest Airlines Crazy Recipe for Business & Personal Success (Kevin & [16] Jackie Freiberg, Bard Press, 1996) seems to focus more on how to manage and treat employees.

The World on Time—The 11 Management Principles That Made Federal Express an Overnight Sensation (James C. Wetherbe, Knowledge Exchange, 1996) is directed solely at management.

Not JUST a "how-to" customer loyalty book.

There are many customer-loyalty-type books, but most use different descriptions like customer retention, keeping customers, or customer service. None of these ties in one major corporation as the standard-setter. None of these breaks the buying process down into six very basic and easy-to-understand steps. Following are descriptions of four of the better ones. However, none of them will complete directly, and may in fact serve as complementary reading to *How Saturn Reinvented the Customer Loyalty Wheel*.

[17] *Customers for Life: How to Turn That One-Time Buyer into a Lifetime Customer* (Carl Sewell and Paul B. Brown, Pocket Books, 1990). An excellent book in which Sewell shares his recipes for success based on his GM dealerships. Lacks the customer perspective and quotes, and is directed at a more limited management/big company audience.

The Loyalty Effect: The Hidden Force Behind Growth, Profits, and Lasting Value (Frederick F. Reichheld, Bain & Company, Inc., Harvard Business School Press, 1996) offers a great, in-depth look at the principles that connect customer loyalty with growth, profits, employees, and shareholders. Uses examples from some companies including State Farm, John Deere, and Toyota/Lexus.

Customers Mean Business: Six Steps to Building Relationships That Last (James A. Unruh, Addison-Wesley, 1996) is the result of Unisys Corporation's study of 100 world-class companies that have been recognized for their dedication to customers. (Unruh is the chairman and CEO of Unisys Corporation.) The "how-to" is presented in the form of anonymous quotes, but they are from participating company managers telling "here's what we do," and not much in the way of "here's how you can do it." The six steps are more management-directed and are not presented in a before-during-after buying process.

The Nordstrom Way—The Inside Story of America's #1 Customer Service Company (Robert Spector and Patrick D. McCarthy, Wiley, 1995) is just that—an inside story, and not a how-to book.

About the Author

After spending 18 years in sales, marketing, and management positions in the corporate world, Vicki Lenz started her own marketing consulting and training business in 1993. Clients include local and national businesses: consulting firms, environmental companies, architectural/engineering firms, associations, equipment distributors, industrial, commercial, and retail service and product companies.

17. This seems very similar to the proposed book. The author might want to point out the age of the book as a distinguishing factor. It would also be effective to point out how Saturn in particular has revolutionized car sales. Some titles need to be distinguished more extensively so the publisher or agent won't conclude that the subject has already been effectively addressed.

Vicki is the author of *Employees Serving Customers: Your Starring Role in the Big Picture!* (1997, Affordable Marketing Co.) and *Don't Forget Your Customers!— A Marketing Guide for Small Businesses* (1996, Affordable Marketing Co.).

She has written articles for various local, regional, and national publications, and was interviewed for an article in *Entrepreneur* magazine. She has appeared on local television and radio programs. Vicki regularly speaks on marketing and customer-focus to business audiences, and is a member of the National Speakers Association and on the Board of Directors of the Kentucky Speakers Association.

18. This is a very clear and well-thought-out Table of Contents that shows that the author has a solid sense of where she is headed with the material. It would be easier to follow if it had chapter numbers.

Table of Contents

18

The Framework

A Few Words about Saturn

Step 1.   Create Interest   *"I Think I Want to Buy"*

Step 2.   **Help Customers Feel Welcome** *"I'm Ready to Visit"*
Basic Needs: Yours, Mine, & Ours
Pointers Everyone Can Use
The Games People Play
The Messages That You Send—in Person
The Messages That You Send—with Your Business
Show the Way
Pointers for Managers

Step 3.   **Make It Easy** *"I'm Ready to BUY!"*
It Starts with Knowing
          Training Tips
And It Requires Listening
          Listen Tips
Easy to Understand
          Making It Easy to Understand Tips
Easy to Buy
          Tips for Smoothing the Process
Help Make Choices Easy
Show Me the Money!

Step 4.   **Communicate AFTER the Sale** *"Don't Forget Me Now!"*
Why You Shouldn't Fall Down on the Follow-Up
Let Me Count the Ways . . .
When Service Kicks In
The Education Process Continues
Special Things That "Reach Out and Touch"

Step 5.   **Solve Problems** *"I Need Some Help"*
Bad News Travels at the Speed of Light
Creating Problem Solvers
Preventative Maintenance
The Learning Experience
Turning Problems into Loyalty

Step 6.   **Keep Customers Coming Back!** *"Will I See You Again?"*
Showing Appreciation
The "Value-Added" Component
One Plus One Equal More than Two
Relying on Technology
Planning for Future Growth

Implementing the Saturn Style   *"I've Been Saturnized!"*
The Buck Starts Here
Managing People and Processes
TEAMwork: Inside and Outside
The Profitability Picture
Wrap-up Summary

Q's & A's with the Big Wheels
Questions from a Cross Section of Businesspeople
Answers from Saturn's "People in the Know"

Back Material
Customer Acknowledgments
References
Index

19. **The chapter summaries in this proposal (which we have limited here to the framework and step 1) are so comprehensive and well written that no sample chapter was necessary in closing a deal. This technique can be highly effective, but the proposal must be well developed and written in the style best reflective of the book. The assumption will be that what you see is what you are going to get. In some places this proposal is almost too comprehensive. A proposal is a prospectus and should not be a manuscript in disguise. You don't want to defeat your own purposes or bog down the prospective agent or editor with too much information.**

The Framework

19

I had given up on buying American cars in 1980. Four years ago, when my son turned 16, he asked for my help in looking at cars. I didn't even know what a Saturn was. When I heard that it was an American car and you had to pay full sticker price, I said "No way!" My son pointed out that it wasn't right to be prejudiced about something that I didn't know anything about. So, I called the local Saturn retailer and ended up talking to the sales rep for about one hour. She politely and patiently answered my questions. Now, I'm already thinking that this is different! I told her that I'd think about it and call back in about a week.

One week went by, and there was no call from the sales rep that I thought for sure would be hounding me immediately. Strange, because salespeople usually don't want you to get away. Five minutes before closing, I called her, fully expecting that she wouldn't have time for me. Surprise again! She stayed on the phone for a half an hour after closing, answering my questions. There is absolutely no pressure. Now, I'm thinking, "There's something wrong with this!"

We finally went in to meet with her. I told her what we looking for and tried to start haggling. She showed me a price list and pleasantly described their no-haggle, no-hassle way of doing business. When it came time for a test drive, she went over everything about the car first. We ended up taking 3 or 4 cars out for a test drive. Each time, she patiently explained different features about each car. I wondered, "Where's the camera? There has to be some kind of gimmick."

My son wanted the Saturn, but it turned out that he couldn't afford it at that time. Know what happened? I ended up buying a Saturn for myself!

Today, we have six Saturns in the family, counting my brother and sister in another state. Five of us are on our second Saturn. My wife of 25

years feels comfortable taking the car in for service by herself. My younger single sister doesn't have to get her brother to take the car in for service.
     You have to look at the whole pictures: the car, sales, and service. What makes it special is that I feel I'm being treated like a human being. And that they care.

Do you know a Saturn car owner? Chances are that if you ask a roomful of a hundred people, you'll find two or three Saturn customers. And do you know what happens when they're asked to share their experiences as Saturn customers? They get a smile on their face . . . their eyes light up . . . and they can't wait to tell everyone why they are a LOYAL customer!

These loyal, enthusiastic customers deluge Saturn with complimentary letters, e-mail, cards, posters, pictures, and notes of thanks. They write poems and sing songs about Saturn. One guy even had a Saturn logo tattooed on his leg. When was the last time you felt that way about a company you did business with? Or your customers felt that way about your business? Never? Maybe it's like the back of the Saturn CarClub T-shirt that reads, "If you don't own one, you probably wouldn't understand."

Why Customer Loyalty Should Be Important to You

When I told fellow business friends that I was writing about creating customer loyalty, the responses were generally divided into two categories. In the first category were the ones who would roll their eyes and respond with something like, "Good luck—loyalty is dead, or next to impossible." True, customer loyalty is not what is was 50 years ago (so I'm told; I wasn't actually around to experience it myself). The second category, which I'm happy to say represented the majority, responded with more positive statements. "Great! I know we need to work at that, but we're just not sure how." Or, even better, "That's how I've been successful in business all these years."

In today's competitive times, the search really is on for ways to create customer loyalty. Or if it's not, it should be. This is not the latest "management fad." It's a way of doing business—one that has been around for centuries. The sad truth is that many major corporations now lose half their customers in five years. Companies that ignore these losses can expect a future of low growth, weak profits, and shortened life expectancy.

[20] It's like a leaky bucket. As a company loses customers out of the leak in the bottom of the bucket, they have to continue to add new customers (an expensive process) to the top of the bucket. If the company can even partially plug the leak, the bucket stays fuller. It then takes fewer new customers added to the top of the bucket to achieve the same level of profitability. It's less expensive and more profitable to keep those customers already in the bucket.

Smart businesspeople realize that it costs five to ten times more to land a new customer than to keep a customer they already have. They also recog-

20. This seems repetitive. It is an analogy that sticks in your mind, so to see it again so soon makes it seem overused.

nize that increasing the number of customers they keep by a small percentage can *double* profits. And it doesn't matter what type of business you have—the potential for profits can be substantial. A study by Bain & Company, Inc. (Frederick F. Reichheld, *The Loyalty Effect*) looked at a wide range of industries including insurance, advertising, banking, industrial distribution, office building management, and software. The study found that the impact of a 5-percentage-point increase in retention rate represented anywhere from a 35% to a 95% increase in customer net present value. The majority of the numbers were in the 75% to 95% category. For instance, if a credit card company can hold on to another 5% of its customers each year (increasing its retention rate from 90% to 95%), then the total lifetime profits from a typical customer will rise, on average, by 75%. Reichheld expands on the "leaky bucket" comparison with the following example of long term growth:

"Imagine two companies, one with a customer retention rate of [21] 95%, the other with a rate of 90%. The leak in the first firm's customer bucket is 5% per year, and the second firm's leak is twice as large, 10% per year. If both companies acquire new customers at the rate of 10% per year, the first will have a 5% net growth in customer inventory per year, while the other will have none. Over fourteen years, the first firm will double in size, but the second will have no real growth at all. Other things being equal, a 5-percentage-point advantage in customer retention translates into a growth advantage equal to a doubling of customer inventory every fourteen years. An advantage of ten percentage points accelerates the doubling to seven years."

Reichheld's book goes farther in charting the relationship between customer retention and *productivity*, in addition to profitability. The numbers and results are from real companies. And the numbers are very impressive!

Then there's the "lifetime value" factor to consider. Carl Sewell is one [22] of the nation's leading Cadillac dealers (and other makes/models as well). In his book *Customer for Life*, Sewell calculates the amount of revenue an auto dealer could realize from an average buyer if the dealership could keep the customer for life. Would you believe . . . $332,000? That's just ONE customer!

AT&T was spending about $2 billion a year issuing incentive checks to woo former customers back! Now they realize that it's a lot less costly to keep them in the first place. And, as it was announced that Toyota's flagship Camry was the Number 1-selling car in the United States in late 1997, at the same time, news articles were explaining Toyota's new tactics aimed at boosting customer loyalty. Seems they're rated well below industry average in the way they treat customers. Even though sales are up and market share is increasing, Toyota last year was able to retain only about 45% of its customers. Toyota is worried that, unless it can keep more customers in the fold, growth could definitely falter.

21. This example would be just as effective without the leaky bucket. You should always watch for clichés or examples that may seem repetitive. You be the judge, but be objective. Something may seem terribly clever to you but may not actually add to your writing. Otherwise this is a great example that gives support to the author's thesis.

22. This is excellent. It makes the reader want more.

Customer satisfaction programs are weapons that many companies use in fighting the battles in today's marketplace. That's a step in the right direction, but the truth is that customer satisfaction does not necessarily translate into customer loyalty. Research has shown that 60 to 70 percent of customers who defect to the competition responded to a survey that they were "satisfied" or "very satisfied" with their previous supplier!

23 *"It's not enough to meet our customers' expectations, we must exceed them."*
Don Hudler (Saturn president)
(From a banner hanging in Saturn's new Welcome Center)

23. Excellent.

24 The difference between satisfaction and loyalty is that satisfaction is typically concerned only with the initial buying experience, the "how you get it" part. Loyalty focuses on building relationships for the long term. The "secret," if there is one, is to think of customers in terms of relationships, not transactions.

24. It is very effective to include this level of substance in the outline. This will depend on the type of book you are writing, but it doesn't hurt to exceed expectations.

What can customer loyalty mean for your business?

- Loyal customers will spend more with you. Profit margins will increase.
- Loyal customers tend to understand and appreciate value, and are less likely to price-shop.
- Loyal customers mean repeat, long-term business (and those dollars add up!).
- Loyal customers serve as a fantastic marketing force, providing the best kind of advertising available: word-of-mouth and personal referrals.
- Loyal customers stick with you through difficult times.
- Loyal customers can deliver a blow to your competition, because if customers are loyal to you, it means that your competition isn't getting their business!
- Loyal customers are your cheerleaders, and will go to bat for you.
- Loyal customers tend to tell you what they like and dislike (yes, this is good—you want to know both).
- Creating a customer-loyalty atmosphere within your company can be a great recruiting tool, and help the right employees come to you. The same customer-loyalty atmosphere can boost employee morale.

Need one more reason? Okay, it just plain feels good when you treat people right, which is a key ingredient for creating loyal customers.

25. This proposal uses the outline summaries to restate and support the thesis as stated in the overview. It maximizes the persuasiveness of this portion of the proposal.

What You'll Find in This Book

25

This book is not about the car. It IS about all the things combined that customers like, appreciate, and are important to them in creating customer loyalty. And it is about how Saturn has created, and continues to create, the atmosphere necessary for customer loyalty. This is not theory, and it is not complicated. In fact, simplicity is what makes this loyalty style attractive.

How Saturn Reinvented the Customer Loyalty Wheel shows how to plug the "leaky bucket" and turn one-time customers into repeat-purchasing loyal customers, with the "Saturn style" of business as the role model. It progresses along the basics of a six-step Saturn buying experience—before, during, and after the purchase. It tells how a buying process *should be*—for any product or service, from any size or type of business. Plenty of DOs and DON'Ts, straightforward tips and suggestions are offered. Each step of the way, facts, figures, and examples tell how Saturn has created—and continues to create—the atmosphere necessary for customer loyalty. Perspective is provided from the outside looking in, through quotes from customers that help tell the story and emphasize points. A summarized remembrance in the form of a "key tip" is included at the end of each step. The final two chapters offer additional information on managing and implementing "the Saturn style" in your business, with tips from some of the top people at Saturn who have "been there, done that."

Businesspeople in positions ranging from receptionist to customer service rep, from sales rep to manager, and from small-business owner to CEO, will find something useful in this book. You will find points of value that will benefit you directly in your position, *if* you will apply them.

Any business concerned about increasing sales and growth can relate to the observations and helpful analyses, and apply the tips to their own business.

So rather than reinvent the wheel all over again, why not learn what works FOR customers . . . FROM customers, and from the company that has paved the road to serve as the model for customer loyalty?

Why Saturn and Saturn Customers?

"And the winner is . . . for the third year in a row . . . SATURN!"

This young small car unit (wholly-owned subsidiary) of General Motors Corp. is the perennial leader in the J. D. Power and Associates annual sales satisfaction study. And, in the J. D. Power and Associates 1997 survey of driver satisfaction, Saturn was one of only two U.S. cars ranked in the top 10.

The common link among top-ranking companies "'is that they have developed a corporate culture that stresses keeping the customer happy long after the car is sold," said Ron Conlin, J. D. Power's director of research.

In an industry where customer loyalty rates typically range from 30% to

40%, Saturn excels at close to 60%. Pretty good for an auto manufacturer that has had only seven short years to develop repeat-purchasing customers. In 1994, then-president Skip LeFauve was asked, "How exactly do you measure Saturn's success?"

Here's his response:

> *About two years ago I was with another Saturn team member in this really small Mexican taqueria near the Los Angeles airport. Everybody was speaking Spanish, and we're standing in line with our trays, and this guy looks at our shirts and says, "Hey, you guys work for Saturn?" We said, "Yeah." He said, "Was it true about that man flying to Alaska to help that customer?" And we all said, "Yes." And he said, "That was really cool." And I thought to myself then, sure, we can judge ourselves the traditional way, play the numbers game, compare ourselves to everybody else—in fact, we have to. But the real reward comes from a guy like that. It's stuff like that that really means something.*

It's no wonder that close to 13,000 enthusiastic and loyal Saturn customers have formed their own "car clubs" across the country, or that another 97,000 customers have indicated an interest in joining. Or that 44,000 owners and their families made the trip to Spring Hill, Tennessee, in 1994 for a "Homecoming"—just to eat barbecue, see where their cars were made, and meet the people who made them.

Saturn rightly refers to itself as "A different kind of company." In less than one decade of existence, Saturn is emerging as THE role model for customer loyalty. That's not exactly what they set out to do, but "customer enthusiasm" is more than inherent in their mission statement:

Saturn Mission

Earn the loyalty of Saturn owners and grow our family by developing and marketing U.S.-manufactured vehicles that are world leaders in quality, cost, and customer enthusiasm through the integration of people, technology, and business systems.

Saturn's philosophy and values (which you'll read about later) were further developed with this mission statement in mind.

As for Saturn's customers, after talking with so many of them, I can sum everything up in one word: WOW! They are the picture of enthusiasm, excitement, and, of course, loyalty.

NOT a Saturn Production!

If you're thinking that this book was Saturn's idea, the answer is definitely NO. And, no, I am not, nor have I ever been under contract or employed by Saturn Corporation or General Motors, or any company in the automotive or advertising industry. (However, after being exposed to this Saturn style of doing business, I'm ready to submit my résumé!) With that disclaimer out of the way, let me explain what led me to write this book.

I was first exposed to Saturn loyalty several years ago when a friend purchased a Saturn. She was so enthusiastic that you would have thought Saturn was paying her to act that way. (They weren't, but later, the local retailer did invite her to appear in commercials and newspaper advertisements.) In an earlier book, I wrote about Saturn's Homecoming event as a means for showing customer appreciation and creating generations of customers. Later, as I mentioned the Saturn Homecoming to some of my business audiences, interesting things happened. Excited people—loyal Saturn customers—approached me, anxious to share their stories. The more stories I heard, and the more I learned about Saturn, the more I became convinced that the whole Saturn customer experience was really something special. In fact, I became so convinced and excited that I decided to buy a new Saturn for myself!

The folks at the retail facility where I purchased my car weren't aware that I would be writing this book, so I didn't get preferential treatment. Well, that's really not correct to say, since Saturn's standard practice is that *every* customer gets preferential treatment. I'm proud to say that as a Saturn customer, I have been treated just as all other Saturn customers are treated: ROYALLY. One sales manager told me about a prospective customer informing her that since he would be buying two cars, he expected "special treatment." She was gladly informed that "You're in luck, because ALL of our customers get special treatment!" Later, as I began my research for this book, I continued to receive a warm welcome and wonderful treatment from everyone at Saturn and their retail facilities.

So, as I became even more exposed to the Saturn style of doing business, the idea and conviction of spreading the word through this book was born. Also, the business audiences that I speak to like to hear about how other companies manage to be successful. They want REAL examples, things they can use. Most of us can relate to buying a car. Usually, we rate a car buying experience right up there with an IRS audit, or going to the dentist. What I found is that people outside "The Saturn Family" just don't know the story, or understand what all the hoopla is about. Thus, the Saturn-style story just begged to be told! Plus, I get to add a little bit different angle—my perspective as a customer.

Now, the other side of the story has to do with how all of us are treated as customers on a daily basis. Admit it, wouldn't *you* like for all of your experiences as a customer to be pleasant experiences? Unfortunately, that is all too rarely the case. My hope is that reading about the Saturn style will encourage other businesses to become more customer-focused—and make customer experiences nicer for all of us!

So, here's the story. I hope you enjoy it, learn from it, and apply it to your business so that you're wildly successful, and your customers are loyal!

The Mechanics of Customer Loyalty

I think a Saturn team member summed it pretty well when she said, "'This is not rocket science. We're doing a lot of basic, simple things, but what customer loyalty all boils down to is the way that you treat people." Customers loudly echo that sentiment. Tom Peters, in his book *The Pursuit of WOW!*, expressed his opinion that Saturn has created their almost cultlike following "By embracing the customer as a friend—an intelligent friend—from the moment the customer first steps into the showroom."

Oh, you want to know what the reinvented "customer loyalty wheel" is? In my version, Saturn has refined it into this model of simplicity:

It's not a flashy, detailed, polished chrome model, but it CAN shine gold for you!

There is no single solution for creating customer loyalty, just as there is no single car that pleases everyone. It's a combination of lots of little things that add up. Your business is different, customers are different, and there are a world of options from which to choose. But keep in mind it is important that the "combination of lots of little things" fit together. A Jaguar engine in a Saturn SL1 just won't work. One of Saturn's brochures states that, "It's not always easy to define what Saturn is or isn't. But we know it's more than a car. Or a car company. And it's probably more about all of us doing things together than anything else." Amen. In fact, one of the main "spokes" of the customer loyalty wheel, although not labeled in the model above, is enthusiastic, loyal team members (employees). You'll learn more about that in the final two chapters.

Whether you're a one-person business or CEO of a multibillion-dollar conglomerate, it's up to you to create the excitement and the environment that are the building blocks for customer loyalty. It doesn't have to be complicated. In fact, you'll find that many of the customer loyalty ingredients are basic, common courtesies and common sense. But the concepts and practices have to be the core of your business, embraced by everyone in the company. So, where do you start? At the top, with individual attitudes, management philosophy, and example-setting showing that customers do indeed come first. Of course, you have to consider whether the pursuit of loyalty is consistent with your own goals. Is it in your head AND in your heart?

You can't just pick and choose one or two things to try temporarily and hope it works. It won't. For example, you'll read about Saturn's very successful "new owner clinics." A Cadillac dealership tried to duplicate the clinics for their customers and failed miserably. Then there's the Honda dealer that tried the no-haggle pricing on cars—for ONE weekend only. [26]

Be forewarned of four things:

1) loyalty must be *earned,*
2) it's not easy,
3) it doesn't happen overnight, and
4) keeping loyal customers and creating new ones is a continuous process.

If you're in business just to make a quick buck, this style is not for you. But, if you believe in treating people right, developing long-term customers, and growing your business and profits in the process, then read on!

Now, off you go, to the Saturn style of creating customer loyalty. . . .

26. The remaining summaries, which are excluded for our purposes, are consistently effective. It would be better from an organizational standpoint to separate the book outline into actual chapters. Never make more work for the agent or editor than necessary. Use bullets where possible, and number things so they are easy to find. Keep in mind that editors and agents often scan material to determine their level of interest. They may not read in a linear fashion but will skip around. Make their journey as easy as you can.

PROPOSAL 5

The Creativity Toolbox
by Jordan E. Ayan

We sold this book to the Clarkson Potter imprint of Random House, where it has now settled comfortably as a strong backlist title. My initial concern was to what degree the business community would support a book dedicated to creativity. But the author's creativity and credentials persuaded me, and in turn a publisher, that his book would deliver a clear program and substantial sales.

1. This is an excellent Table of Contents. It is clear, organized, and clever without being hokey.

Table of Contents

2

3

2. The writer has used a different format by including the book "Table of Contents" within the outline of the proposal. This is a creative way of presenting the material, which is certainly a good thing considering the subject matter. If you are so inclined, you can use this integration technique in any proposal as long as you are organized and view your proposal as something fluid. You need to make sure the information flows from one section to another. This is somewhat easier with a standard approach, but this is your proposal and you can do anything you want if you cover the basic information.

3. We never recommend mentioning a book delivery date. Your agent will negotiate this for you, or if you go directly to an editor, he or she will work it out with you according to the list schedule. The book business works at least six months ahead or more, depending on the title and genre. When a book is acquired the publishing house has in mind when it would like to see it released. There are many factors entering into this decision, such as what else they have coming out, the season, and promotion possibilities. You also don't want to lock yourself into promises you may not be able to keep. It is best to leave this issue open.

4. Although it is not included for our purposes, this author included an effective sample chapter. Don't forget how important that can be. It is easy to run out of steam when writing a proposal. You may want to write the sample first so you have the energy to do a good job. A sample chapter is the best way for an editor or publisher to assess the quality of your book.

What is *The Creativity Toolbox*℠ all about?

A business and self-help book

[5] *The Creativity Toolbox* is a personal and business self-help book. It offers a series of tools that readers can apply to increase their creative output at whatever they do. The focus is on identifying specific tools from the toolbox that become personalized based on each reader's individual creative and intelligence makeup. The book will help both the scientist and artist use the tools that will maximize their creative output in all areas of their professional and personal lives.

> 5. It is best to choose one audience or another. You do not want to appear unfocused as far as markets are concerned. In this particular case, it works. Don't be afraid to extend beyond the protocols in all areas of your proposal. You should take what you want from each of our samples and decide what works best for you.

The Creativity Toolbox includes a creativity evaluation that will guide each individual in determining their creativity composition. Once recognized, all of the tools in the toolbox are key-coded so that the reader can concentrate on the sections of the book that will work best with his or her individual thinking style.

A business improvement book

[6] Just as the tools contained in each chapter will boost an individual's creativity, they will also increase the creative level within an organization. Managers, professionals, and entrepreneurs are key target buyers and can use *The Creativity Toolbox* to increase idea and innovation output within their work team or organization.

> 6. This is a good explanation of how the book works. It establishes the hook.

A book in bite-size pieces

[7] *The Creativity Toolbox* can be read from cover to cover. Yet it can also function as a useful creativity guidebook to apply to daily problems and situations. It is written in a format that allows a reader to learn about specific tools without reading the entire book.

> 7. In this case the format of the book is significant. The author does an effective job of explaining how the format helps the overall concept.

From the moment the reader begins to browse, *The Creativity Toolbox* is designed to become an essential part of the reader's personal library. Each creativity tool is illustrated with quotations and cases describing how the tools have worked for others. The style and the structure of the book make it the perfect personal and professional guide to creative ideas and innovation.

8. The author restates his Table of Contents. He could follow what appeared to be the format he indicated in his initial outline by including chapter summaries at this stage of the proposal. You do not have to stick with the outline format. If you do it this way, you would probably want to use more abbreviated summaries so as not to bog down the proposal. As you will see, the author includes extensive promotional information. It would be just as effective to show exactly what the book will be about before further persuading the agent or editor through the promotions section. Do what is most effective. A proposal is like a living document. It stands in the place of you making your pitch. You only have a few minutes of attention. How are you going to maximize them?

Table of Contents

8
|

Section 1—Creativity Overview

Chapter 1: *The Creativity Toolbox*—Now that you have it, what are you going to do with it?

Chapter 2: The Creative Difference—An overview of what creativity is doing for others in our changing world

Chapter 3: An introduction to the theory behind this book (by an author who dislikes academic theoretical reading)

Section 2—The Tools[1]

Chapter 4: People—Using the mastermind concept for creative inspiration and new ideas

Chapter 5: Fun—Letting out the creative child

Chapter 6: Intuition—Tapping into the power of "gut feel"

Chapter 7: SHIFT HAPPENS—Breaking the rules and paradigms in your life that practically guarantee creativity

Chapter 8: Travel—Vacation your way to a more creative you

Chapter 9: Reading—Opening new doors with the creativity of others

Chapter 10: Journaling—Opening the door to your creative soul

Chapter 11: Computers—Take your mind in new creative directions

Chapter 12: Power Thinking and Daily Thinking Time—Idea Generation triggers from your mind and soul

Chapter 13: The Arts—Forget what you think—you can draw, play the piano, paint, sing, or do just about anything else creative (and it's good for you, too)

Chapter 14: Visualization, Meditation, Music, and Dreams—Turning off your head and getting inside your mind

Chapter 15: Metaphors—Looking for creative solutions in other solutions

Section 3—Making it happen

Chapter 16: Ideas into Action—Linking the right brain with the left

Appendix I: Creative Sources, a compilation of resources to make the most of the tools

---

1. The tools fall into seven or eight subgroups, depending on how they are broken down (Subconscious Mind Tools, Active Mind Tools, Activity Tools, People Tools, Creativity Enhancement Tools, Brain Tools, and Artistic Tools). Depending on the book structure, we might want to use these breakouts as subsection dividers. All link to different types of intelligence based on Howared Gardner's Multiple Intelligence theory.

Appendix II: Computer Resources, a compilation of computer resources for creative thought

Appendix III: Commercial Creativity Products, a compilation of aids that will help in the creativity process

Bibliography: Including hard-to-find books and extensive articles on creativity

Who Buys *The Creativity Toolbox* and Why?

Target audience

The strongest demand for *The Creativity Toolbox* is from businesspeople who need to increase either their personal output, or that of their organization with new and creative ideas. The need has never been greater. Creativity is the '90s' answer to organizational problems, sluggish sales figures, downsizing, and competing in the global marketplace. It is the perfect primer for corporate managers, senior executives supervisors, business professionals, and entrepreneurs.

The book will have particular appeal to individuals in the following industries or job functions among others:

Accounting	Advertising
Architecture	Art Departments
Automotive	Banking
Chefs	Computer Industry
Writing	Design
Direct Marketing	Entertainment
Food Industry	Franchising
Fund-raising	Insurance
Interior Design	Landscapers
Law	Management
Marketing	Medical
New Product Development	Programmers
Publishing	Real Estate
Recreation	Research and Development
Restaurateurs	Retail
Sales	Teaching
Telecommunications	Computers
Toy Industry	Utility Industry

9. This listing is not that effective, as it might just as easily have said all industries or jobs. If the author wanted to give this list some teeth, he should have indicated why these particular industries could benefit. Even one sentence tying together the relevance of the list would help. He might also have explained why most industries would benefit and just have bulleted a few examples. He could use brief explanations or could let the list speak for itself. He could also categorize by creative industry, finance, and industry so the list would make more impact.

10. This adds to the shotgun approach of markets, which does not add to the proposal.

The book will also appeal to people in other walks of life, including the teaching profession, government, and the nonprofit sector. [10]

The Creative Toolbox is a book designed to help. Both people and organizations grow.

Why this author? [11]

11. This is a strong and effective statement.

My background put me in a unique position to author this book. I have used the tools as well as creative problem solving methods to help people maximize their creative potential in mainline American business. I have a growing reputation for creating corporate successes using Creativity Tools.

My recent accomplishments [12]

12. This is a good example of how business accomplishments can be directly relevant to the proposed book. These credentials are as important as or more important than educational credentials for this type of book.

I start to this book fresh from the corporate mainstream, after a variety business successes and creative experiences. The most recent business I built was for Donnelley Marketing, formerly a division of Dun & Bradstreet. Donnelley is one of the nation's leading database and direct marketing firms.

I started with Donnelley as an account executive in the Direct Marketing Division. Using my own creative selling techniques to grow one of the most successful sales portfolios in company history, I was one of the top sales performers, selling millions of dollars in services every year. My client roster comprised the company's largest clients, including:

Sears

Mutual of Omaha

Hallmark Cards

American Express

Kindercare

Lifetouch Portrait Studios

Stanley Steamer

While selling, in my fourth year with the company, I developed a new product idea based on one of my customer's needs. Employing a variety of creative methods to market the idea inside Donnelley, I was able to initiate a new type of strategic alliance and launch the new product. Donnelley entered into a joint marketing agreement with First Data Corporation (then a division of American Express) to form FastData. Today, FastData is the leading online business database service, providing names, addresses, telephone numbers, and other basic demographics to major corporate clients via the information superhighway.

Within five years of its inception, FastData grew from annual revenues of zero to a successful business with revenue targets increasing at unheard-of rates within the corporation. We did it with virtually no up-front investment, using the creativity and innovation of our team.

By 1993, according to management, FastData was the fastest-growing and most profitable business in the company's business portfolio. The Business Unit was recently licensed to First Data Corporation for fees and a long-term licensing agreement totaling a minimum of close to $50 million.

Professional background

[13] Previously, I worked for Allstate Insurance (during perhaps the least creative period in Sears' history), Pacific Bell (in a staff position during the breakup of the Bell system), as well as a variety of smaller businesses. I also spent six years in the motion picture industry, working at Warner Brothers, Columbia Pictures, and all three major television networks.

I am a computer expert. Major software manufacturers, including Symantec, National Semiconductor, and Macromind, request that I review their products and evaluate prerelease (beta) versions of their software. I have also been involved in the testing phases of most of the leading creativity software currently marketed commercially. Many of my ideas have been incorporated into their final programs.

Personal

The author was born October 23, 1957. He has been married to his wife, Jan, for the past ten years (see attached reprint). The couple have two children, Ashley, eight, and Christopher, five. Both children attend school in Naperville Illinois, and are employed by Create-It! Inc. as assistant vice presidents (Coloring Division).

Travel

I have traveled extensively, and have a variety of creativity anecdotes and examples from around the world. I have lived in Canada and Europe (Holland and Switzerland) as well as six states. I have traveled the breadth of the European continent and speak English, French, and Dutch.

I have crisscrossed the United States over the past five years, between my speaking engagements and FastData responsibilities, to have accrued over 1,250,000 miles on a single airline.

[14] Education

I attended the University of Missouri, majoring in Journalism. I graduated *magna cum laude* from California State University—Northridge with a degree in Business Administration/Marketing. I participate in the State University of

13. Here the author includes skills that add to the mix. These skills are relevant to why he is qualified to write the book. They add to his credibility.

14. His education is impressive. It should be in a bulleted list for greater impact. You can use many graphic devices to highlight important information.

New York Creative Problem Solving Institute, and am a member of the Global Think Tank, an internationally networked group using computer technology and multicultural input to solve problems. I am also a member of The Global Intuition Network, an organization based at the University of Texas—Austin focused on research related to intuition.

My professional and personal experiences with creativity make me uniquely qualified to write this book, and provide me with the rich sources of examples of the tools in action.

My network [15]

15. This table raises the question of whether the contacts have agreed to be included in the book. This should be established before inclusion to maximize their importance.

Additionally, I will also draw examples from my network of personal, business, and creative contacts as well as a large database of examples of creativity in action. Included among them are:

Mark Zimmer, President and Creator, Fractal Paintbrush	**William Hodges, Senior Vice President, Discover Card**
Ric Duques, Chairman First Data Corporation	**Lois Hillier, Senior Vice President, Fingerhut Corporation**
Ron Ziebeck, Originator GM Credit Card Division	**Jack Miller, Chairman and Founder, The Quill Corporation**
Stan Rapp, Chairman Rapp Collins Advertising Author	

16. This is a throwaway. It is more useful to contact people for endorsements and include those who have agreed rather than making a statement that has no real value. If there is no certainty, leave it out. If you have a verbal commitment, that is enough. Just don't fudge if you have no personal relationship with the person and no actual way of assuring and endorsement.

I plan to approach some of these individuals for book jacket [16] endorsements.

My creative knowledge

17. This is not a useful claim unless the author has been on a panel with these authors or has studied or collaborated with them. Although the author may have a strong relationship with the members of this list, this could come across as puffery if not given more substance.

With all of the businesses I have been involved in, creativity has always been the key to success. I always strive to modify, improve, and stretch the limits of any product or service I work with.

While working on the FastData project at Donnelley, I gained formal training by participating in a variety of educational opportunities at facilities like the Creative Leadership Programs in Charlotte, North Carolina, and Creative Learning International, Chicago. These institutions are recognized as leading centers for creativity training, education, and research. I have also conducted extensive personal research and self-education. I have used my creative experience to work as a creativity facilitator for a variety of organizations and companies.

I have met and networked with respected, distinguished, and outstand- [17] ing individuals in the fields of creativity and creativity education, including:

Chick Thompson, Author, Speaker, creativity expert	**Jim Aylesworth, Children's Author**
Dr. Edgar Mitchell, Apollo Astronaut, Founder, Noetic Sciences Foundation, and expert on intuition in business	**Dr. Joel Goodman, President The Humor Project**
Dr. George Land, Author, Speaker, creativity program facilitator, and expert; President, Leadership 2000	**Jon Pearson, Artist Author of book on drawing**
Dr. Theresa Amable, Professor, Brandeis University; Author, Researcher	**Roger Von Oech, Author Speaker, creativity expert**
Dr. Weston Agor, Chairman The Global Intuition Network	**Amanda Goodenough, Author, children' computer software**
Robert Trost, President Global Think Tank; European creativity expert	**Dr. Gilles Rappille, Psychologist, Author**

[18]   I plan to circulate my manuscript to select members of this group, and secure quotes for use on the book jacket.

18. Again, a throwaway.

I have applied my knowledge of creativity to learn how to play the piano, as well as how to draw and paint (all within the past three years). I will draw on this experience for the chapters "Letting out the Creative Child" and "The Arts."

Marketing strength

Beyond my creativity knowledge, the greatest strength I bring to this venture is my sales ability. I have extensive sales and marketing experience, and will apply these skills and the creative process to ensure that *The Creativity Toolbox* becomes a best-selling book.

As the book takes form, I will develop interesting publicity hooks and novel selling approaches to ensure participation in television and radio talk shows once the book is published. I will leverage my extensive travel schedule to ensure high public visibility .

I attended an intensive media training program at Fleishman-Hillard Public Relations in conjunction with my work at Donnelley. I served as a company spokesperson for the FastData product and participated in national and trade media interviews. The Fleishman-Hillard program was designed to prepare an individual for any type of media or interview situation.

Speaking business

I currently own Create-It! Inc., a company that handles and markets my speaking and seminar programs on the topic of creativity. I will actively leverage these speaking opportunities into additional book sales, either to the corporation or trade group hosting me or to the individual participants in the program. Additionally, I am developing an extensive database of program attendees, and a subset of people wanting any information on books I publish in the future. It will be used as the basis of a targeted direct mail effort (with my extensive background in the direct marketing industry, this is just another natural extension of my sales experience).

I currently am working with J. P. Communications, a public relations firm, to develop other PR opportunities, including a newsletter that will circulate to program attendees and others.

I am a member of The National Speakers Association, and Professional [19] Speakers of Illinois. I will promote the book among other speakers to spur "word of mouth" promotion. I also anticipate asking many of the top speaking professionals for book jacket testimonials; among those I will target are:

19. Targeting is used often in this book. The connection with the organization is good, but the term *targeting* is no guarantee of anything. This point cannot be made too many times. He also uses names that may not be commonly known to editors or agents. Never assume an editor or agent is knowledgeable about anything. If you are going to mention names, always explain who they are. It is never a good idea to cause an editor or agent to feel ignorant.

Les Brown	Zig Ziglar
Jim Cathcart	Tom Hopkins
Og Mandino	Rosita Perez
Jeff Slutsky	Nido Quebien
Jeanne Robertson	Harvey McKay
Patricia Fripp	Danielle Kennedy

Promotion

I have a variety of additional plans that will increase book sales in addition to the speaking and media details listed above.

The Creativity Toolbox—box

20. This is a great merchandising idea. It shows "creativity." If you have got it, include it.

As a way to assist the publisher in promoting the book among the bookstores, [20] I will help develop a direct mail campaign. To presell the book among volume buyers, I recommend mailing out a toolbox filled with creativity tools. Ideas include: crayons, kazoos, pocket innovator, Create-It! cards, confetti, sketchpad, seashells, finger paint, harmonica, slide whistle, lightbulbs, creative music tape or CID, sidewalk chalk, Play-Doh, pipe cleaners, Popsicle sticks, and, of course, a copy of the book. This novel approach will be a great hook at bookseller trade shows.

[21] Top ten creative things list

J. P. Communications is developing a project currently to create and distribute an annual Top Ten New Creative Things list. The list will highlight ten new things (ideas, concepts, products, services) each year.

My plan is to tie the list publication and media attention to the book publication, thus creating additional demand for the book.

Creativity Tool workshops

I will develop a creativity workshop specifically to promote the book. The workshop will be presented in shopping malls in a short two- or three-hour format. This calls for a tie-in with a major bookseller located in the mail to sponsor the workshop. I will help develop a mail sales kit to help the retailer promote the workshop. After the workshop, I will hold a book signing at the bookstore that will increase sales of the book, as well as overall traffic to the retail location.[2]

The author has already scheduled presentations with Barnes & Noble and Borders in 1994, just based on the market's interest in creativity. Since there is no book to promote at this time, other books will be discussed, but all booksellers have agreed to formal signings and presentations if they are included in a book tour.

[22] Create-It[SM] cards

I am working with Compendium, Inc., a specialty publisher, to produce a set of specialty cards featuring inspirational quotations on creativity. Each card has a special tear-out window that displays the quotation. (A sample of this type of card is enclosed.)

The cards are to be marketed jointly by Compendium and Create-It! Inc.me. This will give us an opportunity to promote the book using a package insert in the card box. The cards are currently sold through the Compendium catalog and other catalog companies including Nightingale-Connant and Successories. Compendiums' products are also sold through a variety of upscale retailers across the country.

I am also open to the idea of bundling the Create-It[SM] cards with *The Creativity Toolbox*.[3]

---

21. Is this for the author or a general project? If this list is directly related to this book, it should be clarified and not assumed that it will be understood.

22. This is another great idea that even has a prototype.

---

2. I have experience with shopping mall promotions. Donnelley Marketing had several mall programs during the period I was selling for them. I was involved in programs for Hallmark, ABC Saturday Morning Television, Universal Studies, and Apple Computers.

3. Roger Von Oech has been successful in marketing his *A Whack on the Side of the Head* book with his Creative Whack Pack idea generation card deck.

23. Once again, another creative idea that is not out of reach.

The Creativity Toolbox calendar   23

The Creativity Toolbox ideas are a "natural" for incorporation into a calendar. I anticipate two versions of the calendar:

> *The Creativity Toolbox* daily desk calendar
> *The Creativity Toolbox* computer pop-up calendar

The author will grant first rights on both of these products to the book publisher if developed in conjunction with or prior to the book's release.

Online communications

I am a self-proclaimed computer "junkie." I participate in a variety of online computer forums, including the creativity forum on CompuServe. I will make full use of these communications vehicles for promoting the book. Computer networks are effective promotional tools. This is best demonstrated by authors Sarah and Paul Edwards. This couple wrote a series of books on working from home, and are frequent participants, as well as Sysops (system operators who answer or direct users' questions to the right person, and lead online discussions). They have promoted additional demand for books through online network communications forums.

24. It is not necessary to preface the statement. No one is an expert at selling books unless they already have a self-made bestseller. There is no need to water down your statement.

Creative commitment   24

While I am not an expert at selling books, I am an accomplished salesperson, with outstanding creative credentials. The publisher will gain not only a bestselling business book, but a salesperson who will creatively partner to increase book sales. In short, the publisher gains my creative commitment to make it happen.

Competition

25. This is a negative statement that will raise thoughts the agent or editor might not have had on their own. Don't cause yourself any trouble.

Not just another book on how to brainstorm   25

There are several good books that provide insight on the creative process, and offer readers help in thinking more creatively. None has taken the approach of *The Creativity Toolbox* by providing an entire set of tools for creative living. Most focus on the brainstorming process, or creative problem-solving. Few approach it from the multiple intelligence perspective.

This book focuses on the entire individual as the key to creativity. By using an evaluation in the first section of the book, the reader will learn about his/her own creative strengths. The results will help the reader learn which tools are most effective in helping them to develop their creative ability.

Corporations recognize the importance of creativity and innovation as keys to success. Now they are starting to focus more energy and resources on cultivating creative abilities within their organizations. Additionally, when the economy is weak, budgets slashed, and human resources stretched thin, corporations tend to rely upon and support the need to arm managers with the creative tools to compete.

[26] Creativity books

Other books in the field that demonstrate the strength of the topic, yet approach it from a different angle, are:

7 Kinds of Smart: Identifying and Developing Your Many Intelligences (Thomas Armstrong, Dutton/Signet, Plume, 1993).

A Whack on the Side of The Head (Roger Von Oech, U.S. Games Systems, 1990).

It Only Takes One (John Emmerling, Simon & Schuster, 1991).

The Art of Creative Thinking (Gerard Neirenberg, Simon & Schuster, 1982).

Thinkertoys (Michael Michalko, 10 Speed Press, 1991).

Using Both Sides of Your Brain (Tony Buzan, Penguin Books, 1991).

What A Great Idea (Charles "Chic" Thompson, Harper Perennial, 1992).

Book Delivery

There will be three sections and a total of sixteen chapters. Chapters in the first section explore creativity and the creative experience. Each chapter will have several subheadings. The second section of the book will detail the creative tools. Each chapter will represent a section of the toolbox, with each subheading explaining a specific tool. Section three contains the conclusion, as well as three appendices and a bibliography of additional creativity resources.

[27]   The complete manuscript will be delivered within twelve months. A diskette in Microsoft Word is available also.

[28] Chapter Summaries

Section 1—Introduction

Chapter 1: *The Creativity Toolbox*—Now that you have it, what are you going to do with it?

How often has the old adage been repeated, "If you want to do the job right, make sure you have the right tools"? Throughout our life, at almost every turn, we receive the guidance to select the tool needed to do a job.

Remember kindergarten? On the first day, you started with a box filled

26. If you are going to list other books, you need some explanation. These books are not directly competitive because of their age. Those that are more obviously on point should be distinguished more effectively even though they are older. For example, he could distinguish his book as being representative of a societal shift. The other books paved the way, but he is taking the information far beyond what is out there. You want to establish how your book is fresh and original.

27. Once again, leave this out.

28. His chapter summaries are a good example of how you can include parts of the text. He gives the reader a good taste of how the book will be. He also supports his main thesis and the reasons for the book's existence throughout his summaries.

with crayons, paper, glue, scissors, and an assortment of other required odds and ends. Thirteen years later you graduated, leaving with a blue 29-cent Bic pen (or perhaps a fountain pen as a graduation present). Somewhere in this equation you had to surrender most of the fun and creative stuff.

If you attended university, you were probably handed course descriptions listing all the books you would need and the lab materials required. If you were lucky, you even got a list of what you needed to do with the tools to get an "A."

And, when you got married or had a child, friends and family often shower you with many of the tools required to help you as you move into a new direction.

Has anyone ever provided you with the life tools needed to be creative?

Other than in the early days of kindergarten, few people are able to explore or even know that there are many creativity tools they can add to their inventory. It is unfortunate, but most people have very limited exposure (if any at all) to the tools. As a result they may end up living through their entire life without knowing their full creative potential. *The Creativity Toolbox* will focus on creativity based on accepted creativity principles, and expand the theoretical into solid, tangible tools that have great applicability in the readers life. It will start with a layman's review of the concept of Multiple Intelligence developed by Howard Gardner, and move into the application of culture as explored by Dr. Giles Rapille, a Jungian psychologist. Finally the "spokes" are added to the creative wheel. These are the tools available in this book.

Our education system currently falls short in most cases in delivering an all-encompassing set of creative problem-solving tools and methods to increase students' dexterity with creative tools. With budget cuts and staff cutbacks, even first graders in some schools get limited exposure to art or music.

Although change is occurring, learning institutions rarely offer any creativity training at all. They operate from the premise that if you are creative, you already know how, and if you aren't, well . . . too bad. Then they go about the business of arming you with all of the intellectual and quantitative tools you'll need in the world.

This book provides the reader with a set of tools and tool builders that are used to help live a more creative life. The world is filled with all types of people; every tool is not for every person. My hope is to provide each reader with a set of tools that work specifically for him or her.

In this chapter readers will learn:

How to use the book to get the most out of the tools in the future.
About the author's experience with creativity in business and life.
How to overcome the myth that creative people are born that way, and

the rest of us just have to accept it if we aren't born with the "creative gene."

Where their creative strengths fall on a creative spectrum through a self-test.

How to use the results of self-evaluation to select the best tools, perhaps using a color-coded indexing system.

Chapter 2: The Creative Difference—An overview of what creativity is doing for others in our changing world

Competition in life is fierce. One way to stand out from the crowd is to use creativity to beat the competition at whatever your business or personal field is in life. In this chapter, I will draw from the experiences in my professional life where creativity has made the difference between success and failure. I will expand the concept by drawing on positive experiences of others. It is a tickler chapter for the rest of the book on what "creativity" can do (followed by the how-to part).

Using interviews with successful entrepreneurs, corporate executives, and scientists, as well as musicians and artists, I will explore creativity as an integral part of the job, as well as the fundamental basis for one's life's work. I will show how creativity does make a difference.

Key points in the chapter, illustrated through individual, and organizational scenarios, are:

How creativity is the key to customer loyalty.

How employee morale increases dramatically in a creative organization.

How creative employees develop new product and business opportunities, if allowed the freedom to do so.

Common factors in creative organizations.

[29] Chapter 3: An introduction to the theory behind this book (by a person who dislikes academic theoretical reading)

While the bulk of this book focuses on tools to help come up with creative, innovative, novel, or great ideas, some understanding of different problem-solving or brainstorming techniques is required. This chapter will briefly cover several creative problem-solving methods that are used in brainstorming. Since this book provides the reader with tools he or she can use, the focus will not be on the theoretical basis of these methods, but on the use and application within a business or as an individual. The reader will learn:

[30] The basis of multiple intelligence

How to conduct a brainstorming session using a variety of problem-solving methods, including:

The Osborne-Parnes Model

29. This is clever and creative. He sets the tone with his title.

30. Bullets would make this look neater. Don't leave things out in space.

The DeZanger Model
Synectics
The Kepner-Tregoe Methodology
Ideatects
The Ideator process

How to choose one of the described models for a particular problem.
Tips for brainstorm facilitators, including how to get the most out of
group participants during a brainstorming session.

30

PROPOSAL 6

In the Beginning . . .

A Keepsake Record of Before-Birth Memories

**Written and Illustrated by
"Julie Karen"
Julie K. Andres**

This proposal is for an illustrated gift book that will include ample space for the mother-to-be to record and preserve her thoughts and feelings during pregnancy. It was purchased by Longmeadow Press, who liked the proposal so much that they asked the author to do a second book for afterbirth memories.

This kind of specialized proposal requires three basic elements:

1. A clear concept that's marketable (of course, it helps if there's not too much competition).
2. An author who can provide necessary graphics, artwork, and photography—or at least has access to someone who can.
3. An author with the proven ability to conceive and organize almost everything that such a book should include.

This proposal accomplished all those things, and is a perfect example of how a good idea with a strong presentation can offset an author's lack of publishing history.

1. In the original draft, the overview wasn't as direct or persuasive as it is in this rewritten version. It's now concise and clearly conveys all the pertinent information the publisher needs in order to understand the project.

2. The overview does a sufficient job of explaining the author's vision. Writing an overview for this type of book is much more challenging than for standard nonfiction books. It's difficult to categorize this book, and the editorial content is secondary to appearance and usability.

3. This overview is strong because it shows the personality of the project and generates enthusiasm. It's not written in a stuffy, formal tone. While a proposal is a sales pitch, the writing doesn't have to be strictly businesslike to be persuasive. As you read this proposal, you get a feel for the book

4. The informality of the section headings might not work for another type of book, but it works here.

5. This section establishes the writer as an expert on the subject—or at least as being qualified to write the book.

Overview

In the Beginning is a keepsake record book for mothers who have recently discovered that life as they know it will be changed forever. Pregnancy is like a rite of passage that, for most women, brings cherished memories to be shared with loved ones throughout their lives. This unique heirloom-quality record book enables mothers to easily preserve scraps, thoughts, and memories that can be presented to her precious child when the time is just right.

Unlike other baby books that record the statistics, major changes, and accomplishments of babies as they grow, *In the Beginning* is purchased early in pregnancy and completed by the time the baby is brought home from the hospital. It captures a special time of wonder when everything is possible and full of mystery.

The format of the book includes beautifully illustrated pages for writing about the baby's life before birth—choosing names, birth-preparation classes, nursery decorating, the trip to the hospital, labor, etc., until the baby is brought home—everything that happens before the traditional "baby book" kicks in. It also includes blank pages and pockets to give freedom to each woman's individual journey. *In the Beginning* captures the variety of emotion and the brilliant spectrum of change and growth during pregnancy like no other book can. It guides the mother to express the joy and excitement, fears and frustrations—and the sometimes-comic moments—that accompany her unique pregnancy. There are pages for photos, and pockets for special items such as congratulatory notes and cards, ultrasound photos, and shower invitations.

This book begins when the mother first suspects that she might be pregnant and, page by page, takes her through the experience of maternity—from major events to sentimental thoughts and extraordinary feelings.

In the Beginning has the look and feel of an heirloom. It's attractive and substantial without being daunting. It's humorous and sometimes "cute," while also being poignant and purposeful. It is approximately 60 illustrated pages in length.

Why I Am Writing This Book

Sixteen years ago I was pregnant with my first child. I had a strong urge to keep a record of my pregnancy and attempted to do so in one of those bound, blank books. The record is sketchy, but the memories, conjured up by the few entries I did make, are precious. About a year after the birth of my daughter, I was pregnant again and, during that pregnancy, I kept no records at all. When they became old enough, my children asked me questions about

5 their lives before birth and greatly enjoyed hearing my earliest impressions of them. I wished that I had more to share with them than my memories.

Last year I became pregnant with my third child. Right after the test came back positive I rushed out and bought another one of those bound, blank books to write in.

But I wanted something better. That's when the idea struck me: *Mothers want to write about their child's or children's beginnings and a book that encourages this is desirable and valuable.*

In the Beginning meets this preexisting need!

6 Pregnancy is a time of introspection, acute body consciousness, intimate closeness with a person not yet seen . . . mystery and wonder! It's a time when, even though a woman may be working full-time and taking care of other children, she has many quiet moments to think about the new life within her. Most women want to keep a record of their pregnancies. Doing so has immediate rewards as well as providing long-term memories to be cherished with the child, and with other family members. My older children, now 15 and 13, still love to hear me tell stories about their very earliest days.

During my recent pregnancy, I was again immersed in the spell of maternal instinct. I started *In the Beginning* while visiting doctors, getting medical tests taken, feeling the baby exercise within me, attending Lamaze classes, buying maternity clothes, reading stacks of pregnancy books, preparing a nursery, "eating for two," and living through the most amazing body changes a person can experience. *In the Beginning* is based on my own feelings and experiences.

About Me

7 In addition to being a mother, I am a graphic designer and artist. I have exhibited watercolors in a one-woman show, at community galleries, and exhibited illustrations as a graphic arts student at UCLA. My articles on graphic design have been featured in national publications. I have designed numerous newsletters, and illustrated freelance for the past twelve years. I have taught watercolor classes to five-, six-, and seven-year-old children and have given demonstrations on music and art to nursery schools. In April 1991 I began work as a volunteer to help mothers of newborns adjust to the changes and challenges of motherhood through a community outreach program sponsored by the United Way.

Who Will Buy This Book?

8 *In the Beginning* is for mothers who have recently conceived. It's written to be reread by the parents to the child as soon as he or she asks the question "Was

---

6. Here the author makes a compelling statement for why this book should be published. What also counts here is the author's ability to be personal and convey poignant maternal feelings.

7. The author highlights the necessary attributes for a project of this nature: She's an accomplished graphic artist; she can write; and she's a mother who cares about other mothers. All the information is relevant to the project and shows the competence and ability necessary to the goal.

8. This strong and commonsense testimony shows that a large nat-

ural market exists for this project. This type of marketing information is useful because these ideas broaden the potential market considerably and might not have been obvious to the publisher.

9. This observation on today's parents shows careful consideration of the book's commercial viability.

I in your tummy, Mommy?" When completed, it's a written history of the [8] child, beginning at the beginning. It will be a treasured heirloom capturing a magical time as nothing else can.

Every expectant mother will want one *each time she becomes pregnant. In the Beginning* is also an ideal shower gift.

Mothers who have already given birth have excellent memories of what happened during their pregnancies. *In the Beginning* is inviting to them also and they will want to "catch up" their babies' histories and find a place for all of the treasures they have saved.

Today's parents are beginning to have babies at a later age than previ- [9] ous generations; most are in their 30s, many in their 40s. They are people with careers and they have money and time to invest in their children's futures. They conscientiously plan pregnancy and childbirth and cherish their family time. Many parents try for years to conceive—in the last decade fertility clinics have become very busy places. Childless celebrities say, yes, they have it all . . . except . . . a family. Babies are in vogue. *In the Beginning's* time has come.

Why People Will Buy This Book

As soon as a woman's pregnancy is confirmed, she heads to the bookstore! There are multitudes of books on what can be expected during pregnancy. There are picture books about the progression of the baby's growth in utero. There are labor and birth-preparation books. New books—about every aspect of pregnancy and birth you can imagine—are released on a regular basis.

The most closely related books to *In the Beginning* are *The Pregnancy Organizer* by Pamela Eisenberg, and *Pregnancy Day by Day* by Sheila Kitzinger. *The Pregnancy Organizer* is in small looseleaf-binder form and like a Day Timer® in purpose—organizing and planning. *Pregnancy Day by Day* is primarily an informational book with small spaces to write about various aspects of pregnancy. While *In the Beginning* has a slight similarity to these books, it is in a class by itself. It's the only book that focuses on the life of the child before birth—ultimately to share the experience with the child.

There are no pregnancy-related books designed to begin a child's history before birth. So many things happen at the very beginning of life that are lost to posterity without *In the Beginning*.

There are no pregnancy-related books designed to share with your child. *In the Beginning* has room for the mother to write all that she wants to express to her son or daughter. There are lovely illustrations, timeless in quality, as appropriate now as they will be in 25 years.

In the Beginning is unique because it's not just a diary; it gives the mother the opportunity to do much more than just make journal entries. *In the Beginning* is a fertile place, bringing life to the thoughts and details of the mother's entries.

There is nothing like it currently available. It's such a simple idea that when people see it they will say, "Why hasn't someone thought of that before?"

Marketability/Promotion

[10] There is a place for *In the Beginning* in all bookstores, card and gift shops, and stationery stores. Maternity and parenting magazines (*9 Months, Parenting, American Baby, Child, Childbirth*) are ideal for reviews and advertising. Hospital gift shops, especially those in hospitals that offer birth-preparation classes, are also appropriate outlets. Birthing-class instructors will help promote it to attending parents-to-be.

[11] TV shows such as "The Home Show" and "Live with Regis & Kathie Lee" are ideal forums for promotion.

Timing

In the Beginning will be completed within eight months of my signing a contract with the publisher.

[12] Sample Page Subjects

Opening Poem

[13] First Inklings*

I first thought that I might be pregnant when . . .
I decided to get a positive answer . . .
When I told your Dad, he . . .
What our friends said . . .
And our families . . .
I felt . . .

News Traveled Fast*

We got congratulations from . . .
And phone calls from . . .
*Marked pages are illustrated on accompanying art boards.
Here are some of the special wishes that were sent . . .

Pocket

10. The marketability and promotion section shows some innovative ideas. The publishing house might not have thought in terms of the gift market and birth preparation classes.

11. This section's weakness is that there is no indication of the author's ability to promote the book through these avenues. While the ideas are good, there is no practical link between the author and the promotions.

12. This outline presentation shows strong and comprehensive organization. Every emotion and event relevant to the experience appear to be addressed. It's evident that this book will be a real tool for the reader to express and record intimate feelings.

13. Including these poems helps set the "from the heart" tone the book will have.

About Your Mom
I was born
What was happening that year
Stories I liked as a child
Games I played
Pets I had
About my family

About Your Dad
He was born
What was happening that year
His favorite stories
His favorite games
His pets
His family

Doctor Visits
Your estimated time of arrival was . . .
Routine tests
Ultrasound (photo if available)
Special tests (when and why)
When I first heard your heartbeat . . .

Getting a Kick out of You*
I felt the first flutter . . .
You wriggled regularly by . . .
When your movements were stronger, it felt like . . .
Sometimes I wondered if . . .
What your dad thought when he first felt you move . . .

Keeping Busy
At work
At play
While waiting I made you a . . .
Trips I took while pregnant

Diet & Health (2 pages)
I had some crazy cravings . . .
And some favorite treats were . . .
You were worth the weight! I gained . . .

My favorite exercise was . . .
Just before you were born my waist measured . . .

Poem

Photo page

Education
I went to birth-preparation classes at . . .
I learned . . .
The classes made me feel . . .
Books that I read . . .

Wishes and Dreams
Poem

Good dreams/scary dreams
Wishes and hopes

Letters to Our Child
From Mother
From Father

Pockets

The Name Game (2 pages)
Name books I read . . .
Girls' names I liked . . .
     Top five names . . .
Boys' names I liked . . .
     Top five names . . .
The final decision . . .
Why we chose to name you _____

Shopping (2 pages)
Maternity clothes, my favorite ones
Preparing your layette . . .

Your Nursery
Planning and doing
Colors and characters

Photo of your nursery

Shower Time*
When . . .
Where . . .
Friends who came . . .
Family who came . . .
Gifts received . . .

Photo page

Pocket for invitation and cards

Dazed Days
One day I was so clumsy I . . .
One of the funniest things that happened . . .
Sometimes when I couldn't get up . . .

Hospital Preparation
Packing the bag
Practice run
Touring the nursery

Labor and Delivery (2 pages)
False starts
The real thing—when/where
I was in labor (how long) . . .
Who was there to share . . .
To feel comfortable I brought . . .
My thoughts and feelings . . .

On Your Mark, Get Set, You!
Just one look
First hug
Dad's impressions

Your first photo

Special Pockets (2)
ID bracelet
Dad's hospital mask
Bassinet card

Vital Statistics

Weight
Length
Hair, eyes, etc.

Closing Poem

Opening Poem

Your life begins as does a rose
A seed is planted, then it grows
With love and caring, a bud appears
And flowers bloom throughout the years
As the rose began beneath the earth
Our love began before your birth

Health & Diet page

Even when I was tired
At the end of a long day
I always felt happy
That you were on the way

Dreams Poem

"As long as you're healthy . . ." I've often said
As long as you're warm and loved and fed
As long as you smile then I'll smile, too
With my hopes fulfilled and
My dreams come true

Closing Poem

We were together quite a while
Before we really met
And the moment I first saw you
Is one I won't forget
And through the weeks and months and years
I'll keep open my ears and my heart
And let you know I've loved you so
Right from the very start

The following sample pages are important because they show off the author's creative and artistic talents—which are of primary importance for this kind of book. The sample pages also provide an exact visualization of how the project will be executed; they bring everything to life and prove the project's workability.

Getting a Kick Out of You

I felt the first flutter _____

_____

_____

You wiggled regularly by _____

_____

_____

When your movements were stronger it felt like_____

_____

_____

_____

Sometimes I wondered if _____

_____

_____

What your dad thought when he first felt you move_____

_____

_____

_____

_____

_____

_____

_____

_____

_____

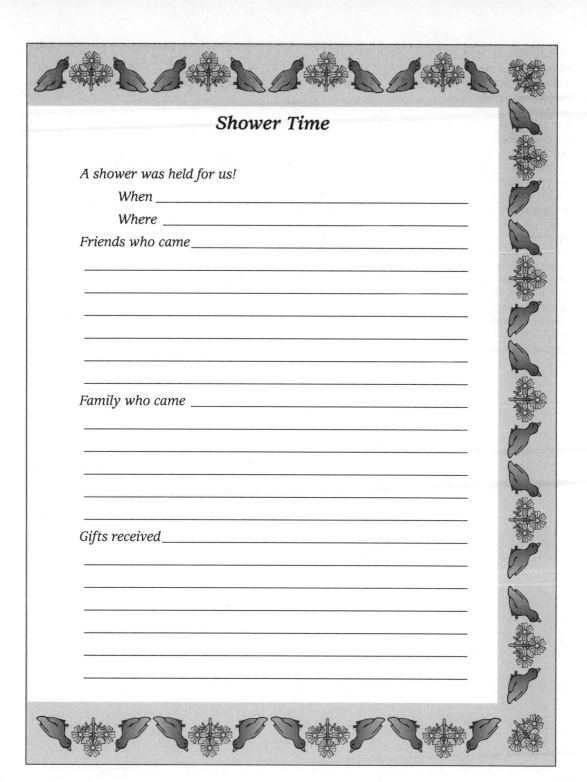

Shower Time

A shower was held for us!

When _____

Where _____

Friends who came _____

_____

_____

_____

_____

_____

_____

Family who came _____

_____

_____

_____

_____

_____

Gifts received _____

_____

_____

_____

_____

_____

_____

_____

We sold this one to the publishing division of the American Management Association (AMACOM Books). Our initial concern was, Is this too "soft" a concept for the traditional business community? But, hey, it was the 90s and things had certainly become more open to new ideas. *Fortune* 500 companies and small businesses all wanted to know more about intuition, and this was an excellent proposal by a mainstream businessman and lawyer as opposed to a New Age guru.

PROPOSAL 7

Trust Your Guts!

Develop Your Business Intuition and Win—Consistently

by Richard M. Contino, Esq.

Trust Your Guts!

Develop Your Business Intuition and Win—Consistently

Proposal Table of Contents

1. For a long proposal, a table of contents for the proposal itself is a good way to show that the writer is well organized. It also makes it easier for the editor or agent to skip to the sections he or she considers to be most vital. Not everyone likes to begin at the beginning.

Trust Your Guts!

Develop Your Business Intuition and Win—Consistently

by Richard M. Contino, Esq.

Book Overview

The moment you touched this proposal your intuitive process was engaged. A particular body sensation, lasting only a fraction of a second, was your signal. Typically, it goes completely unnoticed in the pace of business. If you knew how to take advantage of that special moment, you would have begun a unparalleled journey into releasing your extraordinary intuitive capabilities. That is the point of this innovative, groundbreaking book—to learn how to access and use your innate and powerful sixth sense abilities for business.

Too often we're taught that success in business comes from the prag-

2. Watch out for typos, especially in the first paragraph.

3. The author tells what the book is about in the first paragraph. This is especially important in a proposal for a book that could be considered esoteric within its typical category.

matic application of business principles and theory. If it was that simple, everyone could easily make millions. Clearly, it's not. So what's answer? If you talk to highly successful career people and entrepreneurs you learn that they rely on something most ignore—their intuition. A skill they've honed through years of trial and error.

Albert Einstein was one of many noteworthy individuals who knew [4] how to use his sixth-sense capabilities for success, first intuiting the right answer then proving it through experiment. If you could similarly take advantage of your intuition in business, think about the possibilities. You would be able to:

4. This analogy creates automatic credibility. The author anchors his approach, so he is not dismissed out of hand.

- Uncover hidden personal agendas
- Come up with, brilliant profit ideas
- Creatively solve what others claim to be insurmountable problems
- Accurately predict decision outcomes
- And more

5. This shows a strong how-to element and emphasizes what the reader can get out of the book. It helps to anchor the concept and will inspire the editor or agent to leap into marketing possibilities.

Sound impossible? It's not. By using the simple and unique awareness [5] and unblocking techniques presented in *Trust Your Guts!*, you can unlock your uncanny sixth-sense powers.

Developing your intuition for business is easy—once the mystery is taken out of the process. It is a natural capability everyone has. It can be developed like any other skill, with an open mind, some guidance, and a little practice. And, contrary to what other teachers and authors profess, you [6] don't have to be in an altered state of consciousness, engage in mental contortions, or undergo a mystical or magical experience to access it. All you have to do is remove unfounded and self-imposed limitations.

6. The author again removes his book from what is often perceived by the business community as the "la-la land" genre of New Age. He bridges into the business book arena, which is where this book belongs.

The innovative mind development techniques offered in *Trust Your Guts!* are based on the author's fifteen-year search for ways to predictably increase business success. An extensive educational background in engineering, law, business, and finance was of help, but clearly wasn't enough. So, in his struggle up the success ladder as a Wall Street attorney and businessman, Mr. Contino aggressively sought the advice and insights of business leaders, mentors, entrepreneurs, and management consultants and psychologists. Even with their assistance, he made a lot of wrong turns.

7. The author could briefly explain the example as a sidebar rather than just alluding to it.

A life-changing breakthrough came when, in desperation, he left a [7] mainstream career path to purse a direction that simply "felt" right. It was the most difficult decision in his business career—everyone, including himself, thought the new direction was not only a mistake, but self-destructive. This decision, however, turned out to be the best one he had ever made. And it was the genesis for his development of a new business tool that would successfully and predictably guide his career and business endeavors from that point forward—his intuitive powers. Over time, and through trial and error, he learned to access these intuitive powers on demand. As his sixth-sense capabilities increased, his perceptive abilities also sharpened—dramatically, enabling him, for example, to quickly get to the core of difficult problems and spot manipulative or destructive people. It ultimately became clear that what people thought of as mystical or paranormal abilities were, in fact, natural capabilities, and that accessing these sensing "powers" was merely a matter of getting out of your own way.

Very simply, *Trust Your Guts!* will teach readers how to easily develop their intuitive skills for business success. It demystifies what are often thought of as mystical powers, shows that our intuitive sensing capabilities are a natural and latent gift everyone has, and provides straightforward techniques for unblocking and developing these abilities to their fullest potential. It offers proven techniques that the author and his colleagues apply daily in their business endeavors.

Book Approach

Trust Your Guts! will be a 60,000–70,000-word book aimed at providing people in business with a simple methodology for accessing and using their powerful sixth-sense abilities. Unlike books that offer the promise of developing psychic or paranormal skills through a mystical and, for most people in business, off-putting approach, *Trust Your Guts!* shows how to develop intuitive skills in a groundbreaking and straightforward way. And it does so in plain English.

The book begins by taking the mystery away from our sixth-sense capabilities by leading the reader through common threshold intuitive occurrences that everyone experiences, and typically go unnoticed, much in the same way as in the following paragraph. These very experiences are then used as the basis for developing what is in fact an unparalleled business skill.

For example, most people don't realize that they are *always* in touch with their intuition and that they're unconsciously, and continually, ignoring this source of knowing. As you read this proposal, for instance, you are naturally thinking about the book idea. You may believe that you're drawing solely on your prior market experiences in your evaluation process, but in fact you're also engaging your intuition, possibly without being fully aware of it. Whether you take full advantage of it or not depends on your beliefs about intuitive powers. For example, if you take a moment as you consider the book's reader market potential, you may notice that a part of your mind is "thinking forward," in effect looking for an answer by "reaching" into the future—an intuitive process.

8. It would help to list some of these techniques in the overview. The reader wants to grasp the concept in a concrete way that will help him or her to visualize the book.

You may also be subtly aware that, as your mind is searching for a conclusion, you're trying to connect with a "feeling" in making this market assessment. That sensation is how we confirm our intuitive connection. For example, when confronted with business choices, we mentally review them to see which "feels" right. When one does, and if it's unclouded by any fears, anxieties, or other "rational" negative thoughts, it is your intuitive confirmation. To the extent you work with your sixth sense, your business decisions will improve dramatically. [9]

Once the reader is comfortable and, therefore, receptive to exploring his or her intuitive potential, the next step is to teach him or her how to identify and remove blocks, such as anxieties, fears, and life illusions, that interfere with intuitive thoughts. This requires the reexamination of some basic business and life premises that we accept without question and that cripple our sensing potential. For example, the simple belief that emotions aren't a factor in business decisions will block your powers. They are a factor and they must be acknowledged. Once these invented beliefs are put in their proper perspective, your intuitive channel opens. Next, you must learn how to separate the good messages from the bad messages. That is accomplished by exploring our thought processes to identify possible sources of intuitive information. And finally the reader is taught how to hone his or her intuitive skill so it becomes an effortless and natural part of his or her business assessment and decision-making process. [10]

Throughout the book, the reader is given a wide variety of concrete methods for accessing his or her intuition and is also provided skill-building exercises to reinforce what he or she has learned. For example, the reader is shown how to use "intuition bridges" to help make the intuition connection. And he or she is given simple daily exercises to put into practice the author's intuition-developing methodology. For example, as you walk, simply swinging your arms in an opposite-to-normal direction will begin to force you to clear your mind of thoughts that block your intuitive powers. The reader is also taught how to effectively build his or her new skill by, for example, directly and indirectly verifying his or her sixth-sense messages. At each key development stage, hypothetical business exercises are provided so the reader can measure his or her progress and facilitate intuitive development. [11] [12]

In a nutshell, the *Trust Your Guts!* approach takes learning how to access intuition for business out of the New Age talk arena and puts it into a language a businessperson can understand and relate to based upon his or her own life experiences. It shows the reader that developing and using his or her intuition can be a simple, straightforward, easy-to-relate-to, and natural process. And, finally, it explains how the reader can apply these innovative mind techniques in business situations to increase his or her business progress—and to play the business game as a master. [13]

9. But what if you are just a worrier? If a question is raised naturally, anticipate it in your proposal and confront it directly. Here I would devote an entire paragraph to the process to make it as clear as possible.

10. This could be a bulleted list for emphasis.

11. This is good. It shows the how-to aspect of the book.

12. This is an interesting example, one that the reader will likely try.

13. This is a good way to anticipate objections and confront them directly. It also reinforces the thesis. You know exactly what you are getting.

Book Foreword

[14] The author has arranged for an internationally known and well-respected psychic, Dawn Christie, to write a foreword for the book. Ms. Christie has received considerable media attention over the past 15 years, and actively works with many professionals as well as business and political leaders. She is frequently called upon by police agencies for assistance in solving crimes.

Reader Market

The market for *Trust Your Guts!* are readers of general success books who want to use every possible avenue to improve business performance. They, for example, could be professional negotiators, managers, salespeople, sec-retaries, or entrepreneurs. Inasmuch as developing intuitive capabilities has general applicability beyond business situations, a secondary market would [15] be individuals looking for ways to make life easier or more rewarding. For example, intuition can be used in solving personal relationship or commu-nication problems.

[16] Market Analysis—Competition

Trust Your Guts! would compete with business books offering streetwise advice on how to get ahead using practical, bottom-line suggestions, as [17] opposed to textbook theory. For example, a national best-seller, *What They Don't Teach You at Harvard Business School,* written by Mark McCormack and published by Bantam Books (1986), offers the reader this type of practical business advice. Following behind this successful book, Bantam also pub-lished (1990), a supplemental book by the same author entitled *What They Still Don't Teach You at Harvard Business School,* in which his insights were expanded.

[18] Mr. McCormack, a lawyer who recognized that business school theory can be limiting and that success in business comes from street smarts, advances that a key success factor, whether negotiating, selling, or running a business, is being able to read people—through something he refers to as "applied people sense." He advocates that it is important to learn how to lis-ten to what people actually say. And to determine their underlying motiva-tions. To this end he suggests that you can uncover hidden agendas by "listening aggressively." He also suggests that the reader learn to use his or her intuition—something he claims psychics and fortune-tellers have mas-tered. He, however, does not tell the reader how to "listen aggressively" or access his or her intuition. Nor does he provide any other concrete tech-nique for uncovering the hidden information that can make the difference between success and failure in a business endeavor. He also talks about the

14. This is a risky choice. The author might have wanted to refer to her as intuitive rather than a psychic. The term *psychic* has a specific connotation. You should avoid any-thing that can under-mine your thesis. Here the author invested a great deal of energy in distinguishing this book from New Age material, but this choice of fore-word could backfire. Maintain consistency throughout the pro-posal and objectively view how one section relates to another.

15. There is no need to discuss a secondary market here. Here the strength is a fresh approach to a proven market area. You do not want to dilute the pro-posal by taking the market into an area that is potentially over-done.

16. Just call this compe-tition. No biggie. Just keep things simple.

17. This book is a classic and should be referred to as such. The distin-guishing factor is that the new book offers a fresh and up-to-the-minute approach to the concepts that made this earlier one a classic.

18. You don't need such a lengthy discussion of the book. It is not direct competition, as there is always a self-generating market for business books. This explanation, if necessary at all, should be condensed.

19. The proposed book can really stand on its own without this level of discussion; it is stronger to say in a positive way what the book does. This much discussion sounds defensive.

20. This is not directly competitive. The author appears not to fully understand the purpose of a competition section. It is not necessary to point out every book on a similar subject. If there are books that seem directly on point, they must be addressed and distinguished.

21. It would be better not to point out the limitations of the reader's book-buying dollars. It would be a more positive approach to focus on what *Trust Your Guts* does.

22. This is too much. He could say that his book adds an additional element to classic negotiation books, as it . . .

critical part emotions play in business and the need to be aware of them. [18] Once again, he does not give the reader specific techniques for identifying or handling this potential problem. McCormack is clearly on the right track, but fails to go far enough. He, for example, often leaves the reader with the job of figuring out how to do what he suggests.

Trust Your Guts! takes Mr. McCormack's thoughts a giant step farther, by [19] not only discussing success skills, such as intuition and enhanced perception (Mr. McCormack refers to the latter as "listening aggressively"), that can make a difference, but actually teaching the reader how to, for example, develop and use his or her intuitive capabilities to uncover hidden agendas. The book provides the reader with practical and innovative mind-power business tools, not just concepts, ones the author has been using successfully for years in business and ones never taught in business schools.

Trust Your Guts! would also compete with popular books written by Har- [20] vey MacKay, such as *Beware the Naked Man Who Offers You His Shirt*, published by William Morrow (1990). In this particular book, Mr. MacKay offers get-ahead-in-business tips collected from industry leaders supporting three basic premises: Deliver More Than You Promise, Do What You Love, and Love What You Do. Although his book offers excellent business insights, basic generalizations are difficult, and sometimes impossible, to translate effectively into specific situations. *Trust Your Guts!* takes this type of business advice farther. Not only does it offer basic business survival truths, but it provides a foundation skill that the reader can always turn to to develop his or her own success theories an approaches.

Trust Your Guts! would also vie for the readers' dollars with *Super Self*, [21] written by best-selling author Charles J. Givens and published by Simon & Schuster (1994). The Givens book, in a fashion similar to the preceding MacKay book, is geared toward supplying "commonsense" success strategies (for example: "If the cost is less than your per hour value, hire someone else to do the job."). Once again, generalizations can be helpful, but if they were the complete answer, no one in business would have difficulties. *Trust Your Guts!* advocates that achieving success is far more than a matter of following someone else's directions and offers the reader an innovative way to find his or her own achievement solutions.

Trust Your Guts! would compete with "how to negotiate" books such as [22] *The Persuasive Edge*, written by Myles Martel and published by Fawcett (1989), and *Win-Win Negotiating*, written by Fred E. Jandt and published by John Wiley & Sons (1987). To succeed in negotiations, you have to quickly determine what the other side needs or thinks. Traditional negotiation books such as these offer the promise of negotiation success through posturing techniques and the use of clues to determine an opponent's underlying agenda. Some of it helps, but these approaches aren't the entire answer.

[22] Attempting to apply techniques everyone is aware of, or guessing at underlying agendas based upon general clues, has limited benefits. *Trust Your Guts!* offers a supplemental approach to negotiating success. It teaches the reader specific sixth-sense methods for uncovering information that can make a difference. For example, *Trust Your Guts!* shows the reader how to determine if [23] his or her negotiating opponent is blocked by an irrational emotional issue and, if so, how to handle it.

One more traditional business book worth mentioning is *Idea Power,* written by Arthur B. VanGundy and published by AMACOM Books (1994). Although devoted primarily to teaching group techniques for developing business ideas and solutions, it does offer the reader some mechanical methods of individual problem analysis that, for example, break the grip of mental ruts so creative channels are open for business solutions. The techniques suggested work, but are cumbersome, analytical approaches that rely heavily on past experiences, not always the best source of solid or ready solutions. *Trust Your Guts!* addresses the issue of problem-solving by using an individual's genius—his or her powerful intuitive capability, a less cumbersome and very powerful alternative approach.

[24] *Trust Your Guts!* would compete with a less traditional, but very popular, internationally selling, intriguing, and groundbreaking business book, *The Silva Mind Control Method for Business Managers,* written by José Silva and published by Pocket Books (1986). The Silva Mind Control book's premise is based upon using your mind powers to get information and control business outcomes through, for example, various visualization techniques. It advocates trusting your "Alpha" functioning and using your right brain (intuitive) capabilities though meditative and sleep suggestion approaches. These techniques work, but are based in the somewhat stale, complex, and esoteric paranormal terminology and thinking of the 1960s and 1970s. *Trust Your Guts!* aims at the same result, business success, but approaches connecting with your mind powers for business in a far simpler, less mystical, easier-to-relate-to, and wide-awake fashion, through simply releasing self-imposed intuition blocks.

Two final points about this noteworthy book. Mr. Silva states that he has what are referred to clairvoyant abilities, suggesting again a paranormal basis in his approach. Mr. Contino has the same results capabilities, but has found that these "powers" are a natural extension of removing mental and emotional blocks and should not be considered paranormal (as advanced by the Silva book) or mystical. In addition, the Silva book attempts to specifically offer categorical approaches for virtually all business problems, such as managing time more effectively and handling difficult people. In doing so, it devotes little to the actual process that the reader must learn. *Trust Your Guts!,* on the other hand, is comprehensively dedicated to teaching the

23. He could have dealt with the competition more effectively by listing the classic books and then bulleting what his book does rather than what other books don't do. We suspect this competition section was not a determining factor in the sale of the book.

24. This is the only book he might have wanted to address directly, though in a concise fashion, since it refers to intuition in a business context.

reader how to develop his or her basic mind-power tools to use in improving his or her business progress.

25. This is overkill. He started his proposal by stating that his book is business-oriented, not New Age. He dilutes his points with these comparisons. Sometimes less is more. Don't bog down your proposal. You will sound insecure.

Along the lines of the Silva book, *Trust Your Guts!* would be in competition with nonbusiness books offering mind-power approaches to achieving goals, such as the highly successful book *Creative Visualization,* written by Shakti Gawain and published by Bantam Books (1982). Ms. Gawain suggests that the reader can, through the use of mental energy, improve, for example, his or her prosperity as well as achieve the fulfillment of his or her desires. She offers 1970s-style exercises, meditations, affirmations, and techniques to tap into positive life potentials. As the title suggests, the book focuses on using visualizations, similar to the Silva book in some respects, to create outcomes. It, as with the Silva book, is excellent, but its approach may be unsettling for a pragmatic businessperson because it clouds the development of a natural skill in an aura of mysticism and spiritualism. *Trust Your Guts!* advocates a fresh approach to achieving business desires—one that is simple and natural. And one that does not require elaborate visualizations, affirmations, unusual exercises, or mind-stretching beliefs. **25**

There are two other excellent books of significance along the lines of *Creative Visualization, Sixth Sense,* written by Laurie Nadel, Judy Haims, and Robert Stemson and published by Avon Books (1990), and *Your Nostradamus Factor,* written by Ingo Swann and published by Simon & Schuster (1993). *Sixth Sense* offers to teach the reader how to develop his or her intuitive powers for life and business. Its emphasis, however, is more theoretical, exploring, for example, the theory of intuition, technically how the mind and brain works in the intuitive process, and current and past research about intuition, much like a school course book. Little is offered to generally teach the reader the fundamental steps necessary to release his or her intuitive powers. For instance, its Ten Step Program for intuitive development is two pages in length, and merely scratches the surface of the process with suggestions such as: Define It For Yourself, Identify It, and Trust It. And even less is offered for business application, possibly due to the fact that the book is basically written by a professional writer, Ms. Nadel, rather than, as is the case of *Trust Your Guts!,* an intuitive businessperson who actively uses his sixth-sense capabilities every day.

Your Nostradamus Factor is written by a well-known psychic. Although not geared toward the business market, it offers to teach the reader how to develop future-seeing capabilities. The material offered is very credible; however, it is quite esoteric. For example, one chapter discusses the "linear time trap and time looping" and another chapter examines "nostrafac experiences of the second kind," all of which would clearly be of great interest to the student of parapsychology. It, as with the Nadel book, is written like a thesis. A businessperson reading the book is left on his or her own to integrate the teaching into a business context, something that may be difficult for the sixth-sense novice. *Trust Your Guts!* is simpler to understand, is written in plain English, is geared toward the supersensory novice, and goes far beyond future-seeing, exploring the full range of intuitive potential. It is a bottom-line business book.

[26] And finally, books on body language, like *Body Language* written by Julis Fast (*Books in Print* lists the publisher of this successful book as MJF Books, with a 1970 and second unspecified publish date), showing people how to mechanically look into someone's mind on basic issues, such as defensiveness or self-confidence, by attaching particular meaning to physical gestures or postures, are also worth mentioning. Although mechanical techniques are of value, and, properly used, can springboard your intuitive process, they are limited [27] and not always correct. *Trust Your Guts!* brings the concept of reading people into the twenty-first century, using simple mind-power techniques.

[28] Marketing & Publicity

[29] The author will support the publishing of *Trust Your Guts!* with a comprehensive promotional campaign, including the development of a business intuition seminar. He intends to use Holt & Associates, a public relations firm, to promote the book on national radio and television (Mr. Contino has extensive talk show experience), as well as in the print media. In addition, the author will use his numerous business print media contacts with, for example, *Inc.* magazine, *CIO* magazine, and *Entrepreneur* magazine, to gain publicity for the book. The various intuition development tests offered will lend themselves particularly well to print media promotions.

[30] In connection with one of his previous books, *Business Emotions,* promoted by Penelope Holt of Holt & Associates, the author gained national attention for his innovative concepts and approaches, resulting in appearances on national radio and TV talk shows such as:

Television:

- *NewsNight Update*   CNN, National Network Cable TV Show
- *Business Reports*   Syndicated Cable TV Show

Radio:

- *America in the Morning*   WBZ Radio, Mutual Radio Network
- *Rambling with Gambling*   WOR Radio
- *LaPorte & Company*   KNBR-AM Radio (NBC Affiliate)
- *Vera's Voice*   KMNY-AM Radio Talk Show (Metromedia Affiliate)
- *The Michael Jackson Show*   KABC-AM (ABC Affiliate)
- *Job Seekers*   KRTH-AM/FM Radio Show
- *Salt Lake City Radio*   KSL Radio

---

26. Finally! He should just list these books in his bibliography.

27. It bears repeating that the author took a shotgun approach that can backfire. You don't want an editor and agent to spend so much valuable time considering competition or potential problems when there are so many more persuasive things you can say about your book.

28. This should be called "promotions and publicity."

29. This is too general. How does he have these contacts? Back up your statements with facts.

30. Here the author's experience and proven promotability are huge pluses.

Potential Audio Market Product

31

The techniques for developing intuitive capabilities presented in *Trust Your Guts!* lend themselves to audiocassette formatting. For example, a six-cassette course could be put together which would take the listener step by step through the author's program over a six-week period. One cassette would be used weekly, and each would contain a seven-day program of basic developmental information, personal awareness insights, and enhancement exercises.

About the Author

Richard M. Contino, an attorney and nationally known financial expert, is a businessman, professional negotiator, and writer. He lectures extensively throughout the United States and has been developing and conducting seminars for business during the past 14 years. He has been a guest expert on many radio and TV talk shows.

Mr. Contino has founded or cofounded ten successful businesses, including a corporate law firm, four general equipment leasing companies, two railcar leasing companies, a business advisory firm, a seminar company, a computer sales company, and an online computer network company. Prior to becoming an independent businessman, he was affiliated with two major Wall Street law firms and was a senior executive for an international leasing corporation, where he acquired direct experience in law, finance, marketing, and management.

32

In the pursuit of his interest in the development of his human potential, he has, over the past 15 years, studied Eastern and supersensory philosophies and applications with three nationally known groups. He also studied, and is proficient in, transcendental meditation, the Tarot, the Runes, hatha yoga, and the martial arts. He has read extensively in the supersensory area and has taken an array of mind development courses, such as ones in remote viewing and telepathy. He has also worked with a number of management psychologists and credible psychics specializing in human potential development. Mr. Contino is trained in handwriting analysis. He is a member of the American Society for Psychical Research in New York City.

Mr. Contino has a Bachelor of Aeronautical Engineering degree from Rensselaer Polytechnic Institute, a Juris Doctor from the University of Maryland School of Law and an LL.M. from the New York University Graduate School of Law. He is listed in a number of Who's Who publications.

Publications by the Author

33

In his writing endeavors, Mr. Contino has had the following books published:

Margin notes:

31. This is too vague. It is best not to use "could-bes," as they will be ignored. He should say he is developing an audio series. He is conceptualizing it, and that is enough.

32. In our opinion it might be better not to mention his proficiency in "occult arts," in that he stressed the importance of distinguishing his book from New Age material. Keep in mind that all sections of the proposal can create an impression. Make sure they all fit with each other. The other references, though borderline, are more credible than showing that he accepts the use of oracles.

33. These are strong publication credentials. Don't worry, everybody has to start somewhere. But if you have them, flaunt those that are relevant.

- **McGraw-Hill, 1994:**   **Business Negotiation Book**

  Negotiate the Best Lease Deal—Lessor-Beating Tricks, Tips, and Tactics (working title), a general negotiation strategies and tactics book applied to equipment lease financing.

- **AMACOM Books, 1993:**   **Business How-to Book**

  The Franchising Handbook, a hands-on business reference guide for franchisors, collaboratively written by franchise experts.

- **Wordware Publishing, 1989:**   **Business Psychology/Human Potential Book**

  Business Emotions—Breaking through Barriers To Success, a book of innovative and dynamic approaches for achieving predictable success in business. It received national and local radio, TV, and print media attention.

- **AMACOM Books, 1989:**   **Business How-to Book**

  Handbook of Equipment Leasing—The Deal Maker's Guide, a state-of-the-art book on capital equipment leasing.

- **Prentice-Hall, 1979:**   **Business How-to Book**

  Legal and Financial Aspects of Equipment Leasing Transactions, a comprehensive businessman's book on capital equipment leasing.

Chapter Outline & Synopsis

³⁴ Table of Contents Overview

34. This is a very good table of contents—logical, comprehensive, and compelling.

35. These are very good chapter summaries. They capture the writer's voice, tell the agent or editor what to expect, and use outlines to create and support the structure. The summaries are easy to read and understand.

Chapter I   *Control Your Business Destiny!*   **35**

Imagine the competitive edge you would have in business if you could quickly solve business problems, identify new market opportunities, uncover your opponent's hidden negotiating agenda, and consistently make successful business decisions. It's an exciting thought. And it's an exciting reality. If you're willing to suspend all negative thoughts and self-imposed limitations for a few hours, you will be astonished at what you can learn to do by simply allowing a natural capability to surface—your intuitive powers. You'll see that the human potential limits you thought you had are merely artificial ones others have convinced you exist. And that what you believed was possible, and what is possible, are two dramatically different things.

Clearly, using your intuition in business can be a powerful competitive tool. And one that will dramatically increase business success. Learning to use it effectively, however, is like learning any other skill; it takes a receptive mind, guidance, and practice. First, you must realize this incredible gift is a natural capability everyone possesses, blocked only by self-imposed and limiting beliefs and fears. Since intuition is part of our innate human potential, contrary to popular belief you don't have to be in altered state of consciousness to access it. Nor do you have to undergo a mystical or magical process. Very simply, learning to use your intuitive ability is no different than learning a new language in school. Choosing to add it to your business arsenal will be the most important and beneficial decision you will ever make. It will change your business life forever.

One of the primary reasons developing our intuitive powers in business is often overlooked is that unless these feelings or impressions can be confirmed "by the facts" they're flatly ignored. Add to that the poor track record of most people making decisions based upon on what they think are intuitive messages, gut feelings, hunches, and intuitive flashes, it's no wonder our intuitive potential is rarely explored. However, there is good reason to reexamine this powerful human potential possibility. For example, by understanding our thought process, it's easy to see how unconscious, self-destructive emotional inclinations, such as fears, can mistakenly be interpreted as intuitive information. And it's also easy to see how they actually block our intuitive capabilities and mislead us. There is no doubt that relying on impressions unknowingly based upon anxieties, life illusions and other mental or emotional static will produce bad results. Very simply, not making the effort to explore your intuitive potential is throwing away an uncanny information source that can guide you to predictable business success.

For businesspeople, a major obstacle to considering this extraordinary capability is how the intuitive process has been presented. For many, for example, being told that it is a spiritual process, or that accessing intuition requires entering an altered or mystical state, is off-putting and can be intimidating. As a result, they're not receptive to the learning process. The point that needs to be made at the start is that these abilities are in fact not paranormal or supersensory "powers," but rather natural, innate gifts available to everyone. And accessing them requires nothing more than removing unfounded and self-assumed blocks, such as negative thoughts or unfounded limitations that parents and teachers unintentionally imposed, so information can flow freely into our conscious awareness.

For example, our parents often teach us to believe what we're told and not what we feel. It's not unusual for a child to "sense" when a parent is upset and ask what's wrong. If a parent regularly responds by telling the child that everything is fine, the child is, in effect, taught to distrust his or her impressions. Eventually, to avoid inner confusion, the child learns to disregard feelings and rely only on what is said, cutting off his or her intuitive development.

This chapter is a key chapter. It provides the reader with the foundation necessary to open his or her mind to intuition and its power. Once the reader sees it as a human potential reality and that it can be developed as any other skill, it's possible to teach the reader how to develop and use it in business. This is done by providing insights and guidance that the reader can relate to within his or her own personal experience, not by attempting to offer theory that must be taken at face value. In effect, this chapter's aim is to make the reader comfortable and receptive to exploring his or her natural intuitive capabilities.

The following is this chapter's outline:

Chapter I   *Control Your Business Destiny!*

1. Intuition, a Powerful Business Tool
2. Your Objective: Making Failure an Option
3. A Skill—Not a Mystical Experience
4. Why It's Rarely Discussed or Encouraged
5. A Side Benefit—Personal Growth
6. How To Work with It for Success

Chapter II *Tapping Your Intuitive Powers*

The process of developing your intuitive capabilities for business can be simple and straightforward. It does not require, as suggested by other supersensory or mind-power development approaches, a complex visualization process, putting yourself in altered states of consciousness, going through a mystical or spiritual contortion, or programming yourself at bedtime to activate the process during sleep.

To prove this point, this chapter begins by showing the reader, through example, and with a unique quiz, how he or she is already connecting with his or her intuitive source every day and, without realizing it, actively blocking its profound guidance. Then, to provide a firm basis for going forward, the reader is given an overview of the six-step process, explored in depth in the chapters following, for releasing this extraordinary human potential safely and comfortably at his or her own pace.

The six steps that will allow the reader to clear his or her intuitive channel are:

- Seeing How Random Thoughts Actively Block Sixth-Sense Capabilities
- Controlling and Eliminating Destructive Emotional Blocks
- Clearing Away Distracting Life and Business Illusions
- Putting Past Experience into Proper Perspective
- Letting Go of Self-Sabotaging Control Needs
- Building the Skill Using a Simple Verification Process

The following is an outline of this chapter:

Chapter II *Tapping Your Intuitive Powers*

1. Getting Comfortable with a Natural Ability
   A. It's Available at All Times
   B. How You're Already Accessing Your Intuition—a Quiz
2. Women Have an Edge That Men Can Learn
3. The Six Steps to Developing Your Business Instincts
   A. Stop Thinking
      (1) Feeling Uncomfortable May Be the Price of Knowing
      (2) Accept What's There, Not What You Want to See
   B. Eliminate Emotional Blocks
   C. Clean Out Illusions
   D. Throw Away Past Experiences
   E. Let Go of Control Needs
   F. Verify What Your Hear

4. Kick-Starting Your Intuitive Abilities, Mechanically
5. What's the Best Way to Use Your Business Intuition?

Chapter III *Gut Feelings, Flashes, and Other Intuitive Messages*

This chapter is an important step in the intuition skill-building process. It explores common intuitive feeling and thought messages such as gut feelings, hunches, and intuitive flashes. And it discusses other sensing impressions that parade as intuitive messages that must be identified in the intuition development process but that should never be relied on.

The key to identifying unreliable feelings and impressions is understanding the sources of our feelings and impressions, including where real intuitive messages come from. There are many sources of wrong messages, such as childhood socialized beliefs. On the other hand, true intuitive insights come directly from the thoughts of others and from a universal mind connection. The universal mind connection concept may require the reader to stretch his or her thinking, but developing intuitive skills does not depend on its acceptance. As the reader gains proficiency, he or she will be able to draw his or her own conclusions. One thing, however, will become clear, true intuition is never wrong.

Great emphasis will be placed on the type of messages that appear to be intuitive information, but in fact are coming from self-destructive sources, such defensive thinking or ingrained life illusions. If you don't know how to spot these messages, developing your intuition as a viable business tool is impossible. A simple technique is offered that enables the reader to identify these unreliable messages.

The following is an outline of this chapter:

Chapter III *Gut Feelings, Flashes, and Other Intuitive Messages*

1. The Logical Thinking Dilemma
2. Random Thoughts Confuse Intuitive Messages
3. What Are Gut Feelings, Flashes, and Hunches?
   A. Whose Thoughts Are These, Anyway?
   B. We Are Often Mislead by Anxiety or Fears
   C. Self-Destructive Thoughts Often Parade as Intuitive Messages
4. Do We All Have Gut Knowing?
5. Where Does the Information Come From?
6. Can It Be Trusted?
7. What if It's Wrong?

This proposal is for a career book. Three publishers made offers for it, and it was sold to Prentice Hall, largely because two top honchos from the business books division made a special trip to the authors' offices to explain why PH would be the best publisher.

Publishers don't often fight for books in that way. But this one had some special things going for it:

1. The primary author is the founder and CEO of a multimillion-dollar publicly traded company with more than 100 franchised offices.

2. The company promised to purchase approximately 10,000 units of the book—a volume that makes even the largest publishers rather happy,

3. The company had an effective public relations firm on retainer to promote the book.

Don't get the wrong idea—you don't need such impressive credentials to sell a proposal. If the authors hadn't had so much going for them the book may have been published, but the advance would have been significantly lower, and it's unlikely that personal visits would have been made

PROPOSAL 8

Workstyles to Fit Your Lifestyle

The Hands-On Guide to Temporary Employment

by
John Fanning
and
Rosemary Maniscalco

Overview

There is currently no book that shows people how to take advantage of the growing number of rewarding career opportunities now available in the temporary help industry. *Workstyles to Fit Your Lifestyle* fills that gap by providing all the tools and information readers need to earn money temping, while satisfying their short- and long-term career and lifestyle objectives.

Once the primary domain of fill-in secretaries and people out of work, temping is now a viable option for some 10 million women and men in virtually every industry and professional field. Temporary employment provides unmatched flexibility, as well as a number of unique challenges and career opportunities. It is a particularly desirable choice for people who can identify with one or more of the following statements:

- I prefer working only when it suits my needs and wants.
- I am between positions and need to have money coming in.
- I am a wife and mother who wants to supplement my family's income.
- I am a recent college graduate seeking an entry-level position in a competitive field.
- I am a retired person who wants to remain active and productive.
- I'd like to join the ranks of those who have turned a temporary job into a permanent position.
- I've been out of the job market for a number of years, and would like to ease my way back and update my skills.
- I am a performing or creative artist who requires flexibility and extra income.

Coauthor John Fanning is the founder and president of Uniforce Temporary Services, Inc.—a nationally franchised temporary employment service with offices coast to coast.

Mr. Fanning is a nationally known expert on the temporary services field. He has appeared on such TV programs as *The MacNeil/Lehrer News Hour,* and has been featured in articles in *Forbes* and *Business Week* magazines.

Coauthor Rosemary Maniscalco is executive vice president of Uniforce, and a member of its board of directors. Ms. Maniscalco started as a temp and worked her way up through the ranks. Today, she is one of the few female executives to achieve top management status for a major temporary service in the United States. She has been interviewed on numerous radio programs, including *The Barry Farber Show,* and has been featured in magazine articles in such publications as *Working Woman* and *The Office.*

to the authors. Although it's not indicated anywhere in this proposal, the project has a ghostwriter. It can't hurt to mention this in a proposal, especially if it's an impressive ghost.

1. The title of the book seems clumsy, although its subtitle is just right. Something like "Work to Fit Your Lifestyle" might have been a better choice. This bold first paragraph immediately states the need for the book, how the authors plan to fill it, and what the book's thesis will be.

2. Another effective way to begin this overview would be to reverse the two opening paragraphs. The first paragraph would then feature this impressive statistic that supports the viability of temping as an employment option that has been until now a "well-kept secret."

3. If the subject matter of your book is a little dry, be sure to put your aces up front to keep the editor reading. The author's use of these bullets is effective because it helps the editor visualize the various people who will benefit from the book and generates immediate enthusiasm.
This information

could have been saved for the marketing section. However, there are no absolute laws about proposal writing. Do what you think will work so you can secure a contract.

4. Another example of not holding off until the traditional sequential position to inject a sales point. The authors have excellent credentials, and the ghostwriter wanted the editor to know this immediately. (A full bio section does follow.)

5. Concise and pertinent supporting evidence. The authors are building a very persuasive case with each sentence. There's no fluff here.

6. It helps greatly to support the book's thesis with documented facts and figures organized numerically.

7. This statement indicates that business may be a potentially substantial secondary market for the book—or perhaps indicates a need for a follow-up book geared specifically toward businesses.

8. This indicates that the book will include a practical program in addition to its other claims—a must for any commercial book of this nature.

Mr. Fanning and Ms. Maniscalco have led this publicly held company to a position of national prominence. In separate articles, *Business Week* ranked Uniforce as one of the best small companies in the United States, and cited it among six of "franchising's hot performers."

In explaining why the temporary industry is now America's second-fastest-growing service business, the authors cite five trends:

1. In today's mobile society, more people either require or prefer flexible work hours.
2. The demand for skilled personnel is expanding at a much faster rate than the available labor force.
3. There are an estimated 14 million nonworking women caring for their families at home, and over 3 million men and women who have taken early retirement.* Members of these two large groups are filling an increasing number of the jobs that will continue to become available throughout the 1990s. Temping offers the most practical and comfortable way for many of these individuals to enter or reenter the workforce.
4. The automation of the office has created a need for personnel who can operate computerized equipment on a multitude of software packages. Temporary services are adept at meeting corporate America's growing demand for employees with these and other highly specialized skills.
5. Using temporary help makes it easier for businesses to control hiring, training, and benefits costs, thus enabling them to protect their profit margins.

The authors' primary objective in writing *Workstyles to Fit Your Lifestyle* is to show readers how to navigate the changing currents of today's temporary employment industry. Mr. Fanning and Ms. Maniscalco supplement their collective personal and professional experience with insights and anecdotes from a large cross section of their franchisees, temporary employees, and corporate clients. Checklists, interview tips, and self-evaluation materials are included throughout the chapters to give readers everything they need to:

- Realistically assess their marketable skills.
- Select a service that can best address their needs.
- Maximize earnings.
- Build in such perks as health benefits and vacations.
- Design a personalized temporary-employment game plan.

---

* Source: *Megatrends 2000.*

Market Analysis

9 An extensive search of resources, including *Books in Print,* turned up only three books on the topic of temporary employment: John Fanning's *Work When You Want to Work,* originally published by Collier Macmillan in 1969 and reprinted in 1985 by Pocket Books; *Temp Worker's Handbook* by Lewis & Nancy Schuman, published by American Management Association (AMACOM); and *Professional Temping* by Eve Broudy, published by Collier Macmillan.

10 Of these three books, Mr. Fanning's *Work When You Want to Work* is the only one to give readers a complete guide to temping. It is clear, however, that a new book is needed—one that shows readers how to take advantage of the dramatic changes that have reshaped the temporary help industry.

Today, the pay scale, benefits, and training opportunities in some areas of temporary employment have reached the point where thousands of people are declining permanent positions in favor of career temping. Recent articles and industry surveys reveal the following trends:

11
- Nine out of ten American businesses use temporary help. There are now almost 10 million temporary employees in an industry that has grown by an average of 18.9 percent a year since 1970 (U.S. Department of Labor statistics).
- The use of temporary help is proving to be a highly cost-efficient measure in tight economic times. There has also been an improvement in the quality and the range of services offered by temporary services *(Managers Magazine).*
- Temps are now used by small businesses as well as *Fortune* 500 companies. An estimated 944,000 temps work each week through some 10,000 temporary services. When asked what attracts them to temping, these men and women cite flexible schedules, extra income, and the ability to sample work environments in various businesses *(The Office).*
- Professions that are especially promising now for people seeking temporary employment include law, healthcare, computers, and technical fields *(Nation's Business).*

12 In view of the rapid expansion of the temporary industry and recent economic trends, the proposed book is one that will be useful to a large readership. The number of women and men who will consider temping as a short- or long-range career option in the next few years can be measured in seven-figure terms. These potential readers will need the kind of timely information contained in *Workstyles to Fit Your Lifestyle.*

9. The author tackles the competition head on and makes a strong positive statement in favor of the proposed book. He starts out by showing the competition is slight, which may cause an editor to think that "where there are no books there is no market." The author anticipates this possibility and gives many reasons why it would be a wrong conclusion.

10. When referring to another book by the author of this proposed project, it would have been persuasive to point out that he is a pioneer in the field. The author chose to treat this information as he would any competition—a missed opportunity.

11. These facts and figures effectively show that the book has commercial potential.

12. This statement is eye-catching.

Voice and Scope

The authors plan to write a 50,000-60,000 word self-help book in a readable, straightforward style. The chapters will be targeted toward readers who are considering temping as an interim or permanent career option. The materials will also be useful for those who already have temping experience.

The discussion will begin with an overview of the temporary employment industry, and an exploration of the basics of successful temping. The chapters will emphasize those opportunities and trends that are likely to have the greatest impact on readers throughout the 1990s and into the twenty-first century. *Workstyles to Fit Your Lifestyle* is the only book that helps readers answer the following questions:

- What are the most sought-after and highest-paying temp job skills?
- Why are more people choosing to become career temps?
- When is temping the most practical way to secure a desirable permanent position?
- Why do opportunities for temps increase during a recession?
- Why is temping ideally suited to our mobile society?
- Why is temping the best way for homemakers and retirees to enter or reenter the workplace?

Throughout the chapters, readers will be shown how to customize the information to suit their particular needs. Sample interview questions and skill-assessment tests will be included to help readers prepare for interviews and job assignments.

Firsthand anecdotes and practical advice will help readers navigate unexpected or difficult situations. Time management, financial planning, and other self-evaluation tools will help readers pinpoint and realize their career and lifestyle goals.

Readers will finish the book with a good understanding of the opportunities in temporary employment, an assessment of how well suited they are to take advantage of these opportunities, and a personalized temporary-employment game plan.

Sales and Promotion

John Fanning and Rosemary Maniscalco are an especially strong marketing team. Upon the release of *Workstyles to Fit Your Lifestyle,* the authors will work with the publisher in launching a multifaceted advertising and promotional campaign. To bolster bookstore sales, Uniforce is prepared to purchase a significant number of books to be distributed through its national network of offices.

---

13. This "Voice and Scope" section is usually referred to as "the format." Many proposals skip this altogether, but it's a good idea to state somewhere what your plans are for the book, such as word count. Don't characterize your book as "self-help" if it may limit your market. Sometimes the publishers can best make these types of decisions.

14. This listing gives another good overview of the book's substance, but this section is not entirely necessary, as the editor will shortly be evaluating the chapter-by-chapter outline.

15. The statement "prepared to purchase a significant number of books . . ." makes an editor's antennae stand at attention. If you are able to buy a large number of books and will sign a contract to that effect, you will have substantially more leverage in obtaining a contract and a sizable advance. A "significant" buyback usually begins in the 5,000-unit range, which is why only a few authors are ready to commit to one.

16 *Workstyles to Fit Your Lifestyle* will be an outstanding promotional tool for both print and electronic media exposure. These are some of the timely issues the authors are prepared to address on interviews and panel discussions:

- How to generate more income during tough economic times.
- What it's like to work as a temp.
- How temping is smoothing the path for some 14 million women who are entering or reentering the workplace in record numbers.
- Rewarding second-career opportunities for retired persons.
- Unusual workstyles in changing times.
- The new breed of temps: physicians, attorneys, executives, computer experts.
- Successful people in business and the arts who've worked as temps.

About the Authors

17 *John Fanning*, founder and president of Uniforce Temporary Services, is a nationally recognized innovator in the personnel field. Mr. Fanning's pioneering efforts in the industry began in 1954, when at the age of 23, he founded the Fanning Personnel Agency in New York City. In 1966, Mr. Fanning sold his interest in this highly successful operation to devote his time to building the Uniforce network. The company now has franchise offices nationwide.

Mr. Fanning is one of the most visible and articulate spokespersons in the temporary services field. He is the author of *Work When You Want to Work* (Pocket), and is extensively quoted in the book *Work Smart Not Hard* (Facts On File).

Mr. Fanning is regularly featured in newspapers and national publications, such as *Business Week* and *Forbes*. He has been interviewed on such TV programs as *The MacNeil/Lehrer News Hour* and *The Long Island Report* as well as on numerous radio talk shows.

Rosemary Maniscalco, executive vice president of Uniforce Temporary Services, is a dynamic corporate executive as well as an articulate and attractive public speaker. Ms. Maniscalco joined Uniforce's marketing department in 1981. She rose rapidly through the ranks to become director of corporate development in 1983. The author was promoted to her present position in 1984. To this day, she remains one of the few female executives to hold a top management position for a major temporary service in the United States.

Ms. Maniscalco is primarily involved in the growth and development of Uniforce's national franchise network. She has also been instrumental in creating Uniforce's innovative training and educational programs. Her creative vision is key to the success of Uniforce's national advertising and public relations campaigns with the trade, business, and consumer media.

16. It's beneficial to provide actual publicity "news hooks," or story ideas, in this section. This shows some creativity. It's also a good idea to place relevant media experience with this information.

17. These impressive bio sketches show that the authors have all the requisite credentials to write and promote this book. In this case, though, there was much more that should have been included. For example, The Uniforce Company is publicly traded on the NASDAQ; Uniforce has more than 100 franchise offices throughout the country; it's one of the top ten temp agencies; and it's been a top performer on the *Inc.* 500. This information was included in collateral support materials but would also have been effective in the body of the proposal. Don't count on the editors reading your entire package cover to cover. There's a piece missing. The book is being ghostwritten by Gene Busnar, a New York–based writer who has collaborated or authored more than a dozen nonfiction books. His impressive background should have been included.

Ms. Maniscalco has been featured in magazine articles in such publications as *Working Woman* and *The Office,* and has been interviewed on numerous radio programs, including *The Barry Farber Show.*

18. Editors and agents greatly appreciate a comprehensive synopsis/outline like this one. There's enough material here to prove that the book will provide good information, and the expansive sample chapter that accompanied this proposal eliminated the "but can he write?" feelings editors often have.

Chapter Synopsis   18

Workstyles to Fit Your Lifestyle
The Hands-On Guide to Temporary Employment
by John Fanning and Rosemary Maniscalco

Table of Contents   19

19. It's always a good idea to have a separate table of contents before the chapter synopses. This one appears to be just right. The title for Chapter Nine could raise a few eyebrows. It's too undefined. Otherwise, the table of contents shows logic and is a good blueprint for the book.

CHAPTER ONE: Temporary Services: The Field That's Always Hiring

20. The entries in this bulleted list place emphasis on the advantages for people who temp. Always make your outline conform to your projected market.

The authors introduce themselves, and share with readers vital information [20] about the expanding opportunities in the temporary employment industry. Several recent success stories are described briefly. These include:

- Mark, a recent college graduate, who was offered a permanent position as a junior copywriter by an advertising agency after a three-week temporary assignment.
- Ruth, a forty-six-year-old mother of two college-age children who had not been gainfully employed for fifteen years, was anxious

about reentering the workplace. Temping gave her the opportunity to earn money, improve her skills, and gain confidence.

- Sam, an accountant who took early retirement at age fifty-five, returned to the workplace as a temp after three years of relative inactivity, and now feels more needed and respected than ever before.
- Liz, an aspiring dancer, possesses word processing skills that have enabled her to make a comfortable living as a career temp.
- Phil, age fifty, was fired after eleven years as a middle manager at a major communications company. Temping made it possible for him to generate income while exploring career possibilities at several companies.

The authors proceed to explain how the temporary employment industry operates:

Temporary help firms are paid by businesses to find and screen qualified employees. The client company pays an hourly service charge for each employee placed. There is never a charge to the temporary employee. The service makes its profit by marking up the hourly wage it pays its employees.

More and more businesses are finding that the hourly rate charged by temp services is offset by the savings in recruitment costs, fringe benefits, severance pay, workers' compensation, and unemployment insurance—all of which are handled by the temporary service. Qualified temporary employees have the advantage of being able to work when they want at a competitive rate of pay, while avoiding the time and drudgery of job-hunting.

Temporary employees are, in effect, working for the temporary service—not for the company to which they report. It is the temp service that hires, fires, and withholds taxes and Social Security. Depending on the service, employees may be offered opportunities for training, vacations, and other fringe benefits.

Temporary help services recruit new employees through advertising, word of mouth—and by offering bonuses to current employees for bringing new temps into the company. Before new temps are sent out on an assignment, they are evaluated in terms of skills, personality, attitude, and appearance. This screening is accomplished through appropriate skill evaluations and in-person interviews.

The new temp is then evaluated in terms of skill level, work experience, and availability. This allows the service to quickly locate the right person to fill a business's needs.

Today's temporary positions are proving to be the best choice for working mothers, empty nesters, moonlighters, retirees—and others who want or need to work when they choose. Temping gives unemployed and displaced individuals a way to make contacts and pay their rent while looking for permanent work. It also provides an opportunity for students and recent college graduates to gain valuable experience while testing the waters at a number of companies.

Some readers will use temping as a stepping-stone to permanent positions that would have otherwise been inaccessible. Many others will join the ranks of career temps—those who want or need a more flexible lifestyle that allows more time for family and other outside interests.

"There is a whole new world of opportunity out there," the authors state in concluding this chapter. "Our objectives in the chapters that follow are threefold:

1. To help you assess your particular career and lifestyle needs.
2. To determine how these needs fit with the rapidly expanding opportunities in temporary employment.
3. To map out a personalized temporary-employment game plan."

CHAPTER TWO: Is Temping Right for You?

(Please see enclosed sample chapter.)

CHAPTER THREE: Taking Advantage of Expanding Opportunities in Today's and Tomorrow's Temporary-Job Market

The authors discuss the dramatic increase in the demand for temps in a wide variety of fields. In evaluating why nearly 100 percent of all American companies now use temporary help to complement permanent staffs, the authors cite and discuss the following trends:

- Technological advances—particularly those related to computers and the automated office—have led to a shortage of qualified personnel. The ability to use a PC and up-to-date software is becoming a necessity on most jobs. As a result, companies need employees with higher education and skill levels than in the past. Temp services are responding to that need by offering cross-training programs and providing personnel who are skilled in data processing.
- Using temporary help makes it easier for businesses to control screening, hiring, and benefits costs, thus enabling them to protect their profit margins.
- A judicious use of temporary help allows companies more flexibility in staffing, and relief from higher fixed personnel costs. By using temps during peak periods and for specific projects, companies are

able to operate with a lean permanent staff during normal workload periods.

- Other innovative uses of temps include: hiring back valuable employees lost through mandatory retirement, filling vital jobs during hiring freezes, smoothing the transition of business relocations, and filling in for staff who are on vacation or sick leave.

"As we approach the twenty-first century," the authors observe, "we expect the temporary-help industry to expand as companies meet the challenges of a shrinking labor market, escalating costs, and the overall demand for increased productivity in a global marketplace.

"Temporary help will be an important element in companies' staffing strategies as they seek to cope with fluctuating business cycles and try to get more cost-effective productivity from their operations."

The discussion continues with a look at the different fields and professions that now use the services of temporary personnel. While the largest growth areas for temporary employees are in fields requiring data processing and computerized office skills, there is also an increasing demand for temps in the financial, legal, marketing, education, hospitality, manufacturing, and healthcare fields.

The job opportunities in each of these areas are evaluated in terms of current and future demand, necessary skills, experience, and earnings requirements. Readers are asked to complete a questionnaire designed to evaluate their skills and financial requirements in terms of the realities of the temporary-job market. The chapter concludes with specific suggestions on how to translate the results of this questionnaire into a specific plan of action.

This project was published in 1994.

Every editor who saw this proposal had sincere praise for it, but many felt that their health/spirituality quota was already full and that they would be competing with themselves if they acquired any more such titles.

Market glut is a familiar problem. In many popular categories, it's almost endemic. But if you're prepared for this reality from the outset, you can pave your own road and bypass the competition. Dedicated agents, editors, and writers want important books published regardless of what the publishers' lists dictate. Further, it's not necessary for every publisher to want your book. In the end, you need only the right publisher and a reasonable deal.

1. This title conjures up dramatic images similar to a soulful blues melody, and it has everything to do with what the proposal is about. The subtitle is scientific and provides a clear direction for the patients.

Heart and Soul

A Psychological and Spiritual Guide to Preventing and Healing Heart Disease

**by
Bruno Cortis, M.D.**

Overview

Heart disease is the number-one killer of Americans over the age of 40. The very words can sound like a death sentence. Our heart, the most intimate part of our body, is under siege. Until now, most experts have advised victims of the disease, as well as those who would avoid it, to change avoidable risk factors, like smoking, and begin a spartan regimen of diet and exercise. But new research shows that risk factors and lifestyle are only part of the answer. In fact, it is becoming clear that for many patients, emotional, psychological, and even spiritual factors are at least as important, both in preventing disease and in healing an already damaged heart.

Like *Love, Medicine, and Miracles* by Bernie Siegel, which showed cancer patients how to take charge of their own disease and life, *Heart and Soul* will show potential and actual heart patients how to use inner resources to form a healthy relationship with their heart, actually healing circulatory disorders and preventing further damage.

The author, Bruno Cortis, M.D., is a renowned cardiologist whose experience with hundreds of "exceptional heart patients" has taught him that there is much more to medicine than operations and pills.

Dr. Cortis identifies three types of heart patients:

- Passive Patients, who are unwilling or unable to take responsibility for their condition. Instead, these patients blame outside forces, withdraw from social contacts, and bewail their fate. They may become deeply depressed, and tend to die very soon.
- Obedient Consumers, who are the "A" students of modern medicine. Following doctors' orders to the letter, these patients behave exactly as they are "supposed to," placing their fates in the hands of the experts. These patients tend to die exactly when medicine predicts they will.
- Exceptional Heart Patients, who regard a diagnosis of heart disease as a challenge. Although they may have realistic fears for the future, these patients take full responsibility for their situation and actively contribute to their own recovery. While they may or may not follow doctors' orders, these patients tend to choose the therapy or combination of therapies that is best for them. They often live far beyond medical predictions.

It is Dr. Cortis' aim in this book to show readers how to become Exceptional Heart Patients, empowering them to take responsibility for their own health and well-being.

Although Dr. Cortis acknowledges the importance of exercise, stress

---

2. A powerful lead paragraph immediately distinguishes this book proposal from the many competitive books and draws attention to "new research." Anything that's potentially cutting-edge will catch the eye of a prospective publisher.

3. This paragraph contains the central thesis and could have been used as the first paragraph of the proposal. It also contains a clever comparison to a highly successful book, while indicating how the author's book will merit the same type of attention.

4. It's wise to bring the author's credentials into the overview. A comparison made with Dr. Siegel will immediately raise questions as to whether this author has similar potential. The author anticipates this editorial reasoning and makes some strong statements.

5. This is an exceptional overview—especially where it defines the three patient types. It shows a highly focused and well-thought-out plan. Although writing such a good proposal took effort, there's no struggle for the editor to understand exactly what's being proposed and what the book will be about.

6. A good use of facts, trends, and the public's receptivity to what some would characterize as an unorthodox treatment approach.

7. This section is termed the "market analysis," which differs from the marketing section you see in most proposals. Instead of telling the publisher how to sell the book, the writing collaborator shows special insight into the target audience. This type of in-depth analysis of the potential reader can be very persuasive.

8. It's sometimes helpful to identify this portion of the proposal under a separate "competition" heading.

9. The analysis of the competition highlights the most relevant books on the market without listing each one directly. You might want to use this approach if there are too many similar books in your particular subject area. Notice, though, that the writer confronts the heaviest competition directly by finding specific distinguishing factors that support the strength of his proposed project.

management, and proper nutrition—the standard staples of cardiac treatment—he stresses that there is an even deeper level of human experience that is necessary in order to produce wellness. Unlike other books on heart disease, *Heart and Soul* does not prescribe the same strict diet and exercise program for everyone. Instead it takes a flexible approach, urging readers to create their own unique health plan by employing psychological and spiritual practices in combination with a variety of more traditional diet and exercise regimens.

While seemingly revolutionary, Dr. Cortis' message is simple: you can do much more for the health of your heart than you think you can. This is true whether you have no symptoms or risk factors whatsoever, if you have some symptoms or risk factors, or if you actually already have heart disease.

Market Analysis

Heart and Soul could not be more timely. Of the 1½ million heart attacks suffered by Americans each year, nearly half occur between the ages of 40 and 65. Three fifths of these heart attacks are fatal . While these precise statistics may not be familiar to the millions of baby boomers now entering middle age, the national obsession with oat bran, low-fat foods, and exercising for health shows that the members of the boomer generation are becoming increasingly aware of their own mortality.

This awareness of growing older, coupled with a widespread loss of faith in doctors and fear of overtechnologized medicine, combine to produce a market that is ready for a book emphasizing the spiritual component in healing, especially in reference to heart disease.

Most existing books on the market approach the subject from the physician's point of view, urging readers to follow doctor's orders to attain a healthy heart. There is very little emphasis in these books on the patient's own responsibility for wellness or the inner changes that must be made for the prescribed regimens to work. Among the best-known recent books are:

Healing Your Heart, by Herman Hellerstein, M.D., and Paul Perry (Simon & Schuster, 1990). Although this book, like most of the others, advocates proper nutrition, exercise, cessation of smoking, and stress reduction as the road to a healthy heart, it fails to provide the motivation necessary to attain such changes in the reader's lifestyle. Without changes in thinking and behavior, readers of this and similar books will find it difficult, if not impossible, to follow the strict diet and exercise program recommended.

In *Heart Talk: Preventing and Coping with Silent and Painful Heart Disease* (Harcourt Brace Jovanovich, 1987), Dr. Peter F. Cohn and Dr. Joan K. Cohn address the dangers of "silent" (symptomless) heart disease. While informative, the book emphasizes only one manifestation of heart disease and does not empower readers with the motivational tools needed to combat that disease.

10. *The Trusting Heart,* by Redford Williams, M.D. (Times Books, 1989), demonstrates how hostility and anger can lead to heart disease while trust and forgiveness can contribute to wellness. While these are important points, the holistic treatment of heart disease must encompass other approaches as well. The author also fails to provide sufficient motivation for behavioral changes in the readers.

The best book on preventing and curing heart disease is *Dr. Dean Ornish's Program for Reversing Heart Disease* (Random House, 1990). This highly successful book prescribes a very strict diet and exercise program for actually reversing certain types of coronary artery disease. This still-controversial approach is by far the best on the market; unfortunately, the material is presented in a dense, academic style not easily accessible to the lay reader. It also focuses on Dr. Ornish's program as the "only way to manage heart disease, excluding other, more synergistic methods."

Approach

Heart and Soul will be a 60,000–70,000-word book targeted to health-conscious members of the baby boom generation. Unlike other books on heart disease, it will focus on the facts of the connection between the mind and the body as it relates to heart disease, showing readers how to use that connection to heal the heart. The book will be written in an informal but authoritative style, in Dr. Cortis' voice. It will begin with a discussion of heart disease and show how traditional medicine fails to prevent or cure it. Subsequent chapters will deal with the mind-body connection, and the role in healing of social support systems, self-esteem, and faith. In order to help readers reduce stress in their lives, Dr. Cortis shows how they can create their own "daily practice" that combines exercise, relaxation, meditation, and use of positive imagery. Throughout the book, he will present anecdotes that demonstrate how other Exceptional Heart Patients have overcome their disease and gone on to lead healthy and productive lives.

In addition to a thorough discussion of the causes and outcomes of coronary artery disease, the book will include tests and checklists that readers may use to gauge their progress, and exercises, ranging from the cerebral to the physical, that strengthen and help heal the heart. At the end of each chapter readers will be introduced to an essential "Heartskill" that will enable them to put the advice of the chapter into immediate practice.

11. Through example and encouragement *Heart and Soul* will offer readers a variety of strategies for coping with heart disease, to be taken at once or used in combination. Above all an accessible, practical book, *Heart and Soul*

10. The author convincingly demonstrates the uniqueness of this particular project—especially important when compared with the strong list of competitors.

11. This is a clear summary statement of the book.

12. A very good description of the author. The writing collaborator establishes Dr. Cortis as both an expert in his field and a compelling personality. All of this material is relevant to the book's success.

13. A formal vitae follows. It's best to lead with a journalistic-style biography and follow with a complete and formal résumé—assuming, as in this case, the author's professional credentials are inseparable from the book.

14. Although she wasn't mentioned on the title page, Lance is the collaborator. Her bio sketch is strong in its simplicity. Her writing credits are voluminous, but she doesn't use up space here with a comprehensive listing. Instead she showcases only credits relevant to the success of this particular project. Comprehensive author résumés were also attached to the proposal package as addenda.

15. As we stated in other proposal critiques, a separate table of contents would have been useful.

16. This exceptional outline goes beyond the often lazy and stingy telegraph approach many writers use, often to their own detriment.

will present readers with a workable program or controlling their own heart [11] disease and forming a healthy relationship with their hearts.

The Authors

Bruno Cortis, M.D., is an internationally trained cardiologist with more than [12] 30 years' experience in research and practice. A pioneer of cardiovascular applications of lasers and angioscopy, a Diplomate of the American Board of Cardiology, contributor of more than 70 published professional papers, Dr. Cortis has long advocated the need for new dimensions of awareness in health and the healing arts. As a practicing physician and researcher, his open acknowledgment of individual spirituality as the core of health puts him on the cutting edge of those in traditional medicine who are beginning to create the medical arts practices of the future.

Dr. Cortis has been a speaker at conferences in South America, Japan, [13] and Australia, as well as in Europe and the United States. His firm, Mind Your Health, is dedicated to the prevention of heart attack through the development of human potential. Dr. Cortis is the cofounder of the Exceptional Heart Patients program. The successful changes he has made in his own medical practice prove he is a man not only of vision and deeds, but an author whose beliefs spring from the truths of daily living.

Kathryn Lance is the author of more than 30 books of nonfiction and [14] fiction (see attached publications list for details). Her first book, *Running for Health and Beauty* (1976), the first mass market book on running for women, sold half a million copies. *The Setpoint Diet* (1985), ghosted for Dr. Gilbert A. Leveille, reached the *New York Times* best-seller list for several weeks. Ms. Lance has written widely on fitness, health, diet, and medicine.

Heart and Soul

by Bruno Cortis, M.D.

Chapter Outline

Table of Contents [15]

Introduction: Beating the Odds: Exceptional Heart Patients

See sample chapter.

Chapter One: You and Your Heart [16]

Traditional medicine doesn't and can't "cure" heart disease. The recurrence rate of arterial blockage after angioplasty is 25–35%, while a bypass operation

[17] only *bypasses* the problem, but does not cure it. The author proposes a new way of looking at heart disease, one in which patients become responsible for the care and well-being of their hearts, in partnership with their physicians. Following a brief, understandable discussion of the physiology of heart disease and heart attack, further topics covered in this chapter include:

[18] *Heart disease as a message from your body.* Many of us go through life neglecting our bodies' signals, ignoring symptoms until a crisis occurs. But the body talks to us and it is up to us to listen and try to understand the message. The heart bears the load of all our physical activity as well as our mental activity. Stress can affect the heart as well as any other body system. This section explores the warning signs of heart disease as "messages" we may receive from our hearts, what these messages may mean, and what we can do in response to these messages.

Why medical tests and treatments are not enough. You, the patient, are ultimately responsible for your own health. Placing all faith in a doctor is a way of abdicating that responsibility. The physician is not a healer; rather, he or she sets the stage for the patient's body to heal itself. Disease is actually a manifestation of an imbalance within the body. Medical procedures can help temporarily, but the real solution lies in the patient's becoming aware of his or her own responsibility for health. This may involve changing diet, stopping smoking, learning to control the inner life.

Getting the best (while avoiding the worst) of modern medicine. In the author's view, the most important aspect of medicine is not the medication but the patient/physician relationship. Unfortunately, this relationship is often cold, superficial, professional. The patient goes into the medical pipeline, endures a number of tests, then comes out the other end with a diagnosis, which is like a flag he or she has to carry for life. This view of disease ignores the patient as the *main* component of the healing process. Readers are advised to work with their doctors to learn their own blood pressure, blood sugar, cholesterol level, and what these numbers mean. They are further advised how to enlist a team of support people to increase their own knowledge of the disease and learn to discover the self-healing mechanisms within.

How to assess your doctor. Ten questions a patient needs to ask in order to assure the best patient-doctor relationship.

Taking charge of your own medical care. Rather than being passive patients, readers are urged to directly confront their illness and the reasons for it, asking themselves: How can I find a cause at the deepest level? What have I learned from this disease? What is good about it? What have I learned about myself? Exceptional heart patients don't allow themselves to be overwhelmed by the disease; rather, they realize that it is most likely a temporary problem, most of the time self-limited, and that they have a power within to overcome it.

Seven keys to a healthy heart. Whether presently healthy or already ill of

---

Here each abstract reads like a miniature sample chapter unto itself. It proves that the writers as a team have a genuine command of their subject, a well-organized agenda, and superior skills for writing about it. Some writers are reluctant to do this much work on speculation. However, if you believe in your project's viability, and you want to maximize acquisition interest and the ultimate advance, you'll be wise to give the proposal everything you've got.

17. In this interesting technique for a chapter abstract, the writer organizes the structure as a listing of chapter topics and elaborates with a sample of the substance and writing approach that will be incorporated into the book. The editor will come away with a good sense of the quality of the chapter and the depth of its coverage.

18. Although the abstracts are directed to the editor who reviews the proposal, the writer incorporates the voice to be used in the book by speaking directly to the reader. An effective way to get her writing style into the chapter-by-chapter outline.

heart disease there is a great deal readers can do to improve and maintain the health of their hearts. The most important component of such a plan is to have a commitment to a healthy heart. The author offers the following seven keys to a healthy heart: respect your body; take time to relax every day; accept, respect, and appreciate yourself; share your deepest feelings; establish life goals; nourish your spiritual self; love yourself and others unconditionally. Each of these aspects of heart care will be examined in detail in later chapters.

Heartskill #1: *Learning to take your own pulse.* The pulse is a wave of blood sent through the arteries each time the heart contracts; pulse rate therefore [19] provides important information about cardiac function. The easiest place to measure the pulse is the wrist: place your index and middle finger over the underside of the opposite wrist. Press gently and firmly until you locate your pulse. Don't use your thumb to feel the pulse, because the thumb has a pulse of its own. Count the number of pulse beats in fifteen seconds, then multiply that by four for your heart rate.

This exercise will include charts so that readers can track and learn their own normal pulse range for resting and exercising, and be alerted to irregularities and changes that may require medical attention.

Chapter Two: Your Mind and Your Heart

This chapter begins to explore the connection between mind and body as it relates to heart disease. Early in the chapter readers will meet three Exceptional Heart Patients who overcame crushing diagnoses. These include Van, who overcame a heart attack (at age 48), two open heart surgeries, and "ter- [20] minal" lung cancer. Through visualization 2 techniques given him by the author, Van has fully recovered and is living a healthy and satisfying life. Goran, who had a family history of cardiomyopathy, drew on the support and love of his family to survive a heart transplant and has since gone on to win several championships in an Olympics contest for transplant patients. Elaine, who overcame both childhood cancer and severe heart disease, is, at the age of 24, happily married and a mother. The techniques used by these Exceptional Heart Patients will be discussed in the context of the mind-body connection.

How your doctor views heart disease: risk factors v. symptoms. Traditional medicine views the risk factors for heart disease (smoking, high blood cholesterol, high blood pressure, diabetes, obesity, sedentary lifestyle, family history of heart disease, use of oral contraceptives) as indicators of the likelihood of developing illness. In contrast, the author presents these risk factors as *symptoms* of an underlying disease, and discusses ways to change them. Smoking, for example, is not the root of the problem, which is, rather, fear, tension, and stress. Smoking is just an outlet that the patient uses to get rid of these basic elements, which he or she believes are uncontrollable. Like-

19. This shows that specific and practical information will be included in the book—which is generally important for nonfiction. Editors look for these "program aspects" because they can be used In promotional settings such as electronic media, as well as in catchy serial-rights selections targeted toward magazines.

20. The authors do not save the good stuff for the book. If you have interesting case studies or anecdotes, include them in your abstract. The more stimulating material you can include, the more you will intrigue your potential editor.

wise high cholesterol, which is viewed by the medical establishment as largely caused by poor diet, is also affected by stress. (In a study of rabbits on a high-cholesterol diet, narrowing of arteries was less in rabbits that were petted, even if the diet remained unhealthful.) Other elements besides the traditional "risk factors," such as hostility, have been shown to lead to high rates of heart disease.

A mind/body model of heart disease. It is not uncommon to hear stories like this: they were a very happy couple, married 52 years. Then, suddenly, the wife developed breast cancer and died. The husband, who had no previous symptoms of heart disease, had a heart attack and died two months later. All too often there is a very close relationship between a traumatic event and serious illness. Likewise, patients may often become depressed and literally will themselves to die. The other side of the coin is the innumerable patients who use a variety of techniques to enlist the mind-body connection in helping to overcome and even cure serious illnesses, including heart disease.

Rethinking your negative beliefs about heart disease. The first step in using the mind to help to heal the body is to rethink negative beliefs about heart disease. Modern studies have shown that stress plays a most important role in the creation of heart disease, influencing all of the "risk factors." Heart disease is actually a disease of self, caused by self, and is made worse by the belief that we are its "victims." Another negative and incorrect belief is that the possibilities for recovery are limited. The author asserts that these beliefs are untrue, and that for patients willing to learn from the experience, heart disease can be a path to recovery, self-improvement, and growth.

The healing personality: tapping into your body's healing powers. Although the notion of a "healing personality" may sound contradictory, the power of healing is awareness, which can be achieved by anyone. The author describes his own discovery of spirituality in medicine and the realization that ultimately the origin of disease is in the mind. This is why treating disease with medicine and surgery alone does not heal: because these methods ignore the natural healing powers of the body/mind. How does one develop a "healing personality"? The starting point is awareness of the spiritual power within. As the author states, in order to become healthy, one must become spiritual.

Writing your own script for a healthy heart. Before writing any script, one must set the stage, and in this case readers are urged to see a cardiologist or physician and have a thorough checkup. This checkup will evaluate the presence or absence of the "risk factors" and assess the health of other body organs as well. Once the scene is set, it is time to add in the other elements of a healthy heart, all of which will be explored in detail in the coming chapters.

Making a contract with your heart. We see obstacles only when we lose sight of our goals. How to make out (either mentally or on paper) a contract with one's heart that promises to take care of the heart. Each individual reader's contract will be somewhat different; for example, someone who is overweight might include in the contract the desire that in six months she would weigh so much. The point is to set realistic, achievable goals. Guidelines are provided for breaking larger goals down into small, easily achievable, steps. Creating goals for the future makes them a part of the present in the sense that it is today that we start pursuing them.

What to say when you talk to yourself. In the view of the author, the greatest source of stress in life is negative conversations we have with ourselves. These "conversations," which go on all the time without our even being aware of them, often include such negative suggestions as "When are you going to learn?" "Oh, no, you stupid idiot, you did it again!" When we put ourselves down we reinforce feelings of unworthiness and inadequacy, which lead to stress and illness. Guidelines are given for replacing such negative self-conversation with more positive self-talk, including messages of love and healing.

21. The chapter abstract in the proposal continued on to the end, but the first two chapters show you why this proposal was effective.

Heartskill #2: *Sending healing energy to your heart.* In this exercise, readers [21] learn a simple meditation technique that will help them get in touch with their natural healing powers and begin to heal their hearts.

PROPOSAL 10

Taxes Made Easy for Home-Based Businesses

The Complete Plain Language Tax Guide for Home-Based Entrepreneurs and Home-Office Workers

by Gary W. Carter, Ph.D., M.T., C.P.A.

This proposal had many things going for it, including clarity of purpose, a ready and growing market base, and strong author credentials. We ended up selling it to the J. K. Lasser imprint (now part of John Wiley & Sons), which was the perfect home for it. This publisher specializes in consumer tax guides. The book gets revised each year and is very successful.

1. This is a straightfor-
ward title that tells you
exactly what you are
getting. This is a useful
book, and the title
shows specifically who
will benefit from the
information.

2. These are impressive
and appropriate creden-
tials.

Taxes Made Easy
for Home-Based Businesses

The Complete Plain Language Tax Guide
for Home-Based Entrepreneurs
and Home-Office Workers

by
Gary W. Carter,
Ph.D., M.T., C.P.A.

Proposal Contents

- Overview
- Market Analysis
- Competition Analysis
- Author Profile
- Table of Contents
- Chapter Summary
- Introduction
- Chapter One
- Chapter Five

Overview

3. This is a clear and
effective thesis state-
ment.

The Need

The federal tax system carries both opportunities and pitfalls that are unique
to the more than 45 million home-based workers in this country. Those who
seek expert written guidance on tax planning and return preparation find little help. The issues specific to home-based workers are given only cursory
review in the general tax guides for individuals. Further, although books
focusing on small business taxation provide more useful information on
some issues, they furnish only partial coverage. *Taxes Made Easy for Home-
Based Businesses* (hereinafter *Taxes Made Easy*) will stand alone as the tax reference written specifically for home-based workers.

4. This is a simple statement that puts the
author's credentials up
front. The credentials
are significant enough
to warrant special
attention.

The Author

Gary Carter is a C.P.A., and holds a Ph.D. and a master's degree in taxation.
He has practiced in public accounting and has worked as a state revenue
agent. As an award-winning teacher, he makes the most complex tax rules
interesting and understandable to accounting students. Through *Taxes Made
Easy* he does the same for the average home-based worker.

The Book's Design

[5] The author's primary focus is to provide clear and precise guidance to home-based workers on how to comply with the income tax laws. For that reason, *Taxes Made Easy* is a nuts-and-bolts guide to be used while actually filling out the forms. For instance, the reporting requirements for Form 8829, "Expenses for Business Use of Your Home," are particularly difficult to deal with. Two full chapters are devoted to this task. Chapter Five explains the legal principles relating to home-office deductions, and Chapter Six explains the form requirements line by line. At the end of Chapter Six is a comprehensive example.

It is also the author's purpose to educate taxpayers on planning opportunities. Tax planning sometimes goes hand-in-hand with compliance, where strategies are conveyed through a discussion of reporting requirements. Tax rules are often vague, however, and some requirements are interpreted differently by equivalent sources of authority. Most tax guides simply make undocumented suggestions in these situations, leaving readers with virtually no defense if they are challenged by the IRS. Taxpayers deserve the opportunity to make informed choices, especially when the IRS and the courts disagree. *Taxes Made Easy* presents readers with a solid framework of tax law authority (Chapter One), and backs each planning suggestion with authoritative support.

This is a reference book that is also intended to be read and enjoyed. The author speaks directly to the reader in a relaxed manner that should be comfortable for the tax novice. The lessons conveyed, however, will equally serve the tax professional. The author is aware that abundant examples are a must. The numerous examples in *Taxes Made Easy* contribute to ease of reading and help to maximize the reader's comprehension.

Market Analysis

[6] The Audience

A demand exists for a book that delivers clear and specific tax guidance to home-office workers. There are more than 45 million home-based workers in [7] the United States according to Link Resources, a New York marketing research firm. The National Association of Home-Based Businesses agrees with this estimate, and says the number has increased by more than seven-fold since 1984. That makes those who run a home-based business, or who want to, a large customer base for products specific to their needs.

The author's general impression in dealing with owners of home-based businesses is that they are independent, eager to learn, and do-it-yourselfers (sometimes by financial necessity). Perhaps this is why they are a popular

5. This concise description of the structure of the book also shows why it is needed despite all the other books on the subject. The author has anticipated and confronted possible objections.

6. This could also be called "markets," as it describes the natural audience for the book even before any promotional efforts are made.

7. This is a wonderful statistic. It instantly shows a potential market base.

8. This shows a limited research effort when compared to the resources available. It would be better not to mention where the information is from unless the statement is more comprehensive. Otherwise the reader might wonder if something might have been overlooked.

9. This is a blending of "markets" and "promotions." This is fine, but it's better to separate them. Although promotions are part of an overall marketing strategy, "markets" occupies a unique place in the proposal, while "promotions" can describe the details of a marketing plan.

market for how-to books. There are many books on the market that address starting, financing, managing, and running a business from home. Nonetheless, a search of *Books in Print* revealed no current titles that deal comprehensively and exclusively with tax planning and compliance for home-based businesses.

Marketing Avenues

Regional and national home-based business associations. Many of these organizations offer a variety of services to their members. Paul and Sarah Edwards, who are the moderators of the Working From Home forum on CompuServe, have compiled a list of about 50 associations. A lot of them publish a newsletter, and some have regular member meetings. If the directors of these associations are made aware of *Taxes Made Easy* during the filing season, they would likely be eager to inform their members. Perhaps one or more of the national organizations would want to purchase the book to offer as a membership premium or to sell at a special discount to their members.

Workshops and seminars on starting a home-based business. There appears to be a growing number of home-business opportunity promoters. The author has received free passes to several of these events in the past few years. One promoter is Ed Beckley's Home Business Technologies, Inc., and another is The Home Business Group. These promoters typically offer a gift, such as a book, just for showing up at their conferences. What would be more appropriate than *Taxes Made Easy*?

Public speaking. The author has been a regular speaker on tax issues to both lay and professional audiences. He would be willing and eager to be an active promoter of the book in this way, as long as his teaching schedule is accommodated.

The World Wide Web. Since the book can be revised and updated on an annual basis, the author would be pleased to establish and maintain a web site that highlights the book and provides an online ordering form. The site could offer various free tax tips, such as the general rules for the business-use tests for home-office deductions. It could also offer current legislative and court developments relating to issues discussed in the book. This site could be linked to dozens of other sites that pertain either to taxes or to home-based businesses.

Competition Analysis

The Competitors (See the chart at the end of this section.)

Similar titles. As noted above, there are no recent titles that deal explicitly with tax rules for home-based businesses. There are two titles published several years ago that still have active records. They are *Home Office Deductions: Tax Tips for Individuals* (Commerce Clearing House, 1993) and *The Home Office Money & Tax Guide: Bringing Professional Business Practices Home* (Irwin, 1992). The author did not obtain a copy of either of these books, but in the dynamic world of taxation a book over a year old is out of date.

General tax guides. The *Ernst & Young Tax Guide 1996* (Wiley), *J. K. Lasser's Your Income Tax 1996* (Macmillan), *H&R Block 1996 Income Tax Guide* (Fireside), *Consumer Reports Books Guide to Income Tax* (St. Martin's, dist.), and *Taxes for Dummies, 1996 Edition* (IDG Books) are not primary competitors. These books offer a great deal of information on completing an individual return, but focus on breadth and simplicity at the expense of depth of coverage. In addition to lacking precision, these guides do not provide authoritative support for what they tell the reader. A taxpayer who is questioned about a particular deduction will have no defense in telling the IRS agent, "I read I could do this in *Taxes for Dummies.*" *Taxes Made Easy,* on the other hand, documents every tax-saving idea with authoritative support. Given the similarity of coverage of these general guides, only the *Ernst & Young Tax Guide* is included in the comparison chart.

Small-business tax guides. The competitors are listed in the chart. *J. K. Lasser's Tax Deductions for Small Business* (Macmillan) concentrates on business organization and specific deductions but is very short on examples. Its discussion of the various topics lacks precision; and it is not a book that one would buy to learn how to fill out the tax forms because it contains no forms. Similarly, *Tax Savvy for Small Business* (Nolo) focuses on tax planning ideas rather than return preparation. Like the general guides, these books contain no authoritative support for what they tell the reader. The chart includes a book that offers general financial advice on starting and running a home-based business, and purports to provide some tax advice: It is *Small-Time Operator* (Bell Springs). As the chart indicates, it offers no practical guidance for the proposed audience.

The primary competitor. This is believed to be *Tax Planning and Preparation Made Easy for the Self-Employed* (Wiley). As shown in the chart, it has the greatest number of yeses in comparing its coverage to *Taxes Made Easy.* It also documents its advice with authoritative support. The author's goal is to improve and expand on the coverage of this book, so that anyone comparing the two will choose *Taxes Made Easy.* For example, *Tax Planning . . .* offers advice only to the self-employed individual who operates as a sole proprietor (Schedule C). *Taxes Made Easy,* while emphasizing Schedule C, provides specific advice to *employees* working from home, as well as to taxpayers operating partnerships and corporations from their home office. *Tax Planning . . .* discusses the home-office business-use requirements, but does not cover the effects of home-office deductions on the sale of the taxpayer's residence. By

10. This creates an issue regarding the author's book. How will he keep his up-to-date? If you don't have a clear answer it might be best not to red-flag the issue.

contrast, *Taxes Made Easy* devotes an entire chapter to this topic (Chapter Ten), and provides specific advice on how to complete the forms. Additionally, while *Tax Planning* . . . is well written, it employs little humor. Professor Carter has found, through years of teaching, that levity is the best way to hold the attention of the audience in this, the driest of subjects. Accordingly, the author includes witticisms throughout the book that will aid the reader in remaining awake and attentive.

The Author

11. This is a very appropriate author section, and the inclusion of the curriculum vitae is a plus. This book needs credibility and is very credential-dependent.

Gary W. Carter is the Associate Director of Graduate Tax Studies at the University of Minnesota's Carlson School of Management. He received a B.A. degree in accounting from Eastern Washington University in 1976, a Masters of Taxation degree from the University of Denver in 1980 and a Ph.D. in Taxation from the University of Texas at Austin in 1985. He has worked in public accounting for both a Bix Six and a regional C.P.A. firm, and was a revenue agent for the state of Alaska. Professor Carter has appeared in radio and TV interviews, and is featured in a video produced by the University of Minnesota for training accounting students in tax research. He has written for various academic and professional publications, and has spoken on tax issues to both lay and professional audiences. A curriculum vitae follows.

Curriculum Vitae

Gary W. Carter

Academic Background

1985	Ph.D. (Taxation), The University of Texas at Austin
1980	M.T. (Taxation), The University of Denver
1976	B.A. (Accounting), Eastern Washington University

Professional and Teaching Experience

1992–Present	Director of Graduate Tax Studies, University of Minnesota
1985–92	Assistant Professor of Taxation, University of Minnesota
1981–85	Assistant Instructor, University of Texas at Austin
1980–81	Tax department Peat, Marwick, Mitchell & Co., Denver, Colorado
1978–80	Tax department, LeMaster & Daniels, C.P.A.'s, Spokane, Washington
1978	Certified Public Accountant (C.P.A.), state of Washington
1977	Revenue Auditor, Alaska Department of Revenue, Juneau, Alaska

Research

Articles:

"A Primer on Home-office Deductions," *Home-Based & Small Business Network,* Spring 1996, pp. 3–5.

"Improved Treatment of Barter Transactions for Accrual-Method Tax-payers," (written for the Tax Accounting Policy Subcommittee of the American Taxation Association), *Tax Notes,* March 20, 1995, pp. 1851–1857.

"Is Bartering Still Business as Usual Under the Economic Performance Regs?" *Taxes,* November 1993, pp. 675–684.

"Donative Transfers of Expensed Property and the Fundamental Inconsistency Rule of *Hillsboro,*" *Tennessee Law Review,* Winter 1991, pp. 151–229.

"Attorney Fee Recoupment in Tax Litigation after the Tax Reform Act of 1986," *The Review of Taxation for Individuals,* Fall 1988, pp. 335–352.

"The Commissioners Nonacquiescence—A Case for a National Court of Tax Appeals," *Temple Law Quarterly,* October 1986, pp. 879–918.

"Nonacquiescence: Winning by Losing," *Tax Notes,* September 19, 1988, pp. 1303–1307.

Notes:

"An Example That Clarifies Section 469(g)(1)(A)," 52 *Tax Notes* 1654 (September 30, 1991).

"Fixing the Passive Activity Rules," 51 *Tax Notes* 247 (April 15, 1991).

Proceedings:

"Comment on: 'Some Evidence on the Demand for Risky Assets,' by Charles W. Swenson," in *Arthur Young, University of Oklahoma Conference on Contemporary Tax Research,* Fall 1987.

Academic Honors

Outstanding Accounting Teacher of the Year, awarded by the Student Accounting and Finance Association, University of Minnesota, 1989

Outstanding Accounting/Finance Teacher of the Year, awarded by the Student Accounting and Finance Association, University of Minnesota, 1988

Doctoral Dissertation Grant, Ernst & Whinney, 1984

Scholarship, Price Waterhouse & Co., 1983

Scholarship, Alexander Grant & Co., 1982

Scholarship, Ernst & Whinney, 1982

Research and scholarship grant ARCO, 1981

Professional Associations

Editorial Board, *Journal of the American Taxation Association,* 1988–1990

Editorial Board, *Advances in Taxation,* 1987–1989

Ad hoc reviewer, *Journal of the American Taxation Association,* 1988

Site Coordinator, Internal Revenue Service—Volunteer Income Tax Assistance program, University of Minnesota, 1995–present

Chairperson, Tax Accounting Policy Subcommittee, American Taxation Association, 1994–1995

Member, Tax Accounting Policy Subcommittee, American Taxation Association, 1993–1994

Member, Tax Manuscript Award Committee, American Taxation Association, 1987–1988

Member, American Accounting Association/American Taxation Association

Member, American Institute of Certified Public Accountants

Member, Minnesota Society of Certified Public Accountants

Chapter Summary

NOTE: The enclosed Table of Contents indicates page numbering for the text that has been written. It is anticipated that the completed manuscript will be 250 to 300 pages.

Introduction: Before We Get Started

See the enclosed sample chapter.

Chapter One: The Lay of the Land

Although federal taxation is a pervasive body of law, it remains baffling to most taxpayers. It holds widespread interest because it affects nearly everyone, but it seldom evokes positive emotions. The prospect of an audit by the Internal Revenue Service (IRS) traumatizes even the most righteous home-based worker. The author's intent in Chapter One is to dispel the mystery, and to instill confidence in the reader.

See the enclosed sample chapter.

Chapter Two: What Does the IRS Consider a Business?

Although the term "trade or business" is used hundreds of times in the Internal Revenue Code and IRS regulations, neither Congress nor the IRS has

[12] provided us with a general definition. This is an important question, however, for several reasons. It not only determines how deductions are reported and classified, but also establishes what deductions are allowable. In addition, only taxpayers engaged in a trade or business are eligible to claim home-office deductions.

The chapter begins with a review of judicial interpretation of the term "trade or business." It then describes the differences between an investment activity and a business. Business deductions are reported by an individual "above the line" on Schedule C. Deductions relating to investment activities are generally "miscellaneous itemized deductions" reported on Schedule A, and must be reduced by 2 percent of Adjusted Gross Income.

The nature of dealing and trading in tangible or intangible assets is then discussed. Each of these could be either a business activity or an investment activity, depending on the frequency of trades and certain other factors. Taxpayers who derive rents from real estate might also be characterized as investors, or engaged in a business, depending on the nature of their activities.

If a taxpayer's activities are classified as a "hobby" by the IRS instead of a business, any loss incurred is disallowed. The factors the IRS uses to distinguish a business from a hobby are therefore explained.

Chapter Three: Choices for Business Organization

[13] Any taxpayer who owns and operates a business has several forms of business organization to choose from. This chapter discusses the advantages and disadvantages of operating as a sole proprietorship, a partnership (including a limited liability company), a C corporation, and an S corporation. Tax factors and important nontax factors are discussed.

For individual business owners, or spouses operating a business jointly, there are surprisingly few advantages to organizing as anything other than a sole proprietorship. A sole proprietorship has the advantages of simplicity and low cost in its formation, operation, and termination. Sole proprietors file Schedule C ("Profit or Loss from Business") with their Form 1040, and report on Form 1040 the entire amount of income or loss. This provides for one level of business taxation, at the individual rates. Sole proprietors must also pay self-employment tax on the entire net income from Schedule C.

A sole proprietorship is not an entity distinct from its owner. A disadvantage of this simple structure is the unlimited liability to the owner for debts and other claims against the business. This is the most common reason some small-business owners believe it is more prudent to incorporate, or to form a limited liability company (LLC).

C corporations, S corporations, and LLCs are entities independent from their owners, and are legally responsible for their own debts and liabil-

12. This is an important statement that automatically alerts the editor or agent that this author is aware of nuances that are meaningful to the market.

13. This sample chapter shows the comprehensiveness of the book and its usefulness to the reader. It is clear what you are getting. It includes detail and shows how well the author explains complex concepts to the layperson.

ity claims. However, creditors of home-based businesses typically require the owners to cosign for any significant debt. Also, if a civil action is brought against a home-based business, the claimant will typically seek action against the individual owner or owners as well. That means the promise of limited liability by these complex forms of business is often illusory.

The taxing scheme of a C corporation is discussed and compared to a sole proprietorship. It is subject to two tiers of taxation, one at the entity level, and one at the shareholder level on wages and dividends. Nevertheless, it can offer tax advantages in limited circumstances over the proprietorship form. Additionally, limited liability for shareholders becomes more of a reality as corporate assets grow. Financing expansion of the business is also easier when corporate stock and bonds can be issued.

Shareholders of a C corporation can elect S corporation status for income tax purposes. This converts the corporation to a pass-through entity, so that its income is taxed only at the shareholder level. It is similar to a partnership in this respect, although there are significant differences. For a start-up corporation that is expected to become large and profitable, it is often wise for the owners to elect S status in the early loss years so the losses can be deducted on their individual returns. When the company becomes profitable they can revoke the S election and take advantage of the lower corporate rates.

A partnership, like a sole proprietorship, also has the attribute of ease of formation, but extra care must be exercised in the partnership agreement to spell out the rights and obligations of the partners. A partnership is an entity distinct from its partners, but it is not subject to tax at the entity level. Each partner's allocable share of income and deductions is reported on his or her individual return, so income is taxed at only one level. Reporting partnership operations, distributions, and liquidations can be extremely complex, however.

Partners are generally subject to personal liability for debts and other claims against the partnership. Limited liability can be achieved by inactive partners who hold only limited partnership interests. Limited liability can also be achieved by general partners if the partnership is organized as an LLC. LLCs are generally treated as partnerships for tax purposes, but can be taxed as corporations depending on their attributes under state law. A necessary condition of a partnership is two or more owners, so home-based business owners typically do not have the opportunity to operate as a partnership.

14. This summary shows the consistent logic the book adopts. The concepts build upon each other, and it creates a sense of order.

Chapter Four: Tax Accounting Methods and Periods

14

After choosing a form of business, a home-based business owner must determine the best accounting method or methods to adopt. Selection and proper use of an accounting method is critical for proper compliance, but is generally given short shrift by current tax guides. Taxpayers have their choice of methods when they begin business as long as the method they choose clearly reflects income. However, once a method is adopted they can change it only with the consent of the IRS.

A method of accounting is a practice that involves the proper time for the inclusion of an item in income or the taking of a deduction. The primary choices for overall methods are the cash receipts and disbursements (cash) method, the accrual method, or a combination of the two, called the hybrid method. Taxpayers who are required to use inventory are faced with options on how to account for these costs. This chapter describes the attributes of the acceptable methods, and the circumstances in which taxpayers are precluded from using the cash method.

The cash method is the simplest and probably the most flexible in controlling the taxable year in which income and deductions are reported. Under the cash method, income is recognized when cash, property, or services are actually or constructively received. An item is constructively received when it is made available to the taxpayer. Deductions are generally permitted in the year of payment. Certain things are not deductible when paid, however, such as prepaid expenses and capital expenditures.

Flexibility is also possible with accrual methods, but the rules are more complex. There is not one acceptable accrual method but many, depending on common practices within a taxpayer's industry. Under accrual accounting, an item generally becomes income in the year in which it is earned, regardless of when it is received. Deductions are generally allowed when the fact of the liability can be established, the amount can be determined with reasonable accuracy, and "economic performance" has occurred. The rules relating to economic performance are complex and are dealt with in detail.

Some corporations, partnerships with a corporate partner, and "tax shelters" are not allowed to use the cash method, but must use an accrual method. Taxpayers are also obligated to use accrual accounting for purchases and sales if they are required to maintain an inventory. Inventories are required whenever the production, purchase, or sale of merchandise is an income-producing factor.

Historically contractors, such as painters, electricians, carpenters, and plumbers, have used the cash method of accounting. Recently, however, the IRS has been successful in requiring contractors to change to an accrual method because they sell inventoriable goods. This is the case even if the contractor purchases the materials for order and has no ending inventory at year end. Since many contractors are home-based, this issue is discussed, along with planning suggestions for dealing with it.

A taxpayer's period of accounting relates to the time when the taxable year begins and ends. Generally, home-based businesses are required to use the calendar year, but there are exceptions to this rule. Some C corporations have a great deal of flexibility in choosing their year end.

Chapter Five: Limitations on Use of Your Home

15 |

This chapter provides a detailed exposé on the use of a home for business. *See the enclosed sample chapter.*

15. Although the sample chapter is not included in this book, it is apparent the author made a good choice of which chapter to include. This chapter is definitely a subject uppermost in the minds of the home-based business owner.

Chapter Six: Form 8829 Line by Line

This chapter picks up where Chapter Five leaves off, with the mechanical application of the home-office deduction rules. Form 8829 is called "Expenses for Business Use of Your Home" and is probably the most complex form that home-based business owners have to deal with. It was decided to make this a separate chapter because of the intricacy of the form and the additional information that is conveyed. The detailed instruction this chapter gives is missing in other tax guides, and is surely information that home-based workers have been seeking.

Part I of the form, which deals with the part of the home used for business, is addressed first. Allocation procedures for office space are discussed, including the special allocation for day-care centers.

Part II of the form is where allowable deductions are computed. The chapter describes how the income limitations are applied, and how expenses are ordered into tiers for determining their deductibility. Tax-planning strategies are revealed for maximizing allowable deductions.

Part III of the form is where depreciation of the business portion of the home is computed. The chapter instructs taxpayers on how to compute basis for the depreciable portion, and how allowable depreciation is determined. The process for determining the carryover of unallowed deductions is then explained.

The chapter concludes with a comprehensive example using Form 8829 and Form 4562, "Depreciation and Amortization." The example ties together the points demonstrated in the chapter.

Chapter Seven: Planes, Trains, and (Especially) Automobiles

Taxpayers are generally curious about what travel and transportation costs are deductible. Home-based workers should be more interested than most, because special transportation rules apply to them. This chapter provides the answers.

Travel costs are distinguished from local transportation costs. Travel costs include meals and lodging while away from home as well as transportation. The concept of the "tax home" is explained, and what constitutes travel away from home. Proper allocation between business and personal travel costs is discussed, and the standard meal allowance is explained.

Local business transportation is deductible if it is ordinary and necessary and does not constitute commuting. Commuting is going from a taxpayer's home to a regular place of work. Transportation from home to a temporary work location is deductible, as is going from one work location to another. It is the IRS position that transportation between a taxpayer's home office and another regular work location is deductible only if the home office constitutes the taxpayer's principal place of business. This makes the principal-place-of-business determination even more important.

Car expenses can be claimed either using the standard mileage rate or actual costs. If actual costs are used the rules become quite complex. There are "luxury" car limitations on the amount of depreciation or lease payments that can be deducted during the year, and allocation must also be made between business and personal use. Depreciation methods and the limitations are explained, and the forms required are described.

¹⁶

Chapter Eight: Other Common Business Deductions

This chapter shows home-based workers how to minimize their tax bill, even if their home office does not qualify under the business-use tests described in Chapter Five. Expenses commonly incurred by home-based workers (that have not been previously discussed) are detailed. Planning suggestions are also made for deducting less common expenses, such as wages for the spouse and children of the home-based business owner.

A large part of the chapter is devoted to the depreciation of personal property, such as office furniture, computers, printers, fax machines, phones, and copiers. The limitations for personal use are covered, and the depreciation methods are shown in detail. Also included are the rules relating to the election to currently expense depreciable business property. Other costs explained pertain to books, subscriptions and supplies, telephone services, meals and entertainment, business liability insurance, health insurance, and retirement plans for the self-employed.

Chapter Nine: Estimated Tax Payments and Self-Employment Tax

Home-based business owners who have had a successful year, but who have neglected to plan for estimated tax payments, might be flabbergasted by the magnitude of the additional tax and penalty they must pay. Particularly vulnerable to this pitfall are recently self-employed taxpayers, or those who are phasing out of an employment position into their own business. This chapter talks about who must make estimated tax payments, how the payments are computed, and the easiest way to avoid a late-payment penalty. Even if the taxpayer is due a refund, a penalty might be assessed if adequate estimated

16. This summary shows that the book will provide information on issues that the reader might not have considered.

tax payments are not made by the due date of each payment period. The author reveals how to achieve maximum deferral while avoiding the penalty.

This chapter also covers the rules for determining who is self-employed, what income is subject to self-employment tax, and how to compute the tax. Self-employment tax is the tax paid by self-employed individuals to finance the Social Security system. The tax is paid at the rate of 15.3 percent on net self-employment income up to $62,700, and 2.9 percent on the rest. One half of the tax is deductible for income tax purposes, so only 92.35 percent of net earnings from self-employment is subject to the tax. Like a self-employed individual's income tax liability, the self-employment tax is paid through estimated tax payments.

Unlike an employee's portion of Social Security tax, the self-employment tax must be computed by the taxpayer along with the income tax. This tax is independent of the income tax, however, and has its own rules. The determination of whether an individual is an employee or is self-employed generally follows the same tests for both income tax and Social Security tax purposes, but there are differences. Some people are classified as employees for income tax purposes but are self-employed for Social Security tax purposes, and vice versa. For example, workers called "statutory employees" are self-employed for income tax purposes, but are considered employees for Social Security tax purposes. Ministers of the Gospel, on the other hand, are usually employees for income tax purposes but are considered self-employed for self-employment tax purposes.

Individuals who have concluded that they are self-employed must then determine what income is subject to self-employment tax. Income is subject to self-employment tax only if it is derived from a trade or business. Even some business income, however, might be exempt.

Chapter Ten: Sale of Your Residence

This chapter presents critical decisions for taxpayers who qualify under one of the business-use tests described in Chapter Five. Home-based business owners who sell their residence also sell their place of business along with it. But for tax purposes, their home and their office are treated differently. For example, taxpayers can roll over the gain to a new house on the sale of a principal residence, and postpone paying tax on it. A home office, however, is considered a separate business asset, and any gain allocated to it is taxed in the year of sale. Although there is an easy way to avoid this, taxpayers may not want to, depending on their situation. Also, taxpayers cannot deduct a loss on the sale of personal-use assets. So if they sell their house and take a bath, tough luck. However, any loss allocated to a home office is deductible. In this chapter readers learn the options for reporting the sale of their residence, and how to fill out the forms.

Chapter Eleven: Records You Better Keep

The cold, hard facts about adequate record-keeping were frozen in case law over 60 years ago when the U.S. Supreme Court said:

> Deductions are strictly a matter of legislative grace, and a taxpayer has the burden of proving that he or she is entitled to any deduction claimed on the return. *New Colonial Ice Co.* v. *Helvering*, 292 U.S. 435, 440 (1934).

Taxpayers should always be conscious of the fact that nothing is deductible unless they can substantiate it. This chapter shows home-based workers how to be confident in their record-keeping procedures.

Substantiation requirements in general are explained, as is the requirement that business owners keep a complete and accurate set of books. The special record-keeping requirements for travel, entertainment, gifts, and listed property are covered in detail. Finally, suggestions are offered on how long to keep various records.

Taxpayers who own and run their own business should maintain a formal set of books, regardless of how small their business is. The law does not specify how this must be done, as long as the method clearly reflects the income of the business. The books should show gross income and all deductions, and should be backed up by supporting documents. Those business owners who do not maintain a set of books are in jeopardy of the IRS disallowing losses as "hobby losses" (discussed in Chapter Two) or losing the choice of their desired method of accounting (discussed in Chapter Four).

For certain items that have potential for abuse, there are special record-keeping requirements. No deductions are allowed for travel away from home, entertainment, gifts, or any "listed property" unless taxpayers substantiate the expenditures according to the regulations. This chapter explains the substantiation requirements, and the easiest ways to comply with them.

Taxpayers are often curious about how long records should be kept. This chapter separates income and costs into several categories, and suggests, for each category, the safest period for retaining records and documentation.

Chapter Twelve: A Big Example

Students thrive on examples—the more examples they see, the happier and more confident they become. The readers of this book will be no different. So this chapter is devoted to bringing together as many of the concepts discussed in the book as possible through one comprehensive example.

The situation of a typical home-based sole proprietor is described, with all income, deductions, and other transactions listed. The reader is then shown how each specific item is reported on the various tax forms.

Home-office deductions are computed on Form 8829 ("Expenses for Business Use of Your Home"), depreciation is computed on Form 4562 ("Depreciation and Amortization"), business net income is computed on Schedule C ("Profit or Loss from Business"), and self-employment tax is computed on Schedule SE ("Self-Employment Tax"). The results from Schedule C and Schedule SE are shown on the taxpayer's Form 1040, and the tax is calculated. The taxpayer's estimated tax payments for 1998 are then computed. Although many of the concepts and calculations demonstrated in this chapter are also explained through examples in other parts of the book, the reader gets a complete picture of the tax return from this example.

17. This proposal is a good example of how to present what could otherwise be dry material. The author concentrates on the relevance to the reader and makes it easy to understand. He follows through on his promises.

Readers who have an overriding desire to complete their return as quickly and effortlessly as possible will probably turn to this chapter first and try to mimic the example. When they realize they need additional information on particular issues, they will find cross-references for each item to the chapter in which it is fully explained. For these readers, this chapter serves as **17** a home base. Readers who are more meticulous, and who start at the beginning of the book, will find in this chapter a grand confirmation of all the concepts they have learned in the preceding chapters.

BOOK PROPOSAL TERMS

About the Author(s) section   (see **author biography**)

abstract   In a book proposal, a concise rundown of a chapter (or sometimes a section) of the proposed book. It conveys the essentials in a way that shows what you can write—without your having to write it all. Chapter abstracts may be viewed as miniature chapters fine-tuned to persuade as well as to answer likely editorial questions. An abstract (along with a separate table of contents) is a part of the book's outline, and often features elements of the author's intended writing style, anecdotes, and lists of prospective interviewees.

author background (see **author biography**)

author biography   The author background or About the Author(s) section of a book proposal. It contains any information about the author(s) that may be pertinent to the book project and is typically placed at the end of the main body of the proposal and before the outline. It may be followed by a separate formal résumé or complete vita.

buyback   A situation in which an author buys copies of the finished book from the publisher—the number of which may be stipulated beforehand. This figure may come into play during negotiations for a book-publishing contract, whereby the author agrees to purchase (at least) a predetermined number of copies for a specified price. This provides the publisher with a guaranteed sales and circulation base, and may allow the publisher to print more copies, thereby lowering manufacturing costs per copy. Alternately, an author may simply bargain for the right to buy copies at a hefty discount.

competition   The competition section of a book proposal should cover books comparable to the one being proposed. Competing books are existing titles—those in print or formerly in print—with contents or subject area similar to that of the proposed work or that address the same basic target market. This section gives a rundown of at least the higher-profile competing works and distinguishes the proposed book in such terms as innovativeness of approach, comprehensiveness, or scope of potential readership base.

extract   Basically a sample. In a book proposal, an extract represents the actual contents or style of the book and may be seen in the outline, for instance, as a slice of the fuller version of an anecdote, a chapter opening, or pertinent quotation from an interview source.

hook   A catchphrase (or sometimes just a word) that signifies the essence of your product in the marketing arena: your book's public face, which will be displayed to the agent, editor, publisher, and reader. Just as a hook for a piece of popular music may be a portion of the melody, a lyric line, or a brief instrumental riff, the hook for your book proposal is the power point from which your ideas take flight. Finding a hook for your book is the process of distilling its complex ideas and then depicting them in terms equivalent to a television sound bite.

lead   An opening statement. Its point is to get attention—be it in a query letter, book proposal, book manuscript, news story, sales brochure, political speech, or press release.

market   Marketing is an aspect of book publishing concerned generally with ensuring the distribution of a book so that it will be available for its target audience, or market. Consideration of a book's potential market is addressed in a book proposal's marketing section, sometimes phrased in terms of who will read/need this book.

outline   A charting of a book's contents, most often prefaced by a separate table of contents. The outline may take the simple form of chapter headings followed by an abstract or synopsis of each chapter. Often other pertinent elements are included, such as illustrations (or indications thereof), subheadings, and extracts from interviews, anecdotes, or questionnaires.

overview   Typically, the first section of a book proposal—immediately following the title page. It conveys the book's primary message, usually leading with the book's hook and maybe a punchy thesis statement, followed by a brief synopsis of the projected contents—and anything else that should be placed up front. In this section, power writing really comes into play.

program   A program in a commercial nonfiction book accents the how-to elements of the topic. It provides a progressive (programmatic), often step-by-step goal-directed plan of achievement that is central to the concerns of interested readers.

promotion   The promotional aspects of book publishing include advertising schedules and cataloging, as well as such nuances as coordinating distribution and publicity. Successful book proposals often include listings of the author's promotional achievements as well as a selection of original ideas in this section.

publicity   In book publishing a part of the promotion and marketing wing that concentrates on bringing the book and/or the author to the attention of the media. It's sometimes said that the difference between promotion and publicity is that publicity is free. That observation may be true in the sense that news coverage is not regularly sold like advertising; but a publicist writes the original press release and sets up the interview contacts for television and radio appearances—and, like everything else, good publicists don't come cheap. Noting in your book proposal that you have retained a publicist (or will do so) can give you a leg up.

query   In book publishing, a written communication (usually a letter of introduction, sometimes including ancillary materials such as selected press clips and/or author résumé) geared to entice the publisher, editor, or agent to request a look at the author's book proposal package—or in fiction, the completed outline and manuscript.

query letter   (see **query**)

sales   The actual selling of the completed volumes—to bookstores and ultimately to the reader. Besides the traditional bookstore outlets, many book sales today are accomplished through direct-response techniques such as targeted mailings and telephone 800 numbers, as well as through alternative venues such as specialty stores (that are not primarily bookstores), and back-of-the-room sales kiosks set up in tandem with workshops, symposiums, conferences, and conventions. In a book proposal, qualified authors do well to cite specific and pertinent suggestions for fresh sales avenues as well as their experience relevant to the sales arena.

sample chapter   Book proposal packages most often include a completed portion of the proposed book—this is typically a sample chapter or chapters. Sample chapters allow an editor to get a feel for the author's writing style.

SASE   The ubiquitously requested SASE is a self-addressed stamped envelope the author encloses when corresponding by mail with agents, editors, and publishers—all of whom greatly appreciate this courtesy.

synopsis   A summary of the content and intent of something. In a book proposal, a synopsis of the book as a whole is generally a component of the overview, while chapter-by-chapter synopses, also termed chapter abstracts, are presented in the outline section.

Suggested Reading

Appelbaum, Judith. *How to Get Happily Published,* 5th ed. (New York: Harper Collins, 1998). Beyond the "mere" acceptance of a manuscript, this work provides sensible advice on generating ideas, putting them into words, and maintaining control over the editing, sales, and marketing of one's work.

Appelbaum, Judith, Nancy Evans, and Florence Janovic. *The Sensible Solutions How to Get Happily Published Handbook* (New York: Sensible Solutions, 1981). Provides worksheets and additional information for authors of trade books, designed to be used in conjunction with the above-mentioned title.

The Associated Press. *The Associated Press Stylebook and Libel Manual* (Revised and Updated Edition) (Cambridge, Mass.: Perseus Press, 1998). This easy-to-use, dictionary-format guide is an excellent quick reference to contemporary journalistic and mainstream word usage. It's far from comprehensive, but answers most frequently encountered writing questions. Treatment of issues pertaining to libel is a must-read for investigative and opinionative writing.

The Association of American University Presses Directory (New York: AAUP, published annually). Gives a detailed description of each AAUP member press with a summary of its publishing program, names and responsibilities of key staff, and requirements for submitting proposals and manuscripts.

Balkin, Richard. *How to Understand and Negotiate a Book Contract or Magazine Agreement* (Cincinnati: Writer's Digest Books, 1985). Essential reading for every writer who stands to make a sale.

Bernard, Andre, editor. *Rotten Rejections* (Wainscott, N.Y.: Pushcart Press, 1990). A humorous and harrowing collection of literary demurrals, including such rejects as William Faulkner, Gustave Flaubert, James Joyce, and Vladimir Nabokov. Fine inspiration for writers encountering rejection during any phase of their careers.

Bernstein, Theodore. *The Careful Writer: A Modern Guide to English Usage* (New York: Free Press, 1995). An incomparable, lively, accurate, and exquisitely articulate classic in its field. Mainstream and mass-market writers may view it as too high-toned a tome to grace their shelves, but this work nevertheless addresses their needs accessibly with observations they might well heed.

———. *Miss Thistelbottom's Hobgoblins: The Careful Writer's Guide to the Taboos, Bugbears, and Outmoded Rules of English Usage* (New York: Simon & Schuster, 1984). More apt insights from the author of the above-listed work.

Boston, Bruce O., editor. *Stet! Tricks of the Trade for Writers and Editors* (Alexandria, Va.: Editorial Experts, 1986). A supple, interactive collection of articles that sets the writer inside the heads of editors and publishers.

Boswell, John. *The Awful Truth About Publishing: Why They Always Reject Your Manuscript . . . And What You Can Do About It* (New York: Warner Books, 1986). A view from the other side—that is, from inside the large publishing house.

Bunnin, Brad, and Peter Beren. *The Writer's Legal Companion: The Complete Handbook for the Working Writer* (Cambridge, Mass.: Perseus Press, 1998). The ins and outs of publishing laws, published by specialists in do-it-yourself legal guides.

Burack, Sylvia K., ed. *The Writer's Handbook* (Boston: The Writer, published annually). One of the most respected, clear-eyed, high-quality publications in the writing-for-publication field; a pioneering work, now with a long tradition of success.

Burgett, Gordon. *The Writer's Guide to Query Letters and Cover Letters* (Rocklin, Calif.: Prima, 1992). Sound and pointed advice from an expert perspective on how to utilize the query and cover letter to sell your writing.

The Chicago Manual of Style (Chicago: University of Chicago Press, 1993). In matters of editorial style—punctuation, spelling, capitalization, issues of usage—this book provides traditional, conservative, justifiable guidelines. Long considered by many to be the last word on such matters, the *Chicago Manual* is not, however, set up for ease of use as a quick-reference guide; it's not a handbook of grammar per se and doesn't offer writers ready tips for solving day-to-day creative problems. The manual is, rather, a professional reference work for the publishing and editing trade—and in this area it remains the American standard. Many commercial writers and editors characterize the *Manual* as intricate in organization and arcanely indexed relative to their own stylistic concerns.

Curtis, Richard. *Beyond the Bestseller. A Literary Agent Takes You Inside the Book Business* (New York: Plume, 1990). Incisive and practical advice for writers from a literary agent who is also an accomplished author.

———. *How to Be Your Own Literary Agent: The Business of Getting Your Book Published* (Revised Edition) (Boston: Houghton Mifflin, 1996). Insights and how-to; a personal point of view from one who knows the ropes and shows them to you.

Davidson, Jeffrey P. *Marketing for the Home-Based Business,* 2nd ed. (Holbrook, Mass.: Bob Adams, 1999). For entrepreneurs of all stripes (including writers) who are based in their homes. Digs beneath the obvious and uncovers ways to project a high-level image and transform your computer, telephone, and fax into a dynamic marketing staff.

Goldberg, Natalie. *Writing Down the Bones: Freeing the Writer Within* (Boston: Shambhala Publications, 1998). Offers some thoughts and advice on the art of writing. The author is a Zen Buddhist and writing instructor.

Harman, Eleanor, and Ian Montagnes, editors. *The Thesis and the Book* (Toronto: University of Toronto Press, 1976). A selection of articles detailing revision of the scholarly presentation into one with broader appeal. The discussion of the demands of specialist audiences versus those of a wider market is pertinent to the development of general nonfiction projects—especially those involving collaboration between writing professionals and academics.

Herman, Deborah Levine. *Spiritual Writing: From Journal to XXXX* (XX: Beyond Words Publishing, 2002).

Herman, Jeff. *Writer's Guide to Book Editors, Publishers, and Literary Agents* (Rocklin, Calif.: Prima Publishing, published annually). Gives in-depth advice and how-to tips, featuring extensive directory listings and profiles of literary agents as well as U.S. and Canadian book publishers and acquisitions editors. It's a great way to get acquainted with the likes, dislikes, and priorities of the people who make book publishing happen today; contains essays by literary agent Jeff Herman as well as a wide range of expert contributing writers.

Herman, Jeff, Deborah Levine Herman, and Julia Devillers. *You Can Make It Big Writing Books* (Rocklin, Calif.: Prima Publishing, 2000). The world's most successful authors tell you how to join their ranks.

Horowitz, Lois. *Knowing Where to Look: The Ultimate Guide to Research* (Cincinnati: Writer's Digest Books, 1984). An invaluable tool for anyone who has to dig up elusive facts and figures.

Huddle, David. *The Writing Habit: Essays* (Hanover, N.H.: University Press of New England, University of Vermont, 1994). A serious, useful book on the literary craft from a writer who wants to provide more than a how-to guide; practical, energetic, supportive advice and imaginative approach to learning tricks of the trade.

Kilpatrick, James J. *The Writer's Art* (Kansas City, Mo.: Andrews, McMeel, & Parker, 1984). An opinionated discussion of proper usage, style, and just plain good writing from one of the news business's most popular curmudgeons.

Klauser, Henriette Anne. *Writing on Both Sides of the Brain: Breakthrough Techniques for People Who Write* (San Francisco: Harper San Francisco, 1987). Tells you how to refrain from editing while you write; then how to edit, mercilessly and creatively, what you've just written.

Kremer, John. *Book Publishing Resource Guide* (Fairfield, Iowa: Ad-Lib Publications, 1990). Provides comprehensive listings for book-marketing contacts and resources—contains a vast bibliography and references to other resource guides. Look for newest periodically updated edition.

———. *1001 Ways to Market Your Books—For Authors and Publishers,* 5th ed. (Fairfield, Iowa: Open Horizons, 2000). Sensible, innovative, and inspiring advice on, first, producing the most marketable book possible, and then on marketing it as effectively as possible.

Literary Market Place (New York: R. R. Bowker, published annually). This is the huge annual directory of publishing houses and their personnel, as well as writing, editing, and publishing services nationwide.

Mann, Thomas. *A Guide to Library Research Methods* (New York: Oxford University Press, 1987). A practical guide to the most helpful, time-saving, and cost-effective information sources.

McCormack, Thomas. *The Fiction Editor, the Novel, and the Novelist* (New York: Griffin, 1994). How to fine-tune fiction; every bit as helpful for writers as it is for editors.

Miller, Casey, and Kate Swift. *The Handbook of Nonsexist Writing* (New York: Harper & Row, 1988). An excellent set of guidelines for eliminating sexist terms and constructions from all writing.

Namanworth, Phillip, and Gene Busnar. *Working for Yourself* (New York: McGraw-Hill, 1986). Everything you need to know about both the business and personal sides of freelancing and being self-employed. Great tips applicable to orchestrating a writer's business life.

Parinello, Al. *On the Air. How to Get on Radio and TV Talk Shows and What to Do When You Get There* (Hawthorne, NJ: Career Press). An exciting guide to the electronic media and its use for promotional purposes; ties in marketing aspects of such fields as seminars, social activism, and professional advancement—and is especially appropriate for authors with the entrepreneurial spirit.

Polking, Kirk, and Leonard S. Meranus, editors. *Law and the Writer*, 3rd ed. (Cincinnati: Writer's Digest Books, 1985). A collection of pieces on legal issues that concern writers and their works.

Powell, Walter W. *Getting into Print: The Decision-Making Process in Scholarly Publishing* (Chicago: University of Chicago Press, 1988). An eye-opening, behind-the-scenes look at the operations of two scholarly presses.

Poynter, Dan, and Mindy Bingham. *Is There a Book Inside You? How to Successfully Author a Book Alone or Through a Collaborator*, 5th ed. (Santa Barbara, Calif.: Para Publishing, 1998). A thought-provoking series of exercises to help you assess your publishing potential.

Preston, Elizabeth, Ingrid Monke, and Elizabeth Bickford. *Preparing Your Manuscript*, new/revised ed. (Boston: The Writer, 2000). A contemporary guide to manuscript preparation that provides step-by-step advice for professional presentation of work for submission to editors, publishers, agents, television producers. Covers punctuation, spelling, indexing, along with examples of proper formats for poetry, prose, plays; also offers essential information on copyright, marketing, and mailing manuscripts.

Provost, Gary. *The Freelance Writer's Handbook* (New York: NAL/Mentor, 1982). Invaluable advice, mainly for writers of short pieces.

Rivers, William L. *Finding Facts: Research Writing Across the Curriculum* (Englewood Cliffs, N.J.: Prentice Hall, 1988). A careful inquiry into the research process and the difficulties of achieving objectivity.

Roberts, Ellen E. M. *The Children's Picture Book: How to Write It, How to Sell It* (Cincinnati: Writer's Digest Books, 1981). A savvy and enthusiastic step-by-step guide by an established children's book editor.

Ross, Marilyn, and Tom Ross. *Marketing Your Books: A Collection of Profit-Making Ideas for Authors and Publishers* (Buena Vista, Colo.: Communication Creativity, 1990). Suggests fine-tuned, cost-effective, innovative promotional plans. Authors should note that the marketing strategy begins at the concept stage—before the book itself is written.

Ross, Tom, and Marilyn Ross. *The Complete Guide to Self-Publishing*, 3rd ed. (Cincinnati: Writer's Digest Books, 1994). Up-to-date, step-by-step information and procedures on setting up your publishing business. Shows you how to take your book from the idea stage through production and into the hands of consumers. Not just for entrepreneurs who self-publish—contains valuable tips for commercially published writers to maximize the success of their titles.

Rubens, Philip, editor. *Science and Technical Writing: A Manual of Style*, 2nd ed. (New York: Routledge, 2000). A comprehensive one-stop style guide for writers and editors in scientific and technical fields (including students). Addresses fundamental issues of style and usage, discusses specialized terminology versus technobabble, and provides guidelines for communicating effectively to one's audience.

Seidman, Michael. *From Printout to Published* (New York: Carroll & Graf, 1992). Engaging and unvarnished consideration of the writer-publisher relationship from first draft through finished book. Details nuances of manuscript submissions, working with agents, contract negotiation, advances, editing, cover design, book marketing, promotion—and more.

Strunk, William Jr., and E. B. White. *The Elements of Style*, 4th ed. (Needham Heights, Mass.: Allyn & Bacon, 2000). This highly respected, widely read, and well-loved classic is seen by some contemporary writers as sheer stuffed-shirt punditry. It is, however, a slim volume and doesn't take up much space or time to read—and modern writers may well find themselves following the Strunk-and-White principles in spite of themselves.

Todd, Alden. *Finding Facts Fast* (Berkeley: Ten Speed Press, 1979). Detailed basic, intermediate, and advanced research techniques; hundreds of ideas for those stuck in a research dead end.

Writer's Market (Cincinnati: Writer's Digest Books, published annually). A directory of thousands of markets and outlets; best known for its listing of the hundreds of consumer and trade periodicals. Also includes book publishers, book packagers, greeting-card publishers, syndicates—and more.

Zinsser, William. *On Writing Well*, 6th ed. (New York: Harper Reference, 1998). Shows you how to simplify nonfiction writing and deliver fresh, vigorous prose. An excellent book to keep on hand.

WEB SITES

A Web of On-Line Dictionaries
http://www.yourdictionary.com/
This index of online dictionaries includes 230 different languages and gives preference to free resources. A new feature allows the user to translate words from any European language to any other.

ACQWeb
http://www.library.vanderbilt.edu/
The site is the "gathering place for librarians and other professionals interested in acquisitions and collection development." It provides a directory of publishers and vendors and "Web News for Acquiring Minds."

American Booksellers Association
http://www.bookweb.org/
The American Booksellers Association is a trade association representing independent bookstores nationwide. The site links members to recent articles about the industry and features Idea Exchange discussion forums.

Association of American Publishers, Inc.
http://www.publishers.org/
The Association of American Publishers "is the principal trade association of the book publishing industry." The site includes information and registration for annual meetings and conferences, industry news, information about book publishing, industry statistics and issues, and copyright data.

Association of Authors' Representatives, Inc.
http://www.publishersweekly.com/aar/
The Association of Authors' Representatives, Inc., is "an organization of independent literary and dramatic agents." It is a member-only site that offers information about finding an agent, Internet links, a newsletter, and a canon of ethics.

@writers: For Writers on the Internet
http://www.geocities.com/Athens/Acropolis/6608
The @writers site includes information about markets, links to myriad Internet resources, and reviews of writing-related books. It also provides a technical Q&A section to answer questions about hardware, software, and the Internet. Also available are a chat room and monthly newsletter subscription.

Authorlink

http://www.authorlink.com/

This information service for editors, literary agents, and writers boasts more than 165,000 loyal readers per year. Features include a "Manuscript Showcase" that contains 500+ ready-to-publish, evaluated manuscripts.

The Authors Guild

http://www.authorsguild.org/

For more than 80 years the Guild has been the authoritative voice of American writers and the foundation of the American literary community. This site features contract advice, a legal search, information on electronic rights, how to join the organization, an index to the Guild's bulletins, a list of publishers, a listing of board members, and current articles regarding the publishing field. There is also a link for Back-in-print.com, an online bookstore featuring out-of-print editions made available by authors.

Authors Registry

http://www.webcom.com/registry/

The Authors Registry is an extensive directory of authors with contact addresses, phone numbers, fax numbers, and e-mail addresses. Authors are free to list the contact information of their choice in this searchable database. This site contains instructions for accessing the registry.

Aylad's Writer's Group

http://www.publication.com/aylad

This site provides a forum for "people to get their work read and critiqued by fellow writers in a friendly atmosphere." The service is free, and all writing forms are welcome. The site includes links to other resources for writers.

Booklist

http://www.ala.org/booklist/index.html

This is a "digital counterpart of the American Library Association's *Booklist* magazine." In the site are a current selection of reviews, feature articles, and a searchable cumulative index. Review topics include books for youth, adult books, media, and reference materials. The site also includes press releases, the best books list, and subscription information.

Booknotes

http://www.booknotes.org/right.htm

Based on C-SPAN's *Booknotes,* this site has information on the authors who have appeared on the program, transcripts from the program, RealVideo clips of authors, the upcoming *Booknotes* schedule, recent *Booknotes* programs in RealAudio, and information about the publishing industry in general. The site also features message boards and a link to the C-SPAN bookstore.

Bookreporter

http://www.bookreporter.com/brc/index.asp

Bookreporter offers book reviews and a perspectives section that deals with topics such as when a book becomes a movie. It also features a daily quote by a famous author.

Booktalk
http://www.booktalk.com/
This site is a publishing insider's page where you'll find out who's hot and what's up. It features links to get in touch with authors, agents, and publishers, as well as a slush pile and bookstores.

BookWire
http://www.bookwire.com/
Partners with *Publishers Weekly, Literary Market Place* and the *Library Journal,* among others, BookWire is a site that offers book industry news, reviews, original fiction, author interviews, and guides to literary events. The site includes publicity and marketing opportunities for publishers, authors, booksellers, and publicists, plus a list of the latest BookWire press releases.

BookZone
http://www.bookzone.com/
BookZone was created "to increase book sales and profits for publishers." The site features a Super Catalog of books, thousands of book-related links, industry insights and resources, publishing news, site hosting and development, and online marketing.

The Children's Book Council
http://www.cbcbooks.org/
"CBC Online is the web site of the Children's Book Council—encouraging reading since 1945." It provides a listing of articles geared toward publishers, teachers, librarians, booksellers, parents, authors, and illustrators—all those interested in the children's book field.

Critique Partner Connections
http://www.petalsoflife.com/cpc.html
Users of Critique Partner Connections pay a one-time fee of $15 to be matched with a fellow writer for the purpose of critiquing one another's work. Maintainers of this site strive to match people with similar interests and critique styles.

The Eclectic Writer
http://www.eclectics.com/writing/writing.html
This site is an information source for those interested in crime, romance, horror, children's, technical, screen, science fiction, fantasy, mystery, and poetry writing. It features articles, a fiction writer's character chart, resources by genre, reference materials, general writing resources, online magazines and journals, writing scams, awards, and a writing-related fun page.

The Editorial Eye
http://www.eei-alex.com/eye/
The Editorial Eye web site consists of a sampler of articles originally printed in the newsletter of the same name. The articles discuss techniques for writing, editing,

design, and typography, as well as information on industry trends and employment. The *Eye* has been providing information to publications professionals for 18 years.

The Editor's Pen

http://www.pathway.net/dwlacey/default.htm

The Editor's Pen site exists to connect "sites for and about Writer, Editors, and Indexers." It includes links to lists of freelancers and online dictionaries. Other interesting links include an "Edit challenge" and "Quotable words of editorial wisdom."

Encyclopaedia Britannica

http://www.eb.com/

This service is subscription-based and allows the user to search the *Encyclopaedia Britannica*. New users can try a "sample search."

Forwriters.com

http://www.forwriters.com/

This "mega-site" provides numerous links to writing resources of all kinds. It lists conferences, markets, agents, commercial services, and more. The "What's New" feature allows the user to peruse what links have recently been added under the various categories.

Granta

http://www.granta.com/

The *Granta* web site offers information about the most current issue of this highly regarded literary journal. There is background information about the issue, and the contents are listed. Visitors to the site may read a sample from the issue and obtain subscription and ordering information. It also offers a readers' survey and information about back issues.

Indispensable Writing Resources

http://www.quintcareers.com/writing/

Indispensable Writing Resources offers a categorized listing of Internet writing resources. Categories include online writing labs and centers, general writing/grammar, subject-specific writing, and a miscellaneous collection of writers' resources. It is a searchable site that offers a writing and style library as well as reference material.

Inkspot

http://www.inkspot.com/

Inkspot provides articles, how-to tips, market information, and networking opportunities. Special features include a FAQ section for beginners, classifieds, and a section for young writers. Information is sorted by genre.

Inner Circle

http://www.geocities.com/SoHo/Lofts/1498/circlefaq.htm

The Fictech Inner Circle was started in April 1997 as "a means for writers—especially new and unpublished writers—to correspond through e-mail with others of similar interest." Membership is free and provides the opportunity to communicate with over 1,500 writers from around the globe.

International Online Writers Association

http://www.project-iowa.org/
IOWA's purpose is to "offer help and services to writers around the world through shared ideas, workshops, critiques, and professional advice." Services include real-time monthly workshops, real-time weekly critiques, and periodic round robins. The site also includes a library of essays, poems, short stories, and novel chapters.

Internet Writing Workshop

http://www.manistee.com/~lkaus/workshop/index.html
The Internet Writing Workshop exists to "create an environment where works in progress can be passed around and critiqued, to help us improve these works and to improve as writers," as well as to provide support for writers. The service is membership-based and includes a variety of genres.

Library Journal Digital

http://www.bookwire.com/
Library Journal Digital offers news about the publishing industry, editorials, a calendar of events, video reviews, audiobook reviews, best-seller news, and a job search section.

Literary Market Place

http://www.literarymarketplace.com/lmp/us/index_us.asp
The *Literary Market Place* web site offers information about U.S. book publishers, Canadian book publishers, and small presses, as well as literary agents including illustration and lecture agents. The site also offers trade services and resources.

Local Writers Workshop

http://members.tripod.com/~lww_2/introduction.htm
The Local Writers Workshop is an Internet forum for works in progress, especially those "in the early stages of revision." The creators of this membership-based site pride themselves on its community ethic.

Merriam-Webster Dictionary

http://www.m-w.com/netdict.htm
Like its paper counterpart, this web-based dictionary provides definition to words and phrases sought by users. For word lovers, features like "Word of the Day" and "Word Game of the Day" are included as well.

Midwest Book Review

http://www.execpc.com/~mbr/bookwatch/mbr/pubinfo.html
Responsible for *Bookwatch,* a weekly television program that reviews books, videos, music, CD-ROMs, and computer software, as well as five monthly newsletters for community and academic library systems, and much more. The *Midwest Book Review* was founded in 1980. This site features its reviews.

Misc.writing

http://www.scalar.com/mw

"Misc.writing is a Use Net newsgroup that provides a forum for discussion of writing in all its forms—scholarly, technical, journalistic, and mere day-to-day communication." Web site resources include a writer's bookstore and market information.

The National Writers Union

http://www.nwu.org/

The National Writers Union is the trade union for freelance writers of all genres. The website provides links to various services of the Union, including grievance resolution, insurance, job information, and databases.

The Novel Workshop

http://www.ameritech.net/users/novelshop/index.html

The Novel Workshop is an "online writer's colony; a place where writers—from novice to professional—gather to critique, advise, and encourage each other." The site provides links to other resources for writers and a list of suggested books.

1001 Ways to Market Your Books

http://www.bookmarket.com/1001ways.html

1001 Ways to Market Your Book offers a book marketing newsletter, consulting services, and book marketing updates. Other topics include success letters, author bios, sample chapters, and tables of contents.

Painted Rock

http://www.paintedrock.com/

"Painted Rock provides services to nonpublished writers, published writers, and readers." Free features on the site include information on a free twelve-week Artist's Way program, message boards, goal writing groups, writing topics, a book discussion group, a research listserv, and *The Rock* online magazine. In addition to their free services, the site offers paid online writing classes, a subscription-based newsletter, and two bookstores, as well as advertising, promotion for authors, and web-site hosting and design.

Para Publishing

http://www.parapublishing.com/

The Para Publishing Book Publishing Resources page offers "the industry's largest resources/publications guide," a customized book writing/publishing/promoting information kit, and current and back issues of their newsletter. The site also includes research links, a list of suppliers, and mailing lists.

PEN American Center

http://www.pen.org/

PEN is an international "membership organization of prominent literary writers and editors. As a major voice of the literary community, the organization seeks to defend the freedom of expression wherever it may be threatened, and to promote and encourage the recognition and reading of contemporary literature." The site links to information about several PEN-sponsored initiatives, including literary awards.

Publishers Weekly Online
http://www.bookwire.com/
Publishers Weekly Online offers news about the writing industry and special features about reading and writing. The site also includes news on children's books, bookselling, interviews, international book industry news, and industry updates.

Pure Fiction
http://www.purefiction.com/start.htm
Based in London and New York, Pure Fiction is a web site "for anyone who loves to read—or aspires to write—best-selling fiction." The site includes reviews, previews, writing advice, an online bookshop, a writers' showcase, Internet links, and more. They also offer a mailing list.

R. R. Bowker
http://www.bowker.com/
This site of the reference publisher for the entire publishing industry offers a listing of books in print and out of print, an online directory of the book publishing industry, a data collection center for R. R. Bowker publications, and a directory of vendors to the publishing community.

Reference Shelf
http://Alabanza.com/kabacoff/Inter-Links/reference.html
The Reference Shelf site provides quick access to words, facts, and figures useful when writing and fact-checking. A special "words" section features dictionaries, acronym finders, and links to computer jargon.

Ruminator Review
http://www.ruminator.com/hmr/
The *Review* is a national magazine that presents essays, author interviews, children's book reviews, nonfiction reviews, and poetry reviews. *Ruminator Review* is also offered in a print version, where each issue is built around a particular theme.

Sensible Solutions for Getting Happily Published
http://www.happilypublished.com/
This site is "designed to help writers, publishers, self-publishers and everyone else who cares about reaching readers, including editors, agents, booksellers, reviewers, industry observers and talk show hosts . . . and aims to help books get into the hands of the people they were written for." It includes information about finding a publisher, ways for publishers to raise revenues, the self-publishing option, how to boost a book's sales, and sensible solutions for reaching readers.

SharpWriter.Com
http://www.sharpwriter.com/
SharpWriter.Com is a practical resources page for writers of all types—a "writer's handy virtual desktop." Reference materials include style sheets, dictionaries,

quotations, and job information. The "Office Peacemaker" offers to resolve grammar disputes in the workplace.

ShawGuides; Writers' Conferences
http://www.shawguides.com/writing
The Shaw Site for Writers' Conferences allows the user to search for information about 400 conference and workshops worldwide. An e-mail service can be used to get updates about conferences that meet user criteria for dates, topics, and locations. Other resources include "Quick Tips," links to organizations, and information about residencies and retreats.

Small Publishers of North America
http://www.spannet.org/home.htm
Small Publishers of North America is a site for "independent presses, self-publishers, and savvy authors who realize that if their books are to be successful, they must make them so." The site offers pages for "fan, facts, and financial gain." They also offer a newsletter.

U.S. Copyright Office
http://lcweb.loc.gov/copyright/
The U.S. Copyright Office site allows the user to find valuable information about copyright procedures and other basics. In addition, the user can download publications and forms and link to information about international copyright.

Victory Page
http://www.crayne.com/
For fiction writers, this site has articles on writing resources and how to help you write better, a list of links for and about writing, publishers, agents, and science fiction, a science fiction writing workshop, and an opportunity to subscribe to *Victory's Motivational Newsletter.*

The WELL
http://www.well.com/
The WELL (Whole Earth 'Lectronic Link) is an online gathering place that its creators call a "literate watering hole for thinkers from all walks of life."

Western Writers of America, Inc.
http://www.imt.net/~gedison/wwahome.html
"WWA was founded in 1953 to promote the literature of the American West and bestow Spur Awards for distinguished writing in the western field." The site offers information about Old West topics, a listing of past Spur Award winners, and opportunities to learn about WWA and the Spur Award, to apply for membership in WWA, to subscribe to *Roundup Magazine,* and to contact western authors whose work interests you.

Women Who Write
http://memers.aol.com/jfavetti/womenww/www.html
Women Who Write is a "college of women based all over the United States with a

passion for writing." The site provides useful links and a large dose of encouragement to women writers of all experience levels.

WriteLinks

http://www.writelink.com/

The site provides an array of services including workshops, personalized tutoring, and critique groups. "WriteLinks is designed to be of value to all writers, regardless of their experience, genre, or focus."

The Write Page

http://www.writepage.com/index.html

The Write Page is "an online newsletter with over 300 pages of author and book information for readers and how-to information for writers of genre fiction." Genres that the site deals with include science fiction, romance, historical novels, murder mysteries, technothrillers, children's, young adult, nonfiction, poetry, and small press publications. Articles grapple with issues such as how to write and get published, research, tools of the trade, and listings of conferences and contests.

Write Page Author Listing Information

http://www.writepage.com/pageinfo.htm

This site offers authors a chance to create their own web sites with the help of Callie Goble. It answers many of the questions that one might have about such an enterprise, such as "How long can my page be?," "How long does it take to get listed?," "What sort of exposure will my books get?," "What does the competition charge?," and much more.

The Writers' BBS

http://www.writers-bbs.com/home/shtml

The Writers' BBS is intended for "authors, poets, journalists, and readers" and highlights writers' chat rooms, discussion forums, and an e-zine for beginning writers called *Fish Eggs for the Soul*. It also includes games, personal ads, copyright information, mailing lists, Internet links, an adults-only section, and the online King James Bible.

The Writers Center

http://www.writer.org/

The Writers Center is a Maryland-based nonprofit that "encourages the creation and distribution of contemporary literature." On the web site, they provide information on their 200+ yearly workshops and links to their publications *Poet Lore* and *Writer's Carousel*.

Writers' Exchange

http://writerexchange.miningco.com/

Writers' Exchange offers links to various topics from agents to humor, writers' resources, interviews, information about upcoming writing conferences, writing classes, information about markets, bulletin boards, chat rooms, newsletters, and opportunities to shop in their bookstore, video store, and marketplace.

Writers Guild of America West

http://www.wga.org/manual/index.hml

The WGA West site provides information about the Guild and its services such as script registration. Other links to writing resources are provided as well.

Writers Net

http://www.writers.net/

Writers Net is a site that "helps build relationships between writers, publishers, editors and literary agents." It consists of two main sections, the Internet Directory of Published Writers, which includes a list of published works and a biographical statement, and the Internet Directory of Literary Agents, which lists areas of specialization and a description of the agency. Both are searchable and include contact information. It is a free service that hopes to "become an important, comprehensive matchmaking resource for writers, editors, publishers and literary agents on the Internet."

Writers on the Net

http://www.writers.com

"Writers on the Net is a group of published writers and experienced writing teachers building an online community and resource for writers and aspiring writers." A subscription to the mailing list provides a description and schedule of classes provided by the site and a monthly newsletter.

The Writer's Retreat

http://www.angelfire.com/va/dmsforever/index.html

The objectives of The Writer's Retreat are "to provide a meeting place for writers everywhere, to provide market information, to list relevant Internet links, to list inspirational and motivational information and quotations for writers of all races, creeds, and backgrounds, and to have and provide fun while doing it!"

Writer's Toolbox

http://www.writerstoolbox.com/

The site contains a "diverse and ever-growing collection of Internet resources for writers." The resources are categorized for many types of writers from technical writers and PR professionals to fiction and drama writers. The site also includes links to software for writers and business resources.

Writers Write®

http://www.writerswrite.com

This "mega-site" provides a myriad of resources, including a searchable database of online and print publications in need of submissions. The Writers Write® chat room is open 24 hours a day for live discussion.

Writerspace

http://www.writerspace.com/

"Writerspace specializes in the design and hosting of web sites for authors. We also provide web services for those who may already have web sites but wish to include more interactivity in the way of bulletin boards, chat rooms, contests, and e-mail newsletters." The site also features an author spotlight, contests, workshops, mailing lists, bulletin boards, chat rooms, romance links, a guestbook, and information on web design, web hosting, their clients, and rates.

The Zuzu's Petals Literary Resource

http://www.zuzu.com

The Zuzu's Petals Literary Resource has a comprehensive list of writers' resource links and information. It includes a bookstore, discussion forums, its literary magazine, *Zuzu's Petals Quarterly Online,* news reports on the literary world, and contests.